Dedicated to the memory of my mother,
Alice Wainwright

Printed in England by Flexipress Printing Ltd., Ormskirk, Lancashire.
Tel. 01695 576339 | www.flexipress.co.uk

About This Book

Thank you to everyone who purchased the first volume of *"The Hidden History of St Helens"* and told me that they enjoyed reading it. This follow-up is largely "more of the same", featuring more fascinating stories that I have uncovered from the local newspaper archives.

Many readers have said that they liked being able to dip into the book without having to read a whole chapter. Perhaps, spend five or ten minutes reading in bed before going to sleep.

And so in this second volume I have included more chapters containing compilations of stories – such as *'The Weird and Wonderful Things St Helens Folk Have Said'*, *'"Dear Sir" – A Collection Of Curious Correspondence'*, *'The 19th Century Newspapers That Waxed Lyrical'* and *'Advertising Slogans Of The Old St Helens Stores'*. You'll also find a bit more humour and an increased amount of 20th century stories.

This volume is dedicated to the memory of my mother who passed away in 1991 after developing early-onset Alzheimer's. At the time of publication, my sister Diane Charnock is President of Soroptimist St Helens and the Alzheimer's Society is her chosen charity. Consequently, £1 from the sale of the first 1,000 copies of this book will go to the president's fund.

Much of the content of this book has been sourced from newspapers stored on microfilm at Eccleston Library and I would again like to thank their ever-helpful and cheerful staff *(and those at St Helens Archive Service in the Gamble Building)* for their kind co-operation. **SRW**

Contents

Rumours, Hoaxes And Fake News

"The story took wing in a very connected form, and it flew from point to point so rapidly that the whole town got hold of it."

There may not have been high-speed broadband, social media and 5G mobile telecoms in the 19th century. But there was something else that was also blazingly fast – word-of-mouth! News of some "to do" would spread like wildfire in St Helens and folk would rush out of their homes as fast as their legs could carry them at the prospect of some excitement to brighten their dull day.

And if the incident in question did not have an obvious explanation, some "helpful" individual would invent one. Whether through malice or misunderstanding, a rumour could subsequently take on quite a life of its own.

If the police were quick off the mark they could limit its spread, as in August 1872 when Jane Beecham died. The 59-year-old wife of pills boss Thomas Beecham had been what we would call an alcoholic and had been separated from her husband. The St Helens Newspaper wrote:

> From the period of her death disquieting rumours of a vague character were floating about, which the police endeavoured to have sifted …and the result was that the rumours were shown to have been without foundation.

However, by the time the police investigated the bizarre claims of November 26th 1873, matters were well out of hand and the huge crowds that had gathered in Bridge Street refused to accept a simple truth. A smell from a blocked up sewer had been sensationalised into something much more sinister and rational explanations were seen as cover ups. The St Helens Newspaper described the remarkable chain of events that ensued on that day:

A most extraordinary rumour arose in St. Helens on Wednesday, and obtained a marvellous hold on the public imagination. A tradesman in Bridge-street had nasal demonstration, early in the day, that his sewer was not in the best order, and he sent for the nuisance inspector to have it cleaned. By some means, which it would be impossible to define, the rumour got abroad that the odour arose from a dead body buried in the cellar, and that the dead body was the mortal part of a child belonging to a former tenant, now out of the country. The story took wing in a very connected form, and it flew from point to point so rapidly that the whole town got hold of it. Crowds poured into Bridge-street, and surrounded the house, sniffing the air with the keenness of a pack of hounds.

The rain came down merrily while they stood, but they heeded not the rain, an impression having arised that there was some desire to conceal the tragedy so as to disperse the curious. Therefore the curious, whose name is legion, would not be dispersed, and defied the rain as they surged around the house. The police came to the scene and Inspector Whiteside had a satisfactory explanation from the tradesman; but this was not sufficient, and the crowd held on. The odour was enjoyed, actually enjoyed, because it seemed to furnish an evidence of the existence of a dead body in the vicinity, and persons with powerful imaginations gave very conclusive reasons for their belief. Then little items of a sensational character diversified the monotony.

An invisible express sent the intelligence abroad amongst the mob that a foot had turned up during the excavation which was positively believed to be going on, and terrible was the agitation which the announcement caused. There was a visible shudder, and a swaying of the mass towards the house. The excitement was really serious, however, when a queer looking individual declared that a hand had made its appearance on one of the spades. No one thought much of the scraps of hair and clothing which the imaginary searchers were discovering at every turn; the great interest attached to the human organs which inventive or nervous people were finding from time to time. Nor was the air of reality – horrid reality – dissipated in the slightest degree when the next bulletin revealed the finding of a pair of clogs answering to the size of the supposed deceased.

The absconded tenant had dealt in boots and shoes, and most of the gazers knew that fact well, and yet the idea of his condemning his children to the luxury of clogs did not strike them as at all unreasonable. But the piquant notions which floated through the minds of the crowd in the street bore only a faint resemblance to the raw-head-and-bloody-bones rumours that circulated darkly in more distant places. Quiet people shuddered, as they listened to the dreadful details of another Coram-street tragedy [that had occurred in London last Christmas] which had come to light through the accidental discovery of a human head.

To go through the various graduations of this most extraordinary hoax would give a more vivid idea of human credulity than befits this part of the nineteenth century. All through the evening the grouping continued, and it was late at night before there was a complete dispersal. Even on Thursday timid people looked up at the house eagerly as they passed. It must have been an intolerable nuisance to the tradesman who occupies the premises to have been persecuted by such a silly and ridiculous canard.

THE WHISKY POISONING RUMOUR

In 1864 a rumour that a St Helens pub had served a man poisoned spirits led to concerned crowds gathering near the alleged victim's home. No doubt many wild theories were disseminated as to why Bill Anthony, the landlord of The Queen in Bridge Street, had supposedly given Jimmy Duffy whisky laced with acid. The labourer from Tontine Street was now at death's door fighting for his life and the St Helens Newspaper wrote:

> The affair has created considerable excitement in the town and, of course, suspicion strongly attached to the landlord of "The Queen".

Within 48 hours, the 44-year-old Duffy was dead and so never fully able to explain himself. But although medical science in the 1860s was primitive compared to today, enough was known about the actions of poisonous substances for the man's intent to be uncovered. That was disclosed at James Duffy's inquest, which was held at the Wellington Hotel in Naylor Street in St Helens on August 20th 1864. This is how the newly widowed Margaret Duffy described her husband's movements on that fateful day:

The Wellington Hotel in Naylor Street

> He got up at seven o'clock on Sunday morning, and did not go out until he and I went to church together. When we returned he took a walk up to his brother's while I got the dinner ready. He came back again between two and three o'clock, and as dinner was not yet ready he walked out again, and I saw him go into "The Queen." He came in again

4

at five minutes to five. I saw him coming, and as he staggered in his walk I laughed at him, for I thought he was doing it in a joke. There was a woman sitting on the door step, and he asked her how she was. He walked straight through the kitchen, upstairs, and as he passed through, his brother was sitting in the house, and deceased said, "That's the only brother I have." On going up stairs he made a slight stumble, but got up himself. He had scarcely got upstairs when I heard a scream. I instantly ran upstairs to see what was the matter, as I thought he might have got into bed with a lodger who was upstairs, and they were fighting.

On getting upstairs I found the deceased laid on the top of the bed with his clothes on. He was rolling about, screaming, and appeared to be in great pain. I called his brother upstairs, and he came immediately. I asked deceased what was the matter, but he could not tell me. His brother (John Duffy) loosed the neckerchief, when we found that his mouth was as though it were burned, and the stuff had ran down his chin and neck and burned it to a blister. On taking the neckerchief off it was all burned in holes, and his shirt, and waistcoat, too. That night, deceased told me he had been to "The Queen," and had two glasses of whiskey, and a share of a quart of beer. He said the second glass of whiskey felt like fire in his mouth, and when he got outside he spit it out. He gradually got worse, and died about twelve o'clock at noon on Tuesday.

Margaret Duffy's testimony supported the popular belief that the landlord of The Queen had served her husband poisoned whisky. Upon being asked if she thought James could have committed suicide, the widow replied that he'd behaved normally throughout that day and she could think of no reason why he would want to "destroy himself".

The licensee Bill Anthony also felt that Jimmy Duffy had not behaved any differently than usual while drinking in his Bridge Street pub – except for one thing. Upon leaving, he claimed Duffy had said: "Good bye, Bill, I shall never see thee again".

The landlord also insisted that the whisky he'd given the dead man had not been tampered with in any way – a statement supported by the evidence of Dr James Ricketts. The Cotham Street medic had analysed Duffy's vomit and firmly believed that he'd consumed sulphuric acid at his Tontine Street home, telling the coroner:

> He could not possibly have walked home and spoken as he did had he taken the poison at the public house. The effect would be instantaneous, and the pain most excruciating.

The immediate disabling consequence of consuming sulphuric acid was something that Duffy in planning his suicide had clearly not known. Not only did he inflict a horrible death upon himself – but his intention of throwing the blame on the landlord of The Queen was undermined by his choice of poison.

But if Duffy had taken his own life, what had been his reason and why did he want the licensee to be held responsible? The answer to the former question was unknown, although his wife described James as a quiet man and he appeared to have been the type that kept his worries to himself.

As to the latter, there was no known acrimony between the landlord and Duffy – indeed they appeared to have been friends. But someone had to take the blame for his death and Bill Anthony had seemingly just been the unlucky one. Everything fell into place when the coroner explained to the jury that Duffy had been a member of the St Patrick's United Association Burial Society.

Their rules had a clause that stated that if any member should "come to death by his own hand" no payments would be made. And so the evidence strongly suggested that James Duffy had decided to commit suicide but needed to hide the manner of his demise so that his wife would receive the "club" money. The St Helens Newspaper in concluding their report wrote:

> The Jury then considered their verdict, and in delivering it, remarked that they were perfectly satisfied no blame or suspicion could be attached to anyone but the deceased himself. It was quite clear, as the medical gentleman very properly observed, that the poison from which he died could not have been given him at "The Queen." It would be instantaneous in its effects, and from the fact of the deceased screaming out when he got upstairs, it was evidence sufficient that he took the poison himself immediately on getting upstairs.

The only outstanding matter was why no bottle of sulphuric acid had been found in the man's bedroom. It seemed that in planning his suicide, James had taken pains to leave no evidence behind – although a woman visiting the house shortly after his death had found a cork that burned her mouth on putting it to her tongue.

The lengthy report of the inquest hearing in the St Helens Newspaper contained no police statement and it appears that the room had not been thoroughly searched for clues.

Jimmy Duffy had clearly attempted an insurance scam naming his wife as beneficiary. That was unusual, as rumours would normally allege that individuals had committed scams for their own financial benefit, particularly when fires were involved.

In March 1870 rumours swept Prescot that George Lucas's insurance company had paid him the huge sum of £200 as a result of a fire. Presumably, the gossip was implying that the wholesale confectioner had set fire to his Eccleston Street premises in order to benefit from a massive pay-out. So on March 19th, Lucas paid for a notice to be published on the front page of the Prescot Reporter in order to squash the claims.

FIRE.

AN erroneous impression prevailing that I have received £200 from the Manchester Insurance Company, as compensation for damage done to my property, by fire, on the 19th February, I desire to make known that the whole sum received by me from the company was £17 10s., of which sum I have to pay £2 12s. for the expenses of the Fire Engine. Fire Brigade, &c. The Insurance company denied that they were liable to make good the damage, alleging that the policy of insurance did not allow me to keep straw in the cellar.

(Signed)   GEORGE LUCAS,
Eccleston-street,
March, 1870.   Prescot.

He stated that the amount that he had received from the insurance company had only been £17 10 shillings – and from that he'd had to pay a fire brigade £2 12 shillings for their call out. That was often the case if a brigade attended from outside of the immediate area.

The St Helens Reporter on December 27th 1918 described a rumour of a more ridiculous kind that was spreading about the town. People had been saying that the person who had come second in the recent Tradesmen's Tombola had been given a toy yacht instead of the promised prize of £100 *(around £7,000 in today's money)*.

The tombola had been the centrepiece of a huge fundraising drive in aid of the Mayor's War Relief Fund, with a woman from Boundary Road having won the first prize of a £300 house. Peter Haycock, a railway platelayer from Moss Bank, was the runner-up and he was able to confirm to the Reporter that he'd received the promised £100 in the form of War Savings Certificates – and not a toy boat substitute!

HEARTLESS HOAXES

What was described as a "heartless hoax" was reported in local newspapers in October 1929. A number of unemployed men in St Helens had received anonymous postcards inviting them to attend a building site in Dentons Green where they would be given work. The "lucky" men had been unemployed for years and could ill-afford the tram fares – but made the journey only to discover that they had been cruelly tricked.

The Liverpool Weekly News of October 15th 1898 described how another "cruel hoax" had been played on a woman from Parr:

On Monday some evil-minded person, or the victim of some delusion, perpetrated a very cruel hoax on a woman in the Havannah district of Parr, St. Helens. The woman's husband is a fireman employed at the Southport Pit, belonging to Messrs. Richard Evans and Co., and in the course of the day a man, who had apparently come from the colliery, called upon her and told her that her husband had met with a serious accident in the pit, and she must get the bed ready at once to receive him. The poor woman was, of course, terribly shocked, and frantically inquired the nature of the accident. She was unceremoniously told that her husband had been buried by a fall of roof.

The ghastly news soon spread, and almost the entire inhabitants were soon at their doors awaiting the arrival of "the victim" on a stretcher. In the meantime the poor wife was prostrate with the shock, and one of the officials at the colliery, hearing the report, at once came and assured her that it was absolutely false, and that her husband was perfectly safe and sound. Nothing, however, could satisfy her until her husband came home and demonstrated by his presence the falsity of the base report. The woman, however, was so completely overcome with the terrible news that Dr. O'Keefe had to be sent for, and she is still confined to bed under his care. It is to be hoped that the author of this freak may be discovered.

A SCENE OF EXCITEMENT AND WONDER

Some people would put a remarkable amount of effort and expense into their hoaxes. On August 10th 1869, the Cork Examiner described how a prank had recently been staged in Liverpool that had a Rainhill connection. Placards had been posted all over the city describing how a new bridge at Hotham Street was being opened over Lime Street Station.

Trains were to run from Rainhill and a host of dignitaries, along with the band of the 11th Fusiliers, were going to be present. An immense steamroller would cross the bridge followed by a procession and, at the time appointed, a thousand people patiently waited for the event to start. The newspaper explained that after a long time waiting:

> ...a hoax was scented, and the crowd dispersed, many of them vowing vengeance against the perpetrators.

One might have thought that the poster's reference to there being a "celebrated lunatic asylum" at Rainhill might have been a clue that all was not well. But, people will, of course, allow themselves to be fooled if there is something in it for them.

On one day in February 1849, St Helens was chock-a-block with hoteliers and other tradesmen from Liverpool and Manchester, all eager to cash in on a grand ball that was supposedly going to take place. Most of the fooled arrived by train and at that time such travellers had to disembark at St Helens Junction station to switch trains or to commute into the town by other means. This is how the Liverpool Mercury described the scene:

SHAMEFUL HOAX. – Some individuals of St. Helen's have been playing off a practical joke upon some of our tradesmen, which has been productive of great expense, disappointment, and inconvenience. Mr. Radley, of the Adelphi, Mr. Lynn, of the Waterloo, Mr. Whiteman, of the Brunswick, all admirable purveyors and caterers; Mr. Rainford, the upholsterer, Mr. Hausburg, and a host of others, were amongst the victims. They had summonses, per post, to attend at the house of a gentleman, resident near St. Helen's, to receive orders for a grand ball, to be given in that town, to Sir John Gerard, Bart. A multitude obeyed the command, but found that the letters were forgeries. No sooner had one party arrived and been enlightened than another appeared. The trains from Manchester and the surrounding towns brought fresh additions to the stock of the hoaxed, the earlier arrivals enjoying the joke at the expense of those who came afterwards. Such was the influx that, at twelve o'clock, the train from St. Helen's to the junction could not supply carriages enough to accommodate the disappointed visitors. The next train was equally inefficient, and St. Helen's, during the day, was a scene of excitement and wonder. We understand that the perpetrators of this shameful deception can be traced. If so, we hope that such an example will be made as will deter all idle people hereafter from perpetrating similar mischief.

UNINTENDED HOAXES

Over several weeks in the early months of 1973, the St Helens Reporter's *Whalley's World* column (that was written by Alan Whalley) described some ghostly hauntings that had occurred many years before. Readers also related a couple of manifestations that were far from being of supernatural origin. These included the comical tale of "Old Mr Bibby", the sexton at St Helens Cemetery, who had terrified two workmen after seemingly emerging from a grave in the dead of night. Mr Bibby had been bricking up a vault close to the graveyard wall and, in order to finish the job, needed to work well into the night in spite of heavy rain.

To provide some protection for himself, Mr Bibby built a canvas shelter over the grave. At 2 am he heard a horse and cart coming along Abbey Road, which was occupied by the so-called "night soil" men. They were preparing to empty their loads on what is now the East Lancashire Road. The Reporter reader described what happened:

> Mr. Bibby bobbed up with his lantern to ask the men the time. He only got as far as "Hey…" They found the horse and cart wandering round Crank next day and the two men didn't stop running till they got home to Gerrard's Bridge.

Then on March 2nd 1973, under the headline *"At Last – Spooky Secret Leaks!"*, Alan Whalley described how stories of the ghost / naked lady of Carr Mill had finally been explained. Jack Anders had written to the journalist to confess to being one of the jokers who, about 1930, had frightened local folk by placing a white statue in the middle of Carr Mill Road. Mr. Anders said:

> I was a member of a gang of lads from the Woodlands Road area, and while returning from "Owd" Ben's pub – the Black Horse at Moss Bank – we stopped at a house, occupied by the Middlehurst family in the grounds of Carr Mill Dam. In the front garden was a four-foot tall statue of an angel playing a harp. Being ripe for mischief, the joker among us, Tom Brown, suggested pinching it. Together we crept into the garden, picked up the statue and rushed out with it shouting "He's ere neaw – beawt baw!" We managed to carry it fifty yards, and then finding it too heavy to go on, we dumped it in the middle of the road. In those days there was very little

traffic, especially at night, and the statue might have stayed there until morning had not the last bus from St. Helens to Wigan come trundling along, an old-fashioned single decker with back steps and one-candle-power lamps. The driver peered out at what he thought was a child in the road with its hand held high. The figure didn't move and the conductor went to investigate. Suddenly a man with a bike emerged from a hedge by the roadside, cursing and muttering that he'd been cringing there for ten minutes because he thought he'd seen a ghost. It didn't take long for the rumours to start flying, and soon the district was abuzz with the tale of how a "stark nak't woman had stopped the bus".

FAKE NEWS

Newspaper hoaxes were not uncommon. In September 1885 a Liverpool paper described how a humble cotton porter working in a local warehouse had inherited the huge sum of £80,000 as a result of some family interest in St Helens' coalmines. A long-protracted suit in the Court of Chancery had supposedly led to a judgement being made in the man's favour.

The lucky recipient and the solicitors supposedly involved in the lawsuit were named in the piece. Unfortunately, the Liverpool paper failed to check with them before printing the happy story of a poor man who'd become a wealthy one overnight. But other papers did – and gleefully reported a hoax. Or as one put it – that there had not been the "slenderest substratum of truth" in the story.

In August 1899 a Liverpool paper wrote that Ann Ashall from Church Row in Haydock had briefly been resurrected from the dead. A Dr Hayward was supposed to have examined the 63-year-old's body and then declared: "Yes, she has gone at last; let us hope she is in heaven." Then after being "laid out", the dead woman was supposed to have got up and gone for a walk – before eventually laying down and dying for good.

In fact Mrs Ashall was alive and improving and had never been declared dead. The Wigan Observer wrote that "intense amusement" had been created in the district by the publication of the story. Whether its origin had been through misunderstanding, a deliberate hoax or a rumourmonger with a vivid imagination, was not known.

In August 1926, newspapers reported how a man claiming to be Dai Jones, the well-known Welsh international rugby union player, had played a hoax on the St Helens Rugby League club. The conman was actually William Roslyn from Warrington, who the police dubbed an "inveterate liar".

Roslyn told Saints that he had decided to turn professional and switch codes. The Knowsley Road club paid the bogus Dai Jones £5 travelling expenses before learning the truth. Subsequently, in St Helens Police Court, Roslyn was sentenced to three months hard labour.

It didn't cost much to hoax someone in the classified columns of the Liverpool Echo. On December 2nd 1890, an advert appeared in the paper offering an "easy life" to persons of either sex who wanted a job with the Chemical Union of St Helens. One might have thought that such an unusual promise would have rung some alarm bells with the Echo.

Classified advert in the Liverpool Echo of December 2nd 1890

But with extremely few folk then on the telephone, checking on the authenticity of the huge numbers of adverts that the Echo then published was simply not practical.

The ad in their "Persons Wanted" section was supposedly from William Clesham of Duke Street in St Helens, who was the vice-chairman of the local branch of a trade union called the Chemical Union. Sixpence was just the cost of a pre-paid, one-off insertion in the classifieds, as long as the advert did not exceed 24 words.

Two days after the publication of the fake ad, the Echo wrote that Mr Clesham had already received a large volume of letters and applicants – not only from St Helens but also from Liverpool – had turned up at the man's house requesting an interview. This the paper commented had been:

> …much to the annoyance of Mr. Clesham, who disclaims the authorship. Mr. Clesham has evidently been hoaxed, and we should be glad to communicate with the person who sent the advertisement, or with any person who has knowledge of the author.

FAKE NOOSE !!!

On September 19th 1863, a remarkable letter was published in the St Helens Newspaper describing two "pseudo-suicides" that had taken place in Rainford. These were not the village equivalent of faking death by leaving clothes on a beach and wandering off into the sea – like the act committed by former government minister John Stonehouse and the fictional Reginald Perrin.

The first Rainford case was a hanging hoax motivated by a man's desire to play a practical joke on his neighbours. In the other sham suicide, poison was supposedly taken to elicit sympathy from an angry wife upset over her husband's drunkenness. Both were brainless acts that did neither man any favours once the truth came out. Writing under the pseudonym "A. Spectator", the correspondent said the incidents had taken place within two weeks of each other in School Brow and Johnson's Brow. The former is now part of Church Road but used to be the name of the Rainford road leading from Pasture Lane to the Derby Arms. And Johnson's Brow was situated at the corner of Cross Pit Lane and Ormskirk Road. This is the letter published in the Newspaper's edition of September 19th 1863:

PSEUDO-SUICIDES IN RAINFORD – Sir, – Within the last fortnight we have had two of these sham or counterfeit exhibitions. The first transpired at our "Modern Athens," School Brow. A certain sotswhistle maker, who has only lately entered the marriage state, (while his better-half was on a visit to some of her friends) stuffed his holiday clothes, consisting of Wellingtonians, pants, vest, and coat, so as to personate his own identical person, with a pillow-slip or large cap drawn over his pseudo pericranium, suspended this effigy from the ceiling, upsetting a table placed underneath, locked up the door, and went to his avocation [work]. This soon caught the eye of some of those inquisitive School Brow janglers, and in less time than it takes the reader to peruse these few lines, the Brow, like a "hive of swarming bees," was all on the alert with the cry of "Eh, my God! Bill has hung hissel, whot ever ol bekum of his poor wife and choilt." This "posse" soon called in the "peeler," (who was rather too old a bird to be caught with chaff) but the general cries were "Breike 'th dur," "Cut him daane," "Fetch th' docktor, apply he'll bring him reaund agen."

The "bobby" having taken a view of this supposed strangled corpse, cried "away with you out of this; did you hever see a man 'ung with his 'ands in his pockets?" – in which the bottom part of the sleeves had been placed to prevent the perception of the lack of hands. Ingress was soon obtained, and the supposed body got down, and, lo! the disappointment beggars all description, when they found the fraud, and that there was no real suicide. This character was then ten times worse than if he had really committed the deed, and it would not be to the prolonging of his life to try the thing in earnest, in hopes some one would cut him down ere life was extinct – for I'll be blowed if they would.

The other, a young man who has enjoyed connubial felicity something over thirteen lunar months (his better-half having presented him with a pledge of their affection), known as the "Brewery kad mow," and who is possessed of a faculty within the sphere of few, viz, of turning ale into porter, residing at Johnson's Brow, having been pursuing this faculty rather too freely, his crooked "rib" began to read him over the evening lecture, so often read by "matronised madames" to their drunken spouses. He, to alleviate his transgression, or at least to ameliorate her acrimony, fell from his chair, and stretching himself out as if in the agonies of death, feigned reicking or vomiting.

"What ails thee man, thou nasty drunken thing". "Why, Sally, aw've dun it, aw've taan poison." "Oh, my _____," she exclaimed, and immediately aroused the neighbourhood, fetching his brother, father and mother, and neighbours, who, with wringing hands and tearful eyes, came to render what assistance they could in such an emergency, all enquiring with earnest breath, "Eh, Harry! whot has to dun so for; the shud ne'er a do so; whatever kud make thee do so?" "Why, awre Sally dusn't like me. It's awe gammon." "Yas! Yas! Harry, aw do; the shudn't a dun so; whot'll bekum o' me, an thy little babby dust think?" This ended as the other, by his being reckoned a worse man for the deception than for the real offence. **A SPECTATOR**, Sept. 29, 1863.

A SLUR ON ST HELENS

So-called "fake news" can take many forms. It can be a simple error that leads to the media disseminating an inaccurate story. On February 18th 1967, under the headline *"Slur On St Helens – Worst Town For Debt Defaulters"*, the Reporter described how a firm called British Debt Services had lazily compiled figures that gave a false impression about the townsfolk's credit worthiness:

This week St. Helens people became angry after being branded as Lancashire's "top-of-the-table" bad debtors. Only when the story had appeared on BBC news bulletins and in several evening newspapers was it realised that the whole thing was a mistake. The firm who issued the figures, British Debt Services Ltd., based their calculations on summonses issued for debt by the St. Helens County Court. But what they failed to realise was that the St. Helens County Court issues summonses not only to the County Borough of St. Helens, population 104,440, but also to Whiston, Prescot, Huyton, Widnes, and other outlying districts including certain Liverpool postal addresses. The company stated that 1,824 summonses had been issued in St Helens. This is 1.6 per cent of the population. If the figure had been divided into the total populations of the areas covered, the percentage of bad debtors would probably have been a third of that stated, thus putting St. Helens way down the list of bad debtors.

The Mayor (Coun. W. L. Williams) who immediately resented the affront to the town's dignity, spent most of Thursday afternoon in his office answering queries from national newspapers and TV companies. He contacted the BBC to ask for an apology and a representative was rushed to see him before the Rotary Club Dinner in the Fleece Hotel that evening. A report of what the Mayor told him came over on an early-morning B.B.C. sound broadcast yesterday.

The St Helens County Court in East Street

Note how the BBC had "rushed" a representative to St Helens to placate the mayor – something I can't imagine occurring today when a mistake is made by the Beeb!

The St Helens Children That Were Sent To Prison

"When sentence was passed on the elder prisoners the children cried bitterly and one fainted. On hearing their own sentences the little creatures uttered piercing shrieks."

The Kirkdale Court House and Gaol in Liverpool

There is no doubt that during the 19th century, some parents in St Helens sent their children out to steal. That often led to the unfortunate youngsters receiving severe treatment from the authorities, while their more culpable parents escaped punishment. Many children were sent to Kirkdale Gaol in Liverpool – and / or despatched to a reformatory for what was usually a period of five years. Boys could also be birched, with the phrase "well whipped" often used by magistrates and judges.

Of course, it can be difficult to differentiate stealing through need or from greed and know for certain whether child thefts were individual acts or through parental instruction. But not many toys and sweets were taken by the youngsters. Instead their ill-gotten gains were more commonly coal, bread or clothing – items that would benefit the family home and so point to their parents' involvement in their criminal acts.

Coal stealing during the 1860s and 1870s was easily the most common juvenile crime and was driven by poverty. Such thefts often came from colliery waste heaps and were not of saleable coal, although that was of little consequence to the authorities.

Alternatively, coal could be thieved while standing in railway wagons or from heaps on industrial premises. The quantity taken was invariably small and was only as much as a child or a woman could carry – often in a basket, or even an apron. It was an almost exclusive female crime but occasionally boy thieves were caught.

In St Helens Petty Sessions on March 15th 1869, 12-year-old Ann Callaghan was sent to prison for a month for stealing coal from Ravenhead Colliery. The mine was in Burtonhead Road and also known as Groves Colliery. Upon her release from Kirkdale Gaol in Liverpool, the girl was despatched to a reformatory for five years. This was the second time that Ann had been caught stealing coal and her mother Mary had recently served two weeks in prison for the same offence.

It was clearly Ann's mum who was behind the coal thefts but her daughter was much more harshly punished. Later that month Mary Callaghan was charged with breaching the peace in St Helens by "shouting, clapping her hands, and sundry other antics" and told the court that her heart had been broken – presumably a reference to her daughter's predicament.

The magistrates placed a lot of stock on how defendants looked and behaved in court, as well as the attitude of the young defendants' parents. Consequently children from families deemed respectable and well dressed were far less likely to be imprisoned for coal thefts than those from poor backgrounds. So with Ann Callaghan's mother being involved in coal stealing too, her daughter stood little chance of receiving a sympathetic hearing. Six months earlier Anne Rogers had been caught red-handed stealing coal from Ravenhead Colliery. However, the St Helens Newspaper wrote that in court the 14-year-old had been "very decently dressed" and her father politely appealed to the Bench not to send his daughter to prison because of her age. The man offered to pay a fine instead of gaol and the magistrates agreed. His family were perceived as respectable and so leniency was the order of the day.

A HALF-FAMISHED COAL THIEF

Rarely, did the St Helens Newspaper consider the sending of juvenile offenders to prison to be harsh. But criticism was implied – albeit mildly – in their edition of October 15th 1864 when this report of a St Helens Petty Sessions hearing was published:

> **SEVERE PUNISHMENT FOR COAL STEALING.** – William Flannagan, a half-famished looking lad, ten years of age, whose mother was said to be of such drunken habits, that his father had left her some time ago, was charged by Sergeant Fairley, with stealing about a hundredweight of coal. The offence was proved to have taken place on Monday, at noon, from a railway siding. The juvenile offender, though surrounded by everything deplorable at his so-called place of abode, had never been before the magistrates previously. He was sentenced to be imprisoned for seven days, during which period he was to be well flogged.

"Well flogged" was a reference to the number of strokes that boys received in their corporal punishment – and poor William may have suffered as many as twenty. Girls used to be birched as well as lads – but that was stopped in the 1820s.

A FAMILY AFFAIR

Mothers and daughters sometimes took coal together. At the St Helens Petty Sessions on the November 9th 1868, Bridget and Mary Dolan were both sent to prison for seven days for stealing coal from Ravenhead Colliery. No details of their ages or relationship were provided in the report – but checking census records they appear to be mother and daughter, with the child just 7 or 8. A week's imprisonment was the usual punishment for first-time offenders.

Sisters could get involved in coal stealing too. In the St Helens Petty Sessions on January 4th 1869, Betsy and Mary Ann Barnes were charged with taking coal from a wagon in Pocket Nook. Mary Ann was described as a "mere infant" and Superintendent Ludlam suggested to the magistrates that they discharged the child because of her age.

As Ludlam was in charge of St Helens Police and responsible for all prosecutions, the question might be asked as to why the little girl had been brought into court in the first place. Mary's big sister Betsy was not so fortunate and she was sent to Kirkdale Gaol in Liverpool for seven days.

There was an enormous amount of poverty in St Helens at this time, which was exacerbated by a depression in trade. This created much unemployment and short-time working. As a result, women and girls were sent to prison virtually every week during the winter months for helping themselves to small amounts of coal to heat their freezing homes. This report of a court case from an edition of the St Helens Newspaper from November 1870 shows the desperate state of some households:

A charge was brought against Bridget Conway of stealing 50lbs. of coal from the Ravenhead Colliery, the property of Messrs. Bromilow and company. The prisoner stated that her husband was not of employment, in consequence of an injury which he received, and she was very poor, having to support him and four children. She went to the colliery to pick up some cinders, and she met there some women who told her it would be no harm if she took a couple of pieces of coal which were lying about. She did not think that she was doing any wrong in taking them. Mr. Marsh [magistrate] – Which do you prefer, to be tried here, or go to the sessions? Prisoner – Oh, I am guilty of taking them, sir, but I was told it would not be minded. Mr. Ludlam [Police superintendent] stated that the prisoner had been once convicted of stealing timber, but was discharged. Prisoner – It was some bits I found down near the canal. Mr. Marsh – Is anything known about her family? Mr. Ludlam – She is poor, and has four children. Prisoner – If I am forgiven this time I promise not to go there again. The magistrates sentenced her to fourteen days' imprisonment.

It was to Mrs Conway's credit that she did not involve her children in her activities – but who would provide for them while she was spending a fortnight in Kirkdale Gaol? The magistrates were mainly industrialists, with John Marsh the owner of Parr Alkali Works. Coal would have been taken from there too and so it was in his interests to pass deterrent sentences on individuals deemed to be thieves – no matter what dreadful circumstances they happened to be in.

PROTECTION FROM FUTURE CONTAMINATION

Some enterprising kids would not need parental instruction and would steal coal, seemingly, on their own initiative. Their ill-gotten gains would then be sold to neighbours at a discount and the coppers they received would be used to buy sweets. However, that was a dangerous business with heavy penalties for those caught. That is underlined by this St Helens Newspaper report from May 18th 1864 concerning a court case involving three girls:

Catherine Lee, Mary Glynn and Ann Connolly, three girls, were brought up on remand, charged with severally stealing about a cwt. of coal from Messrs. Bromilow and Haddock's Colliery [Ravenhead Colliery, aka Groves], on the previous Monday. Police-constable Hobson was on watch at the time, and during the dinner hour he saw each of the prisoners fill a sack with coal, valued at fourpence. He apprehended Lee the first, the biggest of the lot, and the other two were subsequently taken into custody. The prisoners pleaded guilty. Glynn had been up before for a similar offence and punished, and, as alleged, induced Lee, one of the other girls, to go with her to steal coals, and sell them at 2d. a sack. The Chairman also stated that from what the Bench had been informed, the girl was grossly neglected at home. The sentence was, that she be imprisoned at Kirkdale for one month; at the expiration of which she be sent to a reformatory for five years to save her from future contamination, and probable ruin. The other two prisoners were each sentenced to one month's imprisonment.

From what I can tell from census returns, Mary Glynn was 13 and Ann Connolly 15 or 16 with both living in St Helens in Garden Street (near Liverpool Street) in Greenbank. I have not been able to establishing Catherine Lee's age.

It was curious thinking by the magistrates that placing young Mary Glynn in prison with criminals and then sending her to a reformatory for five years with hundreds of other offenders would protect the child from "contamination" and "ruin". It was, sadly, commonplace for vulnerable children to be punished for their family backgrounds, rather than supported.

THE LITTLE CREATURES' PIERCING SHRIEKS

Although parents could occasionally be brought to book for their children's thieving if their involvement could be proved, it made no difference to the sentences that their youngsters received. At the Liverpool Quarter Sessions on July 12th 1870, two 13-year-old St Helens girls were accused of a number of thefts at the behest of their parents. Sabina Swift was charged with stealing 16lb of cheese from Sephton and Green's premises in New Market Place in St Helens. Her mother Catherine and father Martin were also charged with receiving the cheese, knowing it to have been stolen.

Another girl called Mary Evans was charged along with Sabina of stealing what was described as "two loaves of sugar" off Isaac Newton. No, not the gravity man (!), this Ike also kept a shop in the market. Sabina's Mum and Dad and Mary's Mum were also accused of various receiving offences. The two girls were sent to prison for 14 days, followed by 5 years in a reformatory – despite clearly being the puppets of their parents.

The judge in the case said there could be no doubt that the women had sent their children out to steal and had assisted them in their thefts. Sabina's mother was sent to prison for 8 months and Mary's Mum received a 12-month sentence. Martin Swift *(Sabina's father)* was found not guilty and appears to have been the only one who'd been out on bail – and so it was likely that the two girls would have served a total of 6 weeks in gaol. The Liverpool Daily Post wrote:

> When sentence was passed on the elder prisoners the children cried bitterly, and one of them fainted. On hearing their own sentences the little creatures uttered piercing shrieks.

The St Helens Newspaper added: "They uttered frantic cries, the girl Swift calling loudly on her father".

A CHORUS OF MOST DISMAL HOWLING

It was common for children to scream and cry in court upon being sent to prison for theft. They clearly had no notion of the potential consequences of their actions. It must have been a pitiful sight – although sometimes newspaper reporters seemed more concerned about the noise than the tragic spectacle.

When four "young girls" called Mary Ellen Tickle, Margaret Fitzpatrick and sisters Margaret and Eliza Craymour *(or Creamer)* appeared in St Helens Petty Sessions charged with theft, they were remanded in custody pending further enquiries. The St Helens Newspaper of August 2nd 1873 said they immediately created a "chorus of most dismal howling".

A coat belonging to John Platt from Thatto Heath had figured in the case with his wife having represented him in court. At the resumed hearing, it was stated that Platt and another victim had withdrawn from the prosecution, presumably because of the children's emotional outburst.

For much of the 19th century, St Helens newspapers rarely stated addresses or precise ages of child defendants in court. The spelling of their names was also often inaccurate, which means locating them in census returns can prove difficult. We do know that the four young defendants that made a dismal howling in court were from the Prescot area – but their stealing had taken place in St Helens.

The youngest child was Mary Ellen Tickle who appeared to be 9 and in the 1871 census was living in Rainhill. The Craymour *(or Creamer)* sisters seemed to be 10 and 12 and resident in Bond Street in Prescot and Margaret Fitzpatrick was about 16 and from Prescot's Tea Street. This is the St Helens Newspaper's report of the resumed proceedings from August 9th 1873:

It appeared that the girls were all on a thieving excursion on Tuesday last. Ann Gibson, of Brook street, missed some articles of dress on Wednesday morning and they were subsequently discovered and traced to the prisoners. Emma Johnson, of King street, came into her house, after marketing, on Tuesday afternoon, and placed her jacket on a table in the kitchen. She went from thence to the parlour, where she stayed a few minutes, and on returning to the kitchen missed not only the jacket, but a coat belonging to her husband. These articles also were found and traced to the possession of the prisoners. Mr. Johnson himself saw

Tickle and Eliza Craymour come out of his back yard, while Margaret Craymour stood at the end of the passage. The magistrates sentence the two Craymours and Tickle to be imprisoned for a month, and then sent to a reformatory for five years. Fitzpatrick was sent to prison for six weeks. Immediately the decisions were announced the girls set up a fearful screaming, which their female relatives increased considerably out of pure sympathy, and several police were required to half carry, half push, them out of court.

Combining a short prison sentence with several years in a reformatory was a common punishment for thieving kids – usually for those with more than one conviction. In April 1870 a lad called Thomas Judge was sent to prison for a month followed by a five-year residency in a reformatory for stealing some blacking worth just one shilling. Blacking ink or paste was used to clean and polish shoes, floors and doorsteps.

The 11-year-old had taken the blacking from a grocer's in the St Helens Market Place. However, Thomas had three previous convictions to his name for which he'd been "well whipped" and served prison terms of 3 days, 14 days and one month's duration.

It's difficult to know if the stealing had been at the direction of his parents or not. Although one offence had involved stealing toys from St Helens Market, on other occasions a loaf of bread had been taken from a shop in Church Street and gin stolen from a house in Cotham Street. But the toys offence had been committed at the age of 9 in concert with his 8-year-old brother Michael and another boy. It was believed the threesome had hidden themselves in the market all night with their parents seemingly unconcerned by their absence from home.

But having their child placed in a reformatory did not mean that parents could wash their hands of them. Fathers were required to contribute to the cost of their keep and two months later, Thomas

Judge Senior was summoned to St Helens Petty Sessions for refusing to support his son.

An order of one shilling a week was made against him. If Judge continued to make no payments, he would be brought back to court and probably jailed. Interestingly his boy was confined to the Clarence Reformatory ship, which since 1864 had been run by the Liverpool Catholic Reformatory Association. The converted warship was moored on the Mersey at New Ferry, near Birkenhead, and accommodated around 200 bad lads until 1884. That was when six of the boys set fire to the ship!

Some children probably responded positively to their harsh sentences and abandoned their life of petty crime. However, Thomas Judge Junior was not the only child who continued breaking the law. Perhaps the severe punishments embittered the youngsters and made them more determined than ever to flout the authorities.

On April 26th 1873, the St Helens Newspaper described the punishment that young William Riley had received in court:

Wm. Riley, aged ten years, was charged with stealing fivepence from the till of James Dennet, publican, Raven street. The wife of the prosecutor deposed that on Friday last she found the boy in her place with his hand in the till, and she gave him into custody. Supt. Ludlum said he had been already imprisoned on a similar charge, and his parents seemed to have lost all control over him. The bench ordered him to be imprisoned for fourteen days, and then sent to a reformatory for five years. The mother of the prisoner, who was present, seemed to be indignant at the sentence on her hopeful, and was about to give voice to her indignation, when she was removed.

The boy served his fortnight prison term but did not go to the reformatory because he was considered too young. Yes, old enough for Kirkdale Gaol but not old enough for a young person's reformatory! Perhaps, despite its harshness, such an institution might have done him some good, as by the time William was fourteen he was a recidivist criminal.

The boy had served five terms of imprisonment and been whipped on more than one occasion – all for stealing small amounts of cash. The prison sentences increased in length with each conviction, with the latest in October 1877 being a term of six months for stealing 7s 6d.

STEALING BREAD FROM BOLD

It was so common for magistrates in the St Helens Petty Sessions to send children to prison that newspaper reports on such cases tended to be brief. On October 18th 1873, the St Helens Newspaper described the theft of a loaf of bread from the Bold Heath home of engine driver William Holley:

> Robert McGregor Campbell, a ragged youth, was charged with stealing a loaf, the property of Wm. Holley, Mill-road, Bold. Eliza Holley, wife of the prosecutor, said that on Tuesday, while she was in her garden, she saw the prisoner come out of her house and on inquiring what he wanted, he said he had been seeking some bread. He then went away. She then missed the loaf and had him apprehended. He was sent to prison for a fortnight.

And that was it. So we are left to wonder the age of the "ragged youth" and whether he had any previous convictions. That was probably unlikely, as lads that were repeat offenders were likely to be whipped and sent to reformatories – as well as imprisoned. And the stealing of bread is likely to come under my "need" category, as opposed to "greed" – but there is no way of being sure.

There was certainly little sympathy given for being a poor "ragged youth". Being dressed in little more than rags suggested that you did not come from a respectable family – and that, as previously stated in my coal stealing example – counted against you in court.

In February 1872 Michael Callaghan appeared in St Helens Petty Sessions charged with stealing a pay tally from Pilkingtons – and spent much of his time crying in the courtroom. Or, as the Newspaper put it, he *"...kept up a crying accompaniment to the narrative of his misdeeds"*.

Superintendent James Ludlam of St Helens Police acted as prosecutor and told the court that the 11-year-old's sister was a prostitute; his mother was serving six months for theft and his brother was in a reformatory. Michael's unhappy family circumstances were seen as confirming he was a bad lad in need of punishment. So he was ordered to serve a month in prison and then be placed in a reformatory for five years. The Newspaper headlined their report: *"A Branch of A Bad Tree"*.

However, children from a better-off family able to afford a solicitor and with a caring mother could expect more favourable treatment from the court. Jane Fielding and her husband Thomas ran a furniture shop in Bridge Street in St Helens, although by 1864 the couple were living apart.

On October 25th of that year their eldest child appeared in court charged with theft. Not only was a solicitor hired to plead the mother's case not to send her daughter to prison – but the 33-year-old got down on her knees in the courtroom to beg for leniency. This is how the St Helens Newspaper described what they called a *"Painful Case"*:

Mary Fielding, twelve years of age, whose mother keeps a small furniture shop in Bridge-street, was charged with stealing three brooches and three shirt collars, valued altogether at 8s, the property of George Parr, Cowley Vale. There was a sale at the house of prosecutor, on the previous Thursday, and the girl was seen about the place, and after the articles were missed the collars were found on her. She denied taking the brooches, and as to the collars she said, when apprehended, that a woman in black had dropped them, and she merely picked them up. She now pleaded guilty to taking the collars, when Mr. Beasley informed the bench that the girl had been locked up since the previous Thursday, and hoped for her sake that the bench would never think of sending her to gaol, to mix up with the worst of characters; if they did the responsibility would, in a great measure, rest on them.

He suggested to them — for the sake of the child's nearly broken hearted mother, who was in court — that the bench would order her to be discharged, with a good whipping by her mother, in the presence of an officer, or keep her in gaol another day or two. Whilst the magistrates were conferring together, the mother of the girl was on her knees in the body of the hall. The Chairman having inquired whether the girl had no father, Mr Beasley spoke in the affirmative, adding, however, that he was not living with his wife. The Chairman told the woman to get up, and said that being the first offence, they should — all the circumstances considered — deal leniently with her. She must be imprisoned for three days, and the bench hoped the mother would not only look well after her, but give her a severe correction as well.

Mary had been in police custody for five days and was sentenced to remain in her cell for three days more — and then likely receive a whipping from her mother. As I've previously stated, by the 1860s courts could not order convicted girls to be birched. However, there was nothing to stop magistrates from recommending parents undertake a "severe correction" of their female offspring.

A far less sympathetic hearing was given at the same court hearing to a nine-year-old disabled boy and his mother — both by the magistrates and the Newspaper. Ellen Tierney was not perceived as being respectable and no solicitor could be afforded to plead for her and her boy's case and so they were both despatched to Kirkdale Gaol. Upon arrival at the prison, the pair would likely have been separated with no concern expressed in court about any undesirables they might come into contact with. This is the Newspaper's report of the case:

Ellen Tierney, a dirty looking customer, and her boy, a cripple in her arms, nine years of age, were charged with attempting to rob the till of Mary Tickle, shopkeeper in Bridge-street. Prosecutrix, on Sunday evening, was seated in the kitchen, when she fancied she heard something knock against the scales in the shop. On hearing the same noise a second time, she got up, and looking inside the shop she saw a lad's shadow on the wall. She went in the direction of the money drawer, and there found the young urchin helping himself. The female prisoner, who was watching outside, then went in, pretending to have been looking after him, and said, "He's not taken anything; I've been watching him." She also suggested that the prosecutrix should slap his bottom, and send him off. The lad stated that his mother was begging in the street, and denied positively that the woman (female prisoner) was his mother. After sending the lad away, witness followed at a short distance, to see if the female prisoner took any notice of him, but she did not until they came near to the canal. Witness, on her return home, met a policeman and sent him after them. The female prisoner had nothing to say, only that she was compelled to beg. They were both committed to Kirkdale for 14 days.

St. Helens Newspaper & Advertiser

(FORMERLY "WEEKLY NEWS")

WITH WHICH IS INCORPORATED BY PURCHASE THE

ST. HELENS INTELLIGENCER, ESTABLISHED 1853.

PUBLISHED EVERY TUESDAY AND SATURDAY

SATURDAY, JANUARY 23, 1869.

[THREE HALF]

BAG OF NAILS

On 11th October 1869, ten-year-old Thomas Fearney was charged with stealing 9lb. of nails valued at 2s 7d from Andrew Kurtz's chemical works at Sutton. The boy's father was dead and his mother was living in Newcastle and so Thomas was in the care of his grandfather, who was employed at the Kurtz works.

One might have thought that the magistrates would have shown the lad some understanding and given him a warning. But the little lad was sent to prison for a month and then onto a reformatory for five years. All for nicking nails.

Again there was no mention in the brief newspaper report of Thomas Fearney committing any previous crimes – although the reformatory sentence suggests it had not been the 10-year-old's first court appearance.

The only case of hard labour being imposed on children by St Helens magistrates that I've been able to find within the newspaper archives occurred on October 11th 1864. That was after two lads had helped themselves to a few beans in a farmer's field. Four days later the Newspaper wrote:

> Two boys, named Joseph Lawton and Henry Boardman, of St. Helens, each eleven years old, were brought up charged by police-constable Shaw, with stealing horse beans from a field belonging to Mr. Robert Birchall, farmer, at Rainford and valued at threepence. They were each sentenced - though their first offence – to seven days' imprisonment with hard labour.

It is possible that the governor of Kirkdale prison decided not to impose hard labour on the boys. It was up to his discretion as to whether he considered prisoners sufficiently able to suffer the backbreaking punishment of the infamous treadmill – although exceptions were rare.

SETTING FIRE TO A HAYSTACK

There could be very harsh treatment for those who committed agricultural crimes in the 19th century. In 1852 Thomas Kenwright was sentenced to transportation to Australia for 15 years for setting fire to a barn at Bold. This was in revenge for his employer scolding the married man with 7 children for the careless manner in which he'd fed his cows.

Although Kenwright appears to have committed his crime of arson, there is a strong possibility that John Alcock did not. In the 1861 census the boy is listed as eleven years of age and living in Appleton Street in St Helens. Just over a year later, the lad received severe punishment after being convicted of setting fire to a haystack. The St Helens Newspaper described John's first court appearance on October 22nd 1862:

At the St. Helens Police Court, held at Messrs. Pilkingtons' office, before R. Pilkington, Esq., on Saturday last, John Edward Alcock, 13 years of age, son of Mr. R. Alcock, beerhouse-keeper, Peasley Cross, was brought up on a charge of setting fire to a haystack belonging to Mr. Richard Baxter, of Peasley Cross Farm. Mr. Marsh [solicitor] appeared for the prisoner. Mr. Baxter stated that the stack contained about 18 tons of hay, and there were some four tons damaged, the value of which would be £20; the fire occurred between three and four o'clock; the wind was south-west at the time of the fire; the stack was railed all round. James Edwards, a painter, said he was passing the stack on Friday afternoon, and when opposite he heard a man shout out, "The stack's on fire." He saw a boy, similar in size to the prisoner, a few yards off the stack, running from it towards the railway; he also saw a man running after the boy. In cross-examination, the witness said the stack was not railed all round; it was broken down near the stump where the prisoner was passing; he saw him fully five minutes running, and he was caught at the bottom of the field; it would be about a quarter past three when he first saw the fire. [Questioned] By Mr Thomas – The boy had on dark clothes like the prisoner's.

Mary Harrison said she saw a boy running down the field, and a man named Heward running after him. Cross-examined [she said] – There's a cart road within three yards of the stack, leading to Bournes & Robinson's colliery; it is divided from it by a stone wall. Edward Heward, a boot and shoe maker, living in Peasley Cross Lane, stated that on the previous afternoon, about twenty minutes past three, his attention was called by his wife to the stack, which was on fire. He went to his door, and saw it blazing to the top. He saw a lad running down the field, and ran down the lane after him, to meet him at the gate at the bottom; met him coming out at the gate; when he met him he saw who he was, and the boy began to cry, and said "It wasn't me as struck the match." Witness asked him who it was, the boy replied, "I don't know – it's a lad from Greenbank". In consequence of knowing who the lad was he let him go, and ran off to the engine-house at St. Helens. Cross-examined by Mr. Marsh – Did you not say, "What did you set that stack on fire for?" Witness: No. Haven't you learnt that way of frightening people from being in the police force? I don't know what you mean; I learnt the truth; I did chastise the boy about three or four months ago, for throwing a stone into my shop; the lad might have been coming from Dagger's farm; the land is opposite to the stack; the house is a quarter of a mile distant; it would be a near cut from his house.

Police-sergeant Firth stated that about half-past four he apprehended the prisoner, and charged him with the offence, to which he replied "I didn't do it; I never was in the field at all – no nearer than the foot-walk; I had been in Mr. Dagger's farm to beg some turnip tops, and I saw a boy running from towards the stack; he had a red head, and was without a jacket, and had a dirty face, and was going towards the red water." Witness found nothing in the shape of matches on the prisoner. The prisoner, after being cautioned, said, "I was not near the rick [hay stack]."

He was then fully committed to take his trial at the next Liverpool assizes, on the charge of wilful arson. Bail was accepted – his father in £50 and two sureties in £25 each. On Monday, the depositions of two more witnesses were read over and signed before the magistrates at the Police Court. Ellen Bamber, a little girl about 12 years old stated she saw the boy creep under a gate near the stack, and go to the middle of the stack, and stoop down with his hands in a peculiar position – witness imitated how they were, and represented them as holding a light to keep it from being blown out – immediately after she saw the stack on fire. She told her mother, but she made her go in. Jane Bamber, the girl's mother, said the girl had told her what had been said.

The South Lancashire Winter Assizes took place six weeks later on December 10th 1862 – and there was good news for John Alcock. A witness had come forward to support his claim of another boy having been in the field at the time of the fire.

Surely there was now a strong element of doubt as to John's involvement in the crime? It also appears the prosecution had failed to establish a motivation for him setting the fire.

Prison record for John Edward Alcock whose court sentence included being "once privately whipped with a Birch Rod and to receive twenty strokes".

However, the jury was unimpressed by the new evidence and found the boy guilty. It appears that the testimony of a 12-year-old girl had condemned a boy of a similar age to a terrible punishment. The judge sentenced John to 9 months in prison and to receive 20 strokes of the birch.

THROWING STONES AT A TRAIN

Railway vandalism in St Helens has been a huge problem in the past and, of course, is still an issue today. But there could be harsh penalties in the 19th century for children making a nuisance of themselves on the track – even if no damage or injuries were caused.

On September 7th 1872, 14-year-old Peter Dolan appeared in court charged with throwing stones at a train near Ravenhead on the St Helens to Liverpool line. One of his missiles had struck a carriage within inches of a window. Although there was no reported damage to the train, the lad still received 14 days in prison.

THE ARTFUL DODGER

The girl involved in this next case did not actually serve any prison time – but she did spend at least three days in a police cell. Incarceration could be a terrifying experience for children. Film director Alfred Hitchcock used to relate how as a boy he had once been locked up after committing some minor misdemeanour. To teach him a lesson, Alfred's father arranged for his son to spend a few hours in a police cell. The experience, he said, affected him badly and led to many of the dark themes within his films.

The case from 1862 concerned a girl called Mary Lightfoot who, along with a friend, had designed a cunning way to earn some coppers. The 12-year-old from Arthur Street *(which used to be off Waterloo Street)* in St Helens would "kidnap" toddlers. After a couple of hours she'd return them to their worried mothers claiming she'd found their child wandering the streets. For reuniting the "lost" boy or girl with their parents, Mary would inevitably receive a small reward.

Of course, such frauds had a limited life and Mary was soon in police custody. This is how the St Helens Weekly News of June 21st 1862 reported her subsequent court appearance under the headline: *"Child Stealing – An Artful and Youthful Dodger"*. Note the repeated use of the word "it" to describe a young child, something that was then very common in newspaper reports.

Mary Lightfoot, a girl aged about 12 years, was brought before the magistrates on Tuesday, and remanded successively to Wednesday and Thursday, charged with child stealing under the following circumstances: About ten days ago she was seen near Caldwell's Dam, at the place known as Sutton Lodge, but which is now converted into a number of cottages, with a young child about 18 months or two years old, and which she said she had found in Westfield-street. It appears that upon that occasion the cottagers had some doubt about the truth of her statement, and one of them having heard of a child been lost from the neighbourhood of the "Finger Post," the extreme opposite end of the town, went with the girl Lightfoot, to see whether the child in her possession was the one missing, but found it was not. The child, as the prisoner knew, belonged to a Mrs. Brown, and after keeping it from home several hours, returned it, pretending she had found it, and got twopence as a reward.

On last Monday, the prisoner was again in the neighbourhood of Sutton Lodge with a child, and, on being questioned by the cottagers, she said it was the same she had there a week before; and made many other statements which the women not believing, one of their number went with her, but the prisoner didn't want her, and resolutely refused to carry the child, and when they got near to the railway station she ran away. Fortunately the child could tell that it lived near the "Sefton Arms," and kept telling the woman that its home was "a bit further," and "a bit further," until they reached Mr. Wrigley's shop, when it said, "this is our shop." The woman restored the child to its mother who said it had been sent out with a penny to a neighbour's, to fetch a bottle of nettle beer. It appeared the prisoner had purchased an orange with the penny, and had enticed the child away from near its home by promising to take it to its grandmother's, and give it some flowers.

Sergeant Rowland stated that the prisoner had said that another girl of the name of Carroll, had "put her up" to the dodge, and that Carroll, who was placed before the magistrates on Tuesday, had, a week or two ago, taken one of Mrs. Butler's children and kept it away for upwards of an hour, and then taken it back and said she had found it in Westfield-street, and had got a small reward for her supposed kindness in finding and bringing it back; and that she (Carroll) had suggested to the prisoner that they should go and look for little children that could not talk, and take them away and get some money for bringing them back, and save the money and have a tea-party.

The Sergeant also stated that the father of the prisoner had told him, that she was addicted to staying out till between eleven and twelve o'clock at night, and that he (the father) could do no good with her. On Wednesday the girl's mother attended, but her conduct was such as to draw from the bench a severe reprimand, and the girl was again locked up. On Thursday the prisoner's father attended, and on his promising to take care of her in future, she was discharged.

The private enterprise of Mary Lightfoot and her friend called Carroll reminds me of the activities of Agnes Burns which occurred some 54 years later. One of Agnes's regular stunts during August 1916 was to burst into tears on the street.

When passers-by asked her what the matter was, the 11-year-old would tell them that she'd lost a tanner. Soon the girl from Fern Street *(near North Road)* would have "another" sixpence collected from the passing Good Samaritans who felt sorry for her – which Agnes then spent at the pictures!

ANIMAL VIGOUR

AND LANCASHIRE, CHESHIRE, AND GENERAL ADVERTISER.
PUBLISHED EVERY MONDAY, WEDNESDAY, AND FRIDAY MORNING.
No. 3059.—VOL. XLVII.   WEDNESDAY, NOVEMBER 11, 1857.   PRICE (Unstamped) 1½D. | in the Country, 2d. extra.

In November 1857, the Liverpool Mercury published a lengthy article on Kirkdale Gaol. The newspaper stated that some eight or nine years earlier, a small detached building had been created within the prison walls to accommodate juveniles. This contained 42 cells but as there were insufficient young prisoners to permanently fill the block, the adult shoemakers in prison were placed with them. That was so that if any of the lads were given long sentences, they could be taught the trade of shoemaking.

I expect few of the boys became cobblers, as most received short sentences as part of the short, sharp, shock system of Victorian justice. That's why the 42 cells designated for kids were never filled, in spite of large numbers of young people passing through the prison each year. Kirkdale's own statistics revealed that out of 2,098 prisoners committed to the gaol in 1856, 100 had been aged 14 or under and 369 were between 15 and 19. The majority of inmates were in their twenties, or as the Mercury put it:

It will be seen from this return that by far the most criminal age is between 20 and 30 years, the time when animal vigour and activity are at the highest.

GIVE THEIR CHILDREN A FLOGGING

And finally, although this last example also did not lead to a prison sentence, the case demonstrates the alternative form of justice that awaited many boys convicted of theft. At a hearing of St Helens Petty Sessions on August 9th 1869, seven lads were charged with breaking into an unoccupied house in Peasley Cross Lane.

The boys were aged between eight and fifteen and had stripped the house of gas piping, five bells and "everything else they could well carry off". A miner called James Greene said one of them called Edward Heeney – who appeared to only be 9 – had sold him a bell for a penny. An 8-year-old called John Bennett from Greenough Street was the main witness against the lads but he broke down while giving evidence, as the Newspaper described:

He gave a tolerably circumstantial account of the offence, and then let out that he was amongst them himself. As if the admission of participation was too much for his feelings, he dissolved into sobs at once, and could not proceed until Supt. Ludlam had poured an immense quantity of balmy encouragement into his ear.

The Chairman of the Bench said if the parents would undertake to give their children a flogging in the presence of a police officer they would dismiss the case. The boys were then removed from the court to receive their lashings, the Newspaper writing:

The young delinquents, doubtless, had a keen sense of what was coming, and reflected it in their faces.

The Curious Excuses Given In Court

"I was talking to my 'bacca. I was for sure.
I smokes thick twist, gentlemen."

The magistrates in St Helens' courts heard a lot of dubious excuses over the years as defendants attempted to explain away their criminal behaviour. At times the JPs must have found it hard to keep a straight face! This chapter contains twenty examples of some of the most unlikely explanations.

THE PEEPING TOMS OF SUTTON MANOR

"The Peeping Toms Of Sutton Manor" was the headline to an article in the St Helens Reporter of June 28th 1932 that described a recent court case. When I first saw the newspaper's sub-heading of *"Looking For Larks"*, I assumed that had been the frank admission of the voyeurs; that they'd admitted spying on a pair of lovers but said it had only been a bit of fun with no harm intended.

But in actual fact it had been the men's excuse for lying in long grass near to the courting couple. They denied being so-called "peeping Toms" but instead claimed to have been bird watchers trying to catch larks! This is a condensed version of the lengthy newspaper report:

"Peeping Toms," who turned violent when they were accused of spying on a couple in a field at Sutton Manor, appeared before the magistrates at the Borough Police Court on Friday. They were William Jones, 14, Scott-avenue, George Jones, his brother, 74, Tennyson-street and Cornelius Finch, Wordsworth-street, Sutton Manor, and they were summoned for (1) conduct likely to cause a breach of the peace and (2) assaulting John Roscoe. P.C. Williams told the Bench that on Sunday, June 19, about 10-15 p.m., he was in Jubits-lane, when he received a communication. Returning to his police station at Sutton Manor, he saw John Roscoe and Edith Welsby with two other men. Roscoe had two swellings over each eye, his face was covered with blood, and his suit was covered [in] blood and soil. William Jones said that he had been for a walk when he met his brother and Finch. Walking through the field, they saw some larks "let" in the grass. The three of them dropped down on their stomachs and began to crawl through the grass in search of the birds' nests. "I felt a kick in my ribs and jumped up," continued Jones. "I said to Roscoe, 'What's the kick for?' and struck back in self-defence. After fighting for about five minutes we finished. I began to explain why we were crawling through the grass, and Roscoe gave me a punch in the eye." Defendant denied spying on the couple and declared that he did not know they were there. "I have a wife and family, and do not want to be brought up here for that," he said. "Why did you crawl on your stomach?" asked Mr. T. A. Turton (Magistrates' Clerk). "It was just out of curiosity to see these birds," he replied.

"Is that your idea of the proper method of catching a lark, or finding larks' nests, by crawling on your stomach through long grass on a Sunday night at 10:15?", asked Mr. W. G. Gentry [magistrate]. Jones said it was not. He only wanted to see if there were any nests there. According to George Jones, his brother had crawled about ten yards through the grass when Roscoe ran across the field to him. "Finch and I heard a scuffle and ran forward and endeavoured to part them," he went on. "They continued to fight and it happened that Roscoe received the worst of it. I daresay that is the reason why he brought this case to Court." He denied that they were there for the purpose of spying on the couple.

John Roscoe, joiner, 5, Leicester-street, Thatto Heath, the complainant, said that he was sitting with Edith Welsby by the side of Rimmer's farm at Sutton Manor. "I saw a man crawling through the grass and I went to him," he continued. "He would not answer me when I first spoke to him but continued to lie on the grass with his face covered with his hands. I later found that his name was William Jones. The other two defendants were some yards away and were also lying on the grass." Continuing, Roscoe said that he touched Jones with his foot and defendant jumped up and they began to fight. Jones tripped witness [John Roscoe] up and before he could regain his feet he was kicked and struck by both brothers. Finch stood at one side. In the end William Jones fell to the ground and witness accompanied Edith Welsby to the police station, where the matter was reported.

Mr. W. G. Gentry asked witness if he suspected that defendants were spying as "Peeping Toms" on him and his young lady. "Yes, that is what they were doing," replied Roscoe. Edith Welsby, mental nurse, 10, Victoria-terrace, Rainhill, supported Roscoe's statement. On the first charge defendants were bound over to keep the peace for twelve months, in sureties of £1 each. On the assault charge, the case against Finch was dismissed, but the Joneses were fined £2 each.

COAL CHUCKING AT NOISY CATS

When the Prescot Petty Sessions were held on February 1st 1870 a curious case of coal stealing was heard. Mary Phillips from New Road in Prescot accused her neighbour, Rebecca Andrews, of taking two pieces. The 54-year-old had caught Rebecca at 2 am helping herself to the coal in her husband's yard that adjoined their house. However, her neighbour claimed she'd simply picked up two small pieces to throw at noisy cats! In fact cats played an important part in the 61-year-old woman's defence. Some time ago Rebecca had lost some chickens and she thought that cats had been responsible. So she set a trap for the felines, which caught and killed Mary's cat. This, as might be imagined, led to much animosity between the pair. Rebecca's counsel claimed that her neighbour had threatened revenge and the case showed the woman's "spitefulness and triviality". The Bench appeared to agree as they dismissed the case.

THE NAG THAT DIDN'T LIKE SOLDIERS' UNIFORMS

Thomas Edwardson was a volunteer in the 2nd Lancashire Light Horse. The mounted rifle corps was created as a result of an invasion scare – but only lasted about 15 years. On November 29th 1869, Edwardson was charged in St Helens Police Court with neglecting to pay a 30-shilling subscription. That was essentially a series of fines imposed on him for not attending drills.

Just because your military service was voluntary, did not mean you could pick and choose when you turned up. And Captain Biram, the commander of the corps, gave evidence at the hearing at St Helens Town Hall that Edwardson had only attended four out of sixteen drills.

His main excuse for not turning up was that his horse did not like his military uniform. He said a sack had to be placed over the animal's eyes so he could mount up. However, seemingly adopting the military strategy that the best form of defence is attack, Edwardson had a right old moan about his unit.

The part-time soldier complained of sometimes being ordered to go to Liverpool to drill in order to accommodate half a dozen Liverpool men, "who rode on broken-kneed cab horses". On one occasion, he claimed, one of these nags had fallen over and the rider had torn Edwardson's trousers with his sabre.

He reckoned to have actually attended six drills but that often nobody was present to drill the men and give them credit for their attendance. He said Captain Biram did not attend drills very often and complained of frequently being forced to ride for six hours without food. This he thought unfair, as he said he was not as fat as his captain! The St Helens Newspaper wrote:

[Police] Superintendent Ludlam told him that he ought not to speak in that way about his captain, but he was indifferent to all advice, and kept grumbling until the magistrates had made up their minds. He was then ordered to pay 30s. and costs of court.

SHOOTING A HEN TO MAKE HIS GUN SAFE

Another part-time soldier appeared in the St Helens Petty Sessions on September 12th 1870. George Cox from Queen Street, near North Road, was accused of shooting his neighbour's hen – but claimed he'd done it in order to make his gun safe. This is how the case was reported in the St Helens Newspaper:

George Cox, a volunteer, was charged with discharging firearms in his back yard. He pleaded guilty. A witness [the neighbour] said he went upstairs to clean himself before going to church when he heard two shots let off. He looked out and saw Cox in his own yard. With one of the shots he knocked a hen of mine down. It was not dead, but we had to kill it afterwards. The prisoner, in defence, said he had been at the review and his rifle was loaded; he only discharged it to render it safe in the house. Fined 1s and costs and 2s 6d for the witness.

WATCH OUT FOR THE BANJO MEN!

The Monday morning sitting of the St Helens Petty Sessions in the 1870s always had a long list of weekend drunks to deal with. The St Helens Newspaper's report on the cases heard on June 6th 1870 bore the headline "The Drunk and Disorderly Roll". The unusual excuse given by a young woman called Jane Rose for committing a breach of the peace in Liverpool Road was that she was only defending herself after being attacked by a "banjo man". Jane was bound over to keep the peace for a month and no doubt kept her distance from banjo men in the future.

That was probably sensible, as the banjo fraternity seemed a peculiar lot with some not being too fussy about where their strings came from. In September 1870 the Liverpool Courier would ask: "What punishment can said to be adequate for a miscreant caught in the act of skinning a live cat to make a banjo?" The answer was seemingly three months, as that was the maximum penalty, much to the disgust of the Courier as they reported on a recent case.

TALKING TO TOBACCO

Countless individuals have appeared in court in St Helens over the years to face charges of threatening their neighbours. However, William Holland must be the only one who claimed that he had not been talking to a person – but to his tobacco! Even more remarkable is that the magistrates appeared to accept his claim.

Under the headline *"A Shindy Between Neighbours"*, the St Helens Newspaper of July 15th 1871 published this report on the dispute between residents of Bruce Street, off Pigot Street:

> William Holland was summoned for assaulting Ellen Hesketh on the Monday previous. The complainant said that she had been examined as a witness against the wife of the defendant a week previous, and when she returned to her own home Mrs. Holland accused her of having committed perjury. In the evening the defendant [William Holland] came out to his door-step, and began to sharpen a knife upon it. As soon as it was sufficiently keen he went to complainant and told her he would put "a yard of steel through her thorax." A neighbour woman was called, and she gave

confirming evidence, having heard the row from her own bedroom. Defendant: I was talking to my 'bacca. I was for sure. I smokes thick twist, gentlemen. I do for sure. (Laughter) Some women came forward in his behalf, and they bore out the tobacco theory to the fullest extent. He was a very much aggrieved man, according to them, some of the neighbours making a habit of annoying him and his wife. The case was dismissed.

TOBACCO CUTTING

Tobacco was also the excuse used by Thomas Glover in his defence. The labourer from Argyle Street in St Helens appeared in court on June 11th 1918 charged with common assault. However, he had not been talking to his "'bacca" – but claimed to have accidentally wounded his son-in-law while cutting some tobacco.

Glover had for some time been living with his daughter and her husband. But three days before the incident that led to the court case, the couple had asked him to leave. Widows and widowers were then much more likely to live with their adult children than today, which often led to arguments in overcrowded houses.

On the following day, Glover returned to the house for his clothes. He swore at his son John and then produced a pocket-knife. During a struggle, Glover's son-in-law, William Kemp, was stabbed on the back of his hand and it was only after the intervention of a neighbour that the man was disarmed.

However, in court Glover claimed he'd been turned out of the house so that his furniture could be stolen from him and he'd received a *"good hiding in the bargain"*. He also denied wilfully stabbing his son-in-law. Glover claimed that when the row began he just happened to be cutting tobacco and his son-in-law must have accidentally caught his hand against the knife when he attacked him. The Bench was unimpressed and Thomas Glover was fined 20 shillings or 14 days in prison.

The YMCA building in Duke Street in St Helens

BRINGING THE WILD WEST TO ST HELENS

On June 15th 1916, a boy called John Phillips from Brynn Street appeared in St Helens Police Court charged with stealing an £8 tent from the YMCA. Thomas Garner, the solicitor representing the 12-year-old, offered this excuse for his young client's behaviour:

> He is a boy scout, one of the Buffalo patrol, and has
> wanted to bring the Wild West nearer home.

Mr. Garner added that it was *"simply love of open-air life"* which led to the theft. This romantic explanation didn't impress the magistrates, who ordered the boy to be brought back to earth with six strokes of the birch rod!

THE UNFIT TONGUE

On August 21st 1917, Elizabeth Turner appeared in Prescot Police Court charged with "exposing for sale cooked tongue unfit for human consumption". A Mrs Taylor gave evidence that she'd bought a quarter pound of tongue from Mrs Turner's shop in Cook

Street in Whiston. When she got the meat home it smelt so bad that her husband refused to eat it. Without the refrigeration that we have today, shopkeepers had much greater difficulty in preventing food from going off – especially during summer.

Many people waited until Saturday night before buying perishable food, as shops would then sell items off cheap, knowing they wouldn't last until Monday. However, Elizabeth Turner had an unusual excuse for selling unfit food. She told the Bench that she'd had a cold at the time of the sale and hadn't been able to smell that the tongue had gone bad. Her claim of impaired senses through the sniffles didn't impress the magistrates who fined her £2.

THE GENTLEMAN WITH A DIRTY HABIT

On March 5th 1918, in Prescot Police Court, Hugh Williams – who described his employment status as a "gentleman" – was charged with spitting in a railway carriage. As well as being a dirty habit, spitting was then seen as a means of spreading TB. Williams from Huyton claimed he suffered from a condition that caused him to spit and it could come on so suddenly that he couldn't help himself. The Prescot magistrates fined the gentleman £2.

Two months later Williams returned to court. However, the "gentleman" was now describing himself as a "retired estate agent with plenty of money"! A fortnight after committing his first offence, Williams had been travelling in the first class carriage of a train to Huyton. Once again he began spitting in front of passengers, who reported him to the railway company. One disgusted witness even turned up at court to give evidence against the man, who had the maximum fine of £3 imposed on him.

PAWNING A COAT FOR SAFEKEEPING

On June 18th 1918 in St Helens Police Court, James Foster was accused of stealing a raincoat belonging to Harry Knifton of Halefield Street, near North Road, in St Helens. In fact Knifton had lent Foster the coat for a short time. When he failed to return it as promised, the police investigated and found it had been pawned in Liverpool. In court Foster pleaded innocence and said he'd taken Harry's coat to the pawnshop so it would be kept in a safe place! There were a number of previous convictions against Foster and the magistrates fined him twenty shillings.

THE WHEELBARROW BORROWER

Thomas Pickersgill of Berry's Lane in St Helens offered up a similar excuse on May 23rd 1921. He told magistrates that he had taken a wheelbarrow from Ashton's Green Colliery in Parr to stop it from being stolen. Of course, it was just a coincidence that his own wheelbarrow had broken down!

The 58-year-old miner had kept the barrow in his possession for a fortnight but insisted that he had planned to return it. *"If I had not taken the barrow the other men would have had it"*, Pickersgill claimed, as if he expected the colliery to thank him for his kindly act of crime prevention! The police said they had searched high and low for the stolen barrow and the magistrates imposed a fine of twenty shillings.

THE PONY THAT LIKED TO SHAKE HANDS

A magistrate helped William Turton to develop his strange excuse. The Duke Street chimney sweep appeared in court on August 26th 1918 charged with leaving his horse and cart unattended in Dentons Green Lane in St Helens. The sweep told the magistrates that his little pony was very quiet and would even shake hands with anybody who asked it.

Turton's defence to the charge was that the pony had been moved out of a passage while he'd been inside a house sweeping a chimney. To which a magistrate quipped: *"You mean it went out into the road to shake hands with somebody?"* Turton put the blame on women who spoiled his pony through petting it and feeding the animal with sugar. This, he claimed, led to the pony following them about and straying. On being told by the Bench that it was dangerous for a horse and cart to stray, the sweep replied: *"I will have to sell it and get a flying machine."*

OOPS! I'M IN THE WRONG HOUSE!

A curious case was heard in the St Helens Petty Sessions on May 13th 1872, in which Margaret Murphy charged Michael Drennan with threatening to assault her. The woman from Park Road in Parr said that the defendant had burst into her house at 8:30pm on one evening and swore *"with terrible oaths"* that he would take her life.

Drennan told the court he had no ill-feeling towards the woman and did not even know her. He claimed he'd been visiting the house of his sister and had gone into Mrs Murphy's home by mistake. Drennan insisted it had been Margaret Murphy who did the name-calling and he'd not molested her in any way. The magistrates accepted his strange excuse and the charge was dismissed.

THE VERY BUSY SUTTON GROCER'S SHOP

This is Junction Lane in Sutton where William Appleton kept a small grocer's shop. He appeared in court on September 6th 1918

charged with having his premises open at 9:10pm. The wartime regulations forced shops to close early in order to save on coal and gas. Appleton's wife claimed that their premises had been open late as she was serving Annie Smith from Herbert Street who had been waiting 90 minutes to get served. It must have been a very busy little shop! That was an excuse that the magistrates didn't buy and William Appleton, his wife Sarah and 16-year-old Annie Smith, were each fined 10 shillings. Annie was fined for aiding and abetting the offence.

THE FLU BREAK-IN

Whenever I've had a bad case of flu, there's only one place I've ever wanted to go. And that's bed. Strangely enough, I've never felt the urge to go out and rob a house! However, in St Helens Police Court on February 24th 1919, a youth blamed influenza for breaking into Henry Plumley's home. John Arnold admitting taking some money, a mouth organ and a key from the house in Whittle Street – but added, *"Not with the intention of stealing them"*.

Arnold from Duke Street claimed that he had been suffering from influenza and consequently had not known what he was doing. The cash he took belonged to Plumley's children and had been kept in a moneybox, although there was a dispute over the amount. The burglar said there had been less than a shilling, although Mrs Plumley reckoned on four shillings.

The boy's father told the court that he had searched his son upon his return home but had found no money. When asked in court why he had searched John, he replied it was to see if his son had any cigarettes on him, as he did not allow him to smoke.

The Chief Constable said the lad's parents were *"very respectable"* and he had no previous convictions. So the magistrates decided to dismiss the case upon payment of court costs. However John would be placed under the supervision of the Police Court probation officer for twelve months. Justice then did often depend upon your family background.

THE MALARIA EXCUSE

In St Helens Police Court on July 30th 1920, an ex-soldier used malaria to explain his assault on a sixteen-year-old-girl. Ellen Johnson told the court that she had been walking along Chester Lane when a man grabbed her by the waist and attempted to drag her into a field. When Ellen screamed, the attacker placed his hand over her mouth but she continued to resist him and he let her go. By the time the police arrived on the scene they found Ernest Foster from Burrows Lane in Eccleston being detained by the girl's father and some other men.

In court Foster's counsel said his client had spent three years during the war serving in Salonika in Greece and on six occasions had suffered from malaria. He had recently been in hospital in Whiston after enduring a relapse and *"a man suffering from that disease was not responsible for his actions"*.

This was one of the first cases heard by a female magistrate on the St Helens Bench and Evelyn Pilkington and two other magistrates fined Foster £5. The Chairman told the defendant that if it had not been for his malaria he might have been sent to prison.

MOTORING EXCUSES

In the early days of motor vehicles, the majority of drivers used acetylene gas lamps that had a tendency to go out during a journey. Of course, it was the responsibility of motorists to ensure the lights on their vehicle remained lit – but that could be tricky when it was the lamp located at their rear. When hauled into court for not having lights on their vehicle, the excuses poured out.

On October 13th 1916, William Webster was the defence counsel representing a lorry driver accused of driving without a red rear light. The solicitor told the St Helens Police Court that it hadn't been his client's fault that his lamp had not been lit when he arrived at the Lingholme – its going out had been an "act of God". Webster then said perhaps it wasn't right to blame the Almighty for the extinguished light and it would be better to attribute the event to the powers of darkness! The chairman of the magistrates Henry Oppenheim, himself a solicitor, was unimpressed and in fining the lorry driver five shillings replied that the cause was more likely to have been a dirty lamp than the Almighty.

Riding a motorbike and sidecar in Church Street in St Helens

The convoluted lighting systems in use on the early motor vehicles offered plenty of potential for creative defences. On October 22nd 1920, Claude Fillingham appeared in St Helens Police Court charged with failing to illuminate his motorcycle with a red rear light. He told the Bench that his lady passenger in the sidecar must have sat on the gas connecting tube and cut off the supply to the lamp. That surely would have meant a rather uncomfortable ride for the woman and Fillingham was fined 5 shillings.

In another case in the Police Court on November 15th 1920, a car driver was charged with not having a red rear light in Church Street. Frank Foulkes blamed St Helens Corporation for the poor state of the roads, telling the court that they were *"very bumpy, and the jolting must have put the light out"*. The excuse was accepted and the case was dismissed upon payment of costs.

As well as lighting offences, many of the early motorists found themselves in court charged with speeding. With speed guns yet to be invented, assessing the rate that a motor car was travelling was subjective. As a rule of thumb, the driver would insist in court that he had been motoring at half the speed claimed by the police.

When Antonio Valenciennes appeared in St Helens Police Court on September 25th 1908 he offered a curious reason for this disparity. The Swiss manager of a motor works at St Helens Junction was charged with *"furiously driving a motor car"* in Robins Lane in Sutton. Valenciennes told the magistrates that the car was only half-finished and to an onlooker would simply appear to have been travelling faster than it actually was.

The fact that he was driving an un-roadworthy, unfinished car at speeds up to 30mph did not appear to worry him! However, Valenciennes' excuse did not impress the magistrates who fined him £5 and costs, the equivalent for many then of 3 weeks' wages.

THE FEEBLE FEET TICKLING EXPLANATION

Brutal wife-beaters invariably attempted to shift the blame for their violence onto their spouse. The woman could be accused of being a drunkard, of being unfaithful, of using provocative language and of not having their husband's tea on the table upon his return home from work. I think the latter was seen as the more serious offence!

However, the St Helens Examiner of September 26th 1891 described how Martin Mullins of Market Street had blamed something else for his wife Martha's facial injuries. The man had been charged with assault through repeatedly pulling Martha out of bed, striking her about her head and cutting her lips. Although Mullins admitted that he had struck his wife once or twice after she had provoked him "by her conduct and talk towards him", the injuries to his wife's mouth were claimed as having been quite unintentional.

Mullins' solicitor told the court that when his client was asleep, his wife repeatedly woke him by tickling his feet. That led to the husband inadvertently kicking out and accidentally striking his wife on the mouth with his feet. Unsurprisingly, there was much laughter from the public benches in court at that feeble excuse and the defendant was bound over to keep the peace for three months.

The Fighting Women Of St Helens!

*"It was nothing in the world o' goodness
but a jingle amongst women."*

They bred women tough in 19th century St Helens! Life was tough and some females in the poorer parts of the town – particularly in Parr and Greenbank *(the district surrounding Liverpool Road)* – became hard as nails. The women would row, use the foulest of language and fight with their fists, stones, drinking glasses and any other object that came to hand. And they didn't seem to care who their opponents were – with men, their sisters, mothers, neighbours and the police often in their firing line.

In describing what they considered a typical dispute between women, the St Helens Newspaper of September 28th 1869 reported on a recent court hearing. The case concerned a row in Liverpool Road in which Catherine Evans had been charged with assaulting Mary O'Reilly – although the attack had centred on verbal abuse rather than violence. The Newspaper wrote:

> The quarrel was one of the usual character, trivial in its origin, and ridiculous in its nature, but studded with filthy expressions. The defendant was bound over.

Three years later in a separate squabble, the Newspaper commented on the court evidence given by a middle-aged woman called Ellen Rigby from Parr:

> Being a female, of course, the court was treated to a rehash of the most filthy language.

When rows escalated and fists or weapons were employed instead of just tongues, the women were not shy of playing their part –

even against men. On September 14th 1868 in the St Helens Petty Sessions, a woman was blamed for starting a vicious battle in Park Road in Parr.

The combatants were Margaret Reilly, Michael Duffy and Peter Reilly who were all charged with breaching the peace by fighting. Under the headline *"A Parr Shindy"*, the St Helens Newspaper explained that the fight required three constables to put down, before adding:

> The woman, who, it would seem, was the originator of the fight, distinguished herself by her vigorous use of both fists and tongue despite the receipt of some very ugly usage. The fun was somewhat diversified by a tremendous thrashing Duffy gave his wife. They were all bound over.

PRECIPITATED A FISTIC COMBAT

On January 25th 1873 the Newspaper described a three-cornered "fistic combat". The report told how an Eccleston fish dealer called Bridget Whelan had called at the house of Ann Cowan to collect the sum of 1s 4d. However, the debt was denied and Mrs Cowan called Mrs Whelan and Esther Taylor, a watching neighbour, a "bad name". That started a fight between the three women – and a subsequent court case – as the paper related:

> Esther Taylor was charged with assaulting Ann Cowan, on the 11th inst. Mr. Swift defended. Complainant said that there was a dispute between her and another person, a Mrs. Whelan, about a "few coppers," and while it was proceeding defendant ran up and assaulted her severely. Subsequently she brandished a knife and threatened to kill complainant and her pigs as well. In reply to Mr. Swift, she denied that she had struck the first blow, and gave a general denial to all the assertions on the other side. For the defence he called Bridget Whelan, a fish dealer, who said that she called upon

plaintiff for 1s. 4d. which she owed her. Plaintiff said that she did not owe the money and called witness a bad name, which she also applied to defendant, as she stood at her own door. This led to an angry discussion and complainant then precipitated a fistic combat by striking defendant in the eye, and giving her a black eye. The bench convicted, and fined defendant 2s. 6d. and costs.

Of course, women who physically fought with their stronger husbands were likely to come off second best. In this curious court case reported by the Newspaper on October 4th 1873, a couple – who appeared to live in College Street – rowed over a late night peace offering after a row. The husband had not tried to patch things up with his beloved by bringing home flowers. Instead, he offered her a cabbage!

James Rimmer pleaded not guilty to the charge of assaulting his wife Mary. Complainant said that he came home on Wednesday morning at two o'clock, bringing in a red cabbage as a peace offering. She declined it, and threw it on the floor, and then he called her a white cabbage. Some other words led to the production of the poker by the woman, and the exercise of his fists by the man. He went up stairs to bed, and while he was trying to snatch a sleep his amiable spouse broke his watch, smashed the cabbage, disordered his bed, deprived him of bolster [pillow] on which he lay, and finally produced a pail of water with which to perform an unlooked for ablution. Defendant to use his own words, "thought it about time to see who was the master," and gave her a trifle of punishment. The bench fined him 1s. and costs, and the Chairman gave the unhappy couple a serious lecture on their conduct.

Anther case where a pail of water performed an "unlooked for ablution" took place in Thatto Heath during the following month.

The primitive sanitary arrangements then in place in much of the St Helens borough often led to female neighbours falling out and fighting with each other.

On November 22nd 1873, the St Helens Newspaper described how a spat between Marjory Gaskell and Jane Platt over dirty water had led to one of the parties getting drenched with a bucket full of H20 – accidentally, of course!

It appeared that the origin of the quarrel between the parties was a habit practised by defendant [Jane Platt] of throwing dirty water in front of "Dame Margery's" residence. Both live at Thatto Heath, and are neighbours. On the 10th inst the complainant presumed to spread some cinders in front of her house to neutralise the effect of any water that might be thrown on the spot, and the defendant, seeing this precaution taken, came up with her brush to sweep it away. In the little altercation which ensued, the complainant "accidentally" drenched defendant with a bucket of water. It was intended to be thrown out in the ordinary way, but unluckily defendant was in the line of flight and got a bath.

Thereupon, warmed up by the cold application, she rushed at the complainant, knocked her down, stood over her, brandishing the sweeping brush, and made fierce threats to commit homicide at least. The defendant, in her own behalf, said that as the houses, in one of which she lives, were without a sewer, the residents were obliged to dispose of dirty water by casting afar over the surface of the ground; and as the wind sometimes blew it up and down, dissatisfaction was frequently given to a neighbour. In this case she merely resented a deliberate insult, with as little violence as possible. The Chairman [of the Bench] said she would have to pay 5 shillings and costs for taking the law into her own hands.

THE THROWING OF STONES AND GLASSES

The breaking of windows often occurred when rows between women got heated. At the St Helens Petty Sessions on October 12th 1868, Ann Wright was charged with maliciously breaking the window of Nicholas Fletcher in Duke Street.

The woman had asked his wife for a loan and when it was refused took her revenge on their glass. The St Helens Newspaper said Ann Wright accompanied the "projection of each missile with uncomplimentary expressions". The case was adjourned for a month to see if a settlement could be agreed between the parties.

That was the pragmatic solution, as "wrangles" between women that resulted in a court summons often had sequels when revenge was sought. This example is taken from the St Helens Weekly News of August 27th 1862 and also illustrates how stones made handy weapons for women to throw at each other:

Ellen Shaw and Margaret Dunn were brought up on a charge of assaulting Sarah Naylor on Friday, the day previous. It appeared that the parties lived down a court in Tontine-street, and early in the week there was a row in the same place, between the Dunns and Naylors, the former being brought up for an assault on Wednesday; this quarrel originated in some measure from that. According to complainant's statement, she was throwing some water out into the court, when Shaw set upon her and threw a large stone at her, hitting her on the mouth. Both defendants then pulled and dragged her about and she ran into the house.

After being in a short time, she heard a knocking, and on going out found it was them comed again and another assault commenced, Dunn having a knife and threatening to stick it in her, and, Shaw with a pair of pincers pulled her about the head and she had to have it dressed at the doctor's. The policeman said he heard a scream when he was in Tontine-street and on going found complainant bleeding from the head. The magistrates after hearing the whole of the case, sent the parties to try and make a peaceable settlement, which with Sergeant Mather's assistance they did.

Just how long the ladies' ceasefire lasted, was, of course, another matter! But throwing a stone at your foe also came with the advantage of being able to claim that you were chucking it at something else – and your aim was wonky!

At the St Helens Petty Sessions on March 6th 1871, Mary Loughlin of Glover Street *(off Liverpool Road)* faced a charge of assaulting Maria Farmer by throwing a stone that struck her neighbour on the head. Although Mary's version was that she had chucked the stone at a dog and it had accidentally hit Mrs Farmer. Mary Loughlin was fined 2s 6d and costs.

Public rows were great entertainment and huge crowds could rapidly assemble at the onset of a squabble – well, there was no television then! Even in the sparsely populated district of Clock Face, the residents were soon out of their homes to watch their neighbours battle it out.

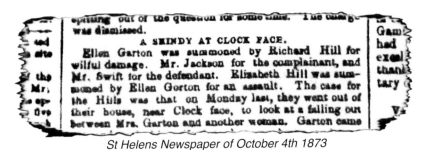

St Helens Newspaper of October 4th 1873

However, the St Helens Newspaper on October 4th 1873 revealed how a 31-year-old engine driver and his wife had got dragged into a dispute – and paid a penalty through having their windows smashed and accusations of immorality showered upon them. The article was published in the Newspaper under the headline *"A Shindy At Clock Face"*:

Ellen Garton was summoned by Richard Hill for wilful damage. Mr. Jackson [acted as counsel] for the complainant, and Mr. Swift for the defendant. Elizabeth Hill was [counter] summoned by Ellen Garton for an assault. The case for the Hills was that on Monday last, they went out of their house, near Clock face, to look at a falling out between Mrs Garton and another woman. [Mr.] Garton came out and took his wife into her own house, and some altercation took place inside which eventuated in the smashing of a window. This set the crowd laughing, upon which Mrs. Garton ran out and assailed Mrs. Hill in violent and insulting language.

Some words having passed, Mrs. Hill and her husband went home. That night, when they were at rest, though not asleep, Mrs. Garton opened a fusillade of stones against the house next to Hill's and belonging to him, breaking a sheet of glass which would take 12s. 4d. to replace. During the examination of the witnesses it was elicited that Mrs. Garton denied to Hill the credit of being the parent of the children which his wife has presented to him since their marriage. There was no direct evidence that defendant had broken the glass in question. It was proved that she went to the front of the house, and threw stones at it, and the supposition was that the broken glass was a portion of the damage done.

For the defence Mrs. Garton was examined. In reply to her advocate (Mr. Swift) she stated significantly, at the very onset, that [Mr.] Garton was the father of her children. On the occasion in question, Mrs. Hill accused her of drunkenness and connubial infidelity. This vexed Garton, who threatened to assault her, and Hill then ran up threatening to perform the extraordinary feat of knocking Garton, into "rooks and heaps, and a cocked hat." She could not have spoken to Mrs. Hill about children, when that lady was not the mother of any, but she called her "a blacklooking thing." The decision of the bench was that Mrs. Hill should be bound over to keep the peace. The other cases would be dismissed.

THIEVES AND LIARS

Pub landladies in St Helens had a reputation for toughness. One even had a street named after her in tribute to her fighting qualities! It is claimed that Elisabeth Seddon was called "Hell Bess" because of her prowess in dealing with rowdy drunks. At some point the name of the Sutton beerhouse took on her own nickname. Then the street followed and before long Hell Bess Lane became Ell Bess Lane – probably because of complaints from the clergy – and in 1902 it was re-named Sherdley Road.

Esther Francis was another landlady who stood for no messing. She and her husband Thomas ran a beerhouse in Park Road in Parr and in August 1873 the 51-year-old appeared in court charged with assault. A miner called Lambert Heaton claimed that Mrs Francis had called him and his wife "thieves and liars" after a dispute over the non-return of a half-gallon bottle that the landlady had lent them.

Then as he was leaving the beerhouse, the furious Mrs Francis had thrown a jug at the 40-year-old, striking him on the face and cutting him severely. However, Heaton's description of what had occurred had – as usual – been rather selective. The St Helens Newspaper of August 30th described what witness Samuel Liptrot told the court:

He said that on the evening in question the defendant was sewing behind the bar, when complainant came in, and addressed her thus: "Well old d_____, fill me a glass of ale." She refused, and asked him about a bottle lent to him. He said it had been returned, and when she denied it, he called her a liar. As he was going out, he called her still more insulting names, and she flung the jug at his head. The Bench considered there was nothing in the defence to justify the throwing of the jug, and they would inflict a fine of £2 and £14 s. 6d. costs.

Note how like "Hell Bess" was ruled unsuitable as the name for a road, the Newspaper felt unable to print the word "devil" in its report.

PULLING OUT CLUMPS OF HAIR

As well as using their fists and throwing stones, hair was routinely pulled in female fights. On September 26th 1868, the Newspaper described a court case in which Ann Woodward was charged with assaulting a neighbour called Catherine Walsh. It was alleged that Mrs Woodward had attempted to bake some bread in an oven belonging to Catherine Walsh's mother. The paper wrote:

No sooner had she made known her intention than the complainant came forward to resist this aggression on what she considered as family property, and an up-and-down fight ensued, in the course of which Mrs. Walsh managed to entwine her fingers most lovingly in Mrs. Woodward's hair, some of which she forcibly extracted.

The magistrates ruled that both women were equally to blame and dismissed the case. Then in the Petty Sessions on March 21st 1870, Mary Fleming's solicitor displayed a large clump of hair, which he claimed Ellen Bowe had yanked out of his client's scalp. This had occurred during a fight in Davis Street in Pocket Nook in which the pair had fought "like bulldogs", as one witness put it.

A woman called Mary McKeegan had attempted to rouse a crowd of 100 people to drive Mary Fleming and her husband "out of the country" and during the row one of them threw a 20lb stone through a window. The magistrates decided to bind over all four involved in the melee, including Mary Fleming.

Sandfield Crescent in the mainly Irish Greenbank district of St Helens

More hair was brought into court on May 16th 1870 when Margaret McCabe was charged with assaulting Johana Hogan from Sandfield Crescent in Greenbank. This is how the Newspaper reported the case:

From the statement of the complainant it appears that the parties are neighbours, and that some ill feeling had arisen through those fruitful sources of quarrelling amongst the women – "the childer". The complainant said on the day in question the defendant commenced to "bullyrag" her about her (complainant's) daughter having struck the defendant's son. The defendant, according to the complainant, digressed from bad language, and made a savage attack on her, tearing her hair out by handfuls, a "specimen" of which she exhibited to the bench. The defendant denied the assault, and said the hair had been got up for the occasion, and wound up by stating that the complainant had attempted to stab her several times with a knife, an assertion which was bitterly, and with much volubility, repudiated by the complainant. The defendant, who throughout considered herself, of course, the injured party, was bound over to keep the peace for 3 months, herself in £5, and one surety of £5.

THE FIGHTING LADIES OF PARR

For some reason Parr bred more female disputes than any other part of St Helens. Writing about a case heard in the Petty Sessions on September 27th 1869, the St Helens Newspaper commented on the deteriorating relations between two Parr residents called Elizabeth Godfrey and Mary Finch:

> Once they were very good neighbours, and now – well the relations common in the district have been established between them.

Miss Godfrey told the court her neighbour had called her foul names, slapped her cheek and spat in her face. Of course, this had not been unprovoked, as the Newspaper explained:

> There had been a regular under-current of slanderous whispering going on for some time previous to the assault, in which both women had borne a fair share. A Mrs. Clare gave corroboratory evidence as to the assault. She said that as the defendant poured forth very abusive epithets, the complainant kept saying "ditto," which was a very agreeable way of throwing them back without actually uttering the words.

Yes, you couldn't get in trouble for being abusive if you simply said "ditto" to your foe! Mrs Clare added that Elizabeth Godfrey was an unmarried mother and caused laughter by adding that there were more mothers than married women in Parr. The magistrates decided that the warring neighbours should be given a chance to settle their differences amicably.

The Newspaper's dim view of the women of Parr was reinforced by their report on a court hearing held on April 11th 1870. Ann Helsby from Johnson Street – "a stout, middleaged woman, whose appearance was in no way improved by a black eye" – was charged with assaulting Mary Ashton in Parr.

The latter had rowed with her mother and after Ann Helsby had heard of the argument, she decided to go into Mary Ashton's house and give the woman a piece of her mind. The Newspaper takes up the rest of the story:

> Having got inside, she began a dissertation on the duties of children towards their parents, which was pretty forcible if not convincing; but she used no violence of a physical kind until the complainant made the apparently vague observation that she did not want any drunken women coming into her house. Somehow it went home very directly, for Mrs. Helsby retorted by a blow. As might be expected this was the signal for a fight, and having transferred operations to the street, the neighbours were delighted with the sight of a real female encounter.

> The complainant got worsted in a short time, and was enabled to escape through the indiscreet sympathy of a friend. One Mrs. Mannion, seeing Mrs. Ashton slow to come up to the scratch, requested a truce, and the next moment she was in full retreat, pursued by the victor, and encouraged by the sweet voices of the crowd. In their absence the complainant retired into her own house, and was repairing damages, when the defendant returned, puffing like a locomotive. This time she changed her tactics,

and vented her ire on the domestic crockery, with the debris of which she overlaid the floor of the kitchen. Some neighbours put a stop to this new mode of mosaic tiling, and got her out of the house, to which, however, she subsequently returned, armed with a basin, which she threw at her opponent's head. We should not omit to state that the language was of a character current amongst a very large class in Parr. The bench requested Mrs. Helsby to pay £2, and 6s. 6d. costs, or put up at Kirkdale [Gaol] for a month.

THE FIGHTING LADIES OF GREENBANK

Neighbours also regularly fell out in Greenbank, the predominantly Irish working-class district around Liverpool Road – which also included Liverpool Street, Sandfield Crescent, Mount Street, Bpld Street etc. Under the heading *"Women Pugilists"* the St Helens Newspaper described a hearing in the Petty Sessions on July 18th 1870 concerning a female battle in Greenbank:

Mary Buckley and Bridget Glen were charged with a breach of the peace by fighting on the 15th July in High-street, Greenbank. Police-constable 638 said the defendants were creating a great disturbance together, with Buckley's husband, by indulging in a "free fight" in the back yard. Glen said the other woman, Buckley, attacked her with a rolling pin, and "she was rolling about in her gores in the gutter". In addition to physical force arguments, the usual amount of un-Parliamentary epithets were launched at each other by the fair belligerents. – They were both bound over to keep the peace.

Then on September 20th 1873, the Newspaper described how two Greenbank women in dispute with a female neighbour had decided to take out their grievance on the woman's husband – using their fists and a poker:

Bridget Martin and Barbara Scarry were charged with assaulting John O'Reilly on the 6th instant. John O'Reilly said that on the 6th instant he was standing at the door of his house in Liverpool street, when the prisoner Martin came up and struck him on the face, giving him a black eye. Shortly afterwards Scully came across the road from her house with a poker hidden under her dress, and hit him on the forehead with it, cutting his head severely. He had it dressed by Dr. Gaskell. He had not been able to go to work since. The plaintiff's wife and daughter corroborated his statement. Bridget Martin was dismissed, and Scarry was ordered to pay £2 and costs. There was a cross-summons issued by Bridget Martin against Mrs. O'Reilly, for using defamatory language. Complainant said that defendant had told several neighbours untruths regarding complainant's character. Two witnesses also supported her statement. The case was dismissed.

No weapons were used in my next Greenbank example from the St Helens Newspaper – apart from tongues, and they could prove to be vicious missiles!

The verbal combatants were all residents in the Liverpool Road / Street area of St Helens and under the heading of *"A Characteristic Female Row,"* the Newspaper of June 14th 1873 described in its own inimitable way the subsequent court case involving the two warring parties:

Elizabeth Bell appeared to answer a charge of having done violence to the feelings of Margaret Baxter, who prayed that the defendant might be placed under the restraint of bail. The complainant, who nursed an obstreperous child while she gave her evidence, told a story in effect that Mrs. Bell had rung the changes on her character and pedigree in very libellous and scandalous language, imputing gross immorality of conduct to her. While she was the victim of this treatment she stood where all women who quarrel seem to stand – on her own doorstep.

And she wound up her statement with this lucid declaration: "I cannot stand to be threatened and called names, first in one house and then in another, which way likewise is not my desire." A young woman who gave the name of Ann Pigott came up to corroborate, and although she was telling a story in favour of one side she put on that expression of rigid impartiality which is so common to the interesting young ladies who are always convenient when a row takes place.

The report then described the remarks of an "aged dame" called Esther Fillingham who in the 1871 census was a 63-year-old widow living in Liverpool Road – but had since moved to Parr:

For the defence an aged dame who acknowledged the name of Esther Fillingham came forward to blacken the complainant's character. She opened with an observation that as she lived in Parr, far removed from the litigants, she had no personal feeling in favour of either; and after this logical assurance she recited her version of the row. It is not exactly such as can be repeated, for although the old woman seemed to labour under a difficulty of breathing, she was enthusiastic enough to struggle through all the nice compliments which had passed between the disputants.

She was too old a woman, she said, to tell a lie, and had therefore told "God's truth." The defendant, before hearing the court decision, appealed deftly to the paternal feelings of their worships by a neat allusion to her maternity of ten children, but it did not save her from being ordered to find sureties to keep the peace.

The St Helens Newspaper did like to have fun at the expense of the Greenbank women when their petty squabbles were told in court. To some extent that was middle-class snobbery of the poorly-educated working class.

However, the latter were responsible for filling up the courts by issuing numerous summonses against their enemies, which could be obtained for as little as 6 shillings. That was a fair sum if your income was only 20 shillings a week – but no doubt the money would be found if your rage required amelioration in court.

In this next case heard in the Petty Sessions on June 24th 1872, the paper's report employed the word "clan" to describe the warring families and commented on the colourful hats that the protagonists from Liverpool Street wore:

Rose Agnes, a smart-looking representative of the house of O'Reilly, was summoned by Margaret, of the clan McDermott, for an assault committed on the 15th June. The injured female found a knight errant in Mr. Swift [solicitor]. Both females were well dressed, and wore wonderful hats and bonnets, trimmed after the latest fashion, and variegated in colouring with green, blue, lavender, crimson, white, yellow, and some less definable tinges. These head-dresses, mounted upon mounds of hair supplied by nature and art, made a pleasant sight in ill keeping with the disgusting expressions which not only the principals but the witnesses made use of quite freely. From the statement of the complainant it would appear that on the date named she observed her mother getting a thrashing in the street from one of the O'Reillys, and she showed her agony by wringing her hands, and wailing vigorously.

Rose Agnes saw the dramatic effort, and stopped it in the middle by a kick in the knee, and some very uncomplimentary epithets which were not intended to assuage the pain of the assault. Miss Riley's cross-examination was aimed at showing that her antagonist had provoked the assault by using language calculated to make the object of it uneasy about her paternity, and suspicious regarding the domestic arrangements of the household some years back. The imputation was denied by the complainant. Miss Drennan, of Mount street, a young woman with a perfect prodigy of a bonnet, and a pyramid of miscellaneous hair to match, deposed to the use of very usual but very disgusting language.

The defendant's version of the matter was that complainant spit in her face, without any preliminary notice, and treated her to some very inelegant language. She called a man named John Greenall to testify in her behalf. The burden of his tale was made up of bad language, delivered with a readiness which showed that no matter what part of a story may be forgotten, memories are wonderfully retentive of such parts of speech. Mrs. Greenall, John's wife, was the last witness, and she tried to do something for her husband by ignoring the relationship, and speaking of him as "that gentleman." When she had finished her evidence, which was a mere collaboration of her husband's, the magistrates dismissed the case.

BLAME THE CHILDREN

Children's arguments were often the sparks that rekindled smouldering antagonism between mothers. One little darling would complain to their parent about the behaviour of another child. The mother of the first would tick off the latter who would complain to his / her own mother – setting the parents off at loggerheads, usually not for the first time. In September 1868, the St Helens Newspaper wrote of a dispute in Parr in which Fanny Welding had issued a summons against Mary Tidswell accusing her of assault:

The evidence in this case showed that, as usual, the row began through the petty quarrels of the children, and led to angry feeling and blows between the women.

Over the Christmas period of that year, Louise Haddock and Elizabeth Pollatt had a big bust up in Rainford that their kids had begun – but which Elizabeth's husband finished off. The Newspaper wrote:

It appeared that the quarrel between the women originated amongst their children, and was marked by the usual features of Billingsgate, screaming, shouting, and hair pulling, with the slight variation of a few vigorous administered taps on the complainant [Louise Haddock] by the defendant's husband.

The Newspaper regularly referred to Billingsgate in their reports on female fights, as the London fish market had a very bad reputation for such goings on.

Then on August 10th 1869, the Newspaper reported on a case brought against three women that had once again been initiated by a child – but in a somewhat different way:

Jane Flynn complained of Sarah Maxwell, Eliza Maxwell, Mary Fitzgibbons, and Ellen Weir, for having assaulted her on the 30th ult. Mr Swift prosecuted. Of course, they pleaded not guilty. The scene of the row was Greenbank. The complainant had gone as a witness to the court against some boy, and the defendants, for that act, appeared determined to be revenged upon her. The collision took place on the 30th ult. and proved very disastrous to very many articles of wearing apparel and fashionable display. Mrs Flynn, who keeps a beerhouse, and is a decent looking widow, was rather wantonly attacked, first by tongue and then by force of arms. One of them accused her of having killed her husband. Another suggested that they should "make bits of her" in the street.

After this they contributed to that result as far as her finery was concerned. Being very hard pressed, in fact in a very disagreeable pickle, Mrs. Flynn caught up a pickle bottle, as a very appropriate missile, and hurled it amongst her assailants, but fortune happily "preserved" them from obstructing its course. The apparition of a police officer finally put an end to the fight, and the defendants retreated from the scene, flourishing pieces of caps, ribbons, remnants of dresses, and other trophies of the fight. We should say that two stones, with which Mrs. Flynn complained of having been struck, were produced, and combined they would have filled a tolerable hat. The defendants were ordered to be bound over [and] pay £1 1s to the complainant.

THE RELIGIOUS DIMENSION

There was often a religious / sectarian dimension to arguments. Calling someone an "orange so and so", does not sound very threatening today – even if the so and so is replaced by an expletive.

However, when Catholics and Protestants rowed, orange *(or more accurately "Orange")* routinely became the adjective of choice for the Catholics. Protestants had their own insults to fling at Catholics, with "Papish so-and-so" being a popular one.

The origin of the dispute usually had no connection with the religion of the combatants – but once name-calling began, they could not resist adding religious and racial slurs. This is how the St Helens Weekly News of July 12th 1862 described a skirmish between two women of different religious creeds:

ORANGEISM AMONG THE WOMEN – Margaret Weir was charged with assaulting Catherine Bevis on the 27th ult., at Pocket Nook. Mr. Marsh appeared for complainant. It appeared that complainant was passing defendant's door and some remarks were passed, which led to the assault, defendant bringing out a poker and saying, "You bloody Orange bitch come up, and I'll do for you." Defendant would have it that Bevis was the assaulting party, but the bench thought otherwise, and inflicted a fine of 41s. with 5s. 6d. costs, or 14 days.

Mrs. Weir also brought her own prosecution against a man called James Owens who she alleged had assaulted her and called her "a bloody Papish bitch", but the Bench dismissed the case.

Another example of religious name-calling featured in the Newspaper's detailed account of a case in the Petty Sessions on July 12th 1869. In this Barbara Skelly pleaded not guilty to a charge of smashing windows in John Hogan's beerhouse. A cabbage rather curiously again features in the Newspaper's account of the court proceedings!

The case was that the defendant [Skelly] went to the beerhouse of the plaintiff, to look for her husband, believing he was there, but the plaintiff denied him. She was angry at this, and she spat upon some cabbage which the complainant was enjoying very comfortably, and the latter, who was furious at the act, jumped up, seized the wholesome vegetables, and dashed them into his antagonist's face. Then ensued some language of the description usually brought into court, in the course of which the defendant was called various names before which "Orange" was invariably used as an adjective. The secret of the row lay in the fact that on one occasion the defendant wrote a private letter to Superintendent Ludlam, informing him that complainant was breaking the Spirit Act on Sunday mornings. One Margaret Littler, a servant woman to the complainant, was called to give evidence, and on being asked the usual question, "What are you?" replied, "A Protestant, sir," to the great amusement of the idlers in the court. Being enlightened as to what was really meant by the question [her job], she went on to give her evidence. The bench fined the defendant 10s.

Upon hearing this decision she [Skelly] became frantic, brandished a child she carried, and abused her antagonist roundly. She screamed out that she would put a stop to the "jerry wagging" on Sunday mornings, gloried in being a "b_____ informer," and otherwise conducted herself in such a disorderly manner that she had to be removed from the court. Her last words (within hearing) were she would not pay one farthing of the fine, if she were to rot in gaol.

THE PUGILISTIC PROSTITUTES

St. Helens Weekly News

AND ADVERTISER.

SATURDAY, APRIL, 26, 1862. [PRICE ONE PENNY]

Prostitution was rife in St Helens in the early 1860s – at least going by the many newspaper references to prostitutes then appearing in the town's courts. Some bore exotic names, such as "Black Diamond", who was sentenced to fourteen days in prison in 1862 for plying her trade.

The poorly regulated beerhouses could serve as brothels with male minders "looking after" the ladies and also, no doubt, looking after their own pockets. There did not appear to be much of a sisterhood amongst the ladies of the night, as they would sometimes end up fighting amongst themselves. On July 16th 1862, the St Helens Weekly News described how such an incident had led to a court appearance:

Mary Ann Caftey and Sarah McCoy, sister to "Crutchey" Ralph, were charged with committing a breach of the peace; and Andrew Spellman was charged with resisting the constable in the execution of his duty. The police-constable stated he saw the two "ladies" fighting in Bridge street, on Saturday night, and on going to them the male prisoner interfered and said he should not let them be taken, and struck him (witness), several times. It was stated he was a sort of bully for the prostitutes at "Crutchey" Ralph's, outside of whose beerhouse the row took place.

Another witness swore to Spellman striking the policeman. Spellman was fined 45s. 6d., including costs, and in default to go [to gaol] for one month. Caftey, (who is well known as a prostitute) was ordered to be bound over herself in £10 and two sureties of £5, to keep the peace for six months, or go to prison for a month, and the other "lady" had to find sureties, herself in £5 and two in £10 to keep the peace for 12 months or go for two months. The two former were taken off to prison but the latter found the sureties required. "Crutchey" Ralph, and another friend appearing for that purpose.

The beerhouse in question was at 18 Bridge Street and "Crutchey" Ralph appears to have been Ralph Woods, who in the 1861 census claimed to be a tailor as well as a beerhouse keeper.

Four persons – all described as "Man N. K." (i.e. Not Known) – were also listed in the census as resident at the beerhouse when the census was taken. Beerhouses were small places and rarely needed staff outside of the family. But Crutchey Ralph was employing three servants – who may have served up much more than beer!

THE HUSBAND BASHER

In Victorian times men hitting their wives was commonplace and only occasionally made the courts. Women were highly dependent upon their menfolk and so rarely complained. And a wife hitting her husband was an even rarer event.

However, Elizabeth Green appeared in the Prescot Sessions on October 4th 1869 facing such a charge, as the St Helens Newspaper described:

> Mrs. Green is a very violent woman – physically the "better half." On Saturday evening, when her help mate came home, he found her conducting a lingual contest with a neighbour; and, feeling displeased at such conduct, he offered her the alternative of ceasing or staying out. She chose neither, and on his attempting to eject her, she caught up a pan and cracked it on his head. She was ordered to be bound over for a month, but not having any friends obliging enough to be responsible for her conduct [i.e. stand sureties for her], she will pass that period in Kirkdale [prison in Liverpool].

THE TAUNTING WOMEN OF ST HELENS

After fist fighting, hair pulling, stone throwing and heated rows, the taunting of individuals by women seems mild! However, the persistency of such insults could drive victims to take out a court summons in the hope their harassers would be bound over. If that happened, sureties guaranteeing good behaviour would need to be provided, which could be lost if their annoying activities continued.

And some of these cases could be amusing – as in Roberts vs. Shaw in September 1873. Their hearing was connected to a Thatto Heath dispute in which two cousins had fallen out over a pigeon. The two men's quarrel led to a fight in which an ear was bitten off.

The Newspaper of September 6th described how the women of the district had subsequently taunting a relative of one of the men:

Elizabeth Shaw was charged with using abusive and irritating language towards Margaret Roberts. It appears that a brother of the complainant has been convicted of biting off another man's ear. Since then sundry neighbours have busied themselves giving her offence by oblique allusions to the circumstances. They ask her if she would like a bit of ear, and also indicate their meaning by pantomime. On the 19th ult., some words arose between the present litigants, and defendant taunted her on the sore subject, by putting her hand to her ear, and asking complainant if she required a new ear. Defendant was bound over for a month.

JUST A JINGLE AMONGST WOMEN

Another case of harassment was heard in St Helens Petty Sessions on January 22nd 1872. On that date Ann Pilkington resumed an action against Betsy Holland in which she accused the widow of defamation. The latter had been a charwoman in Pilkington's beerhouse in Coal Pit Lane (now Merton Bank Lane).

However, Mrs Holland had been sacked and seemingly in revenge had been spreading stories about the landlady. As Ann Pilkington's solicitor, Thomas Swift, put it in court, she had been telling the *most scandalous reports* that any respectable married woman could be subjected to.

However, Mrs Holland denied saying such things and at a previous hearing, the magistrates said the alleged comments appeared little more than gossip. That upset Mr Swift who declared:

If it went abroad in St Helens that one woman might slander another in that way, I do not know what the lower orders would come to.

This is how the Newspaper reported the resumed hearing:

It was now stated that when the parties left the court a week before, the defendant [verbally] attacked her opponent in the street, and continued to scandalise her all the way to Coalpit-lane, to the gratification of a crowd of idlers, to whom a violent-tongued woman is always a treat. Mary Ann O'Neill deposed to having heard the defendant call the complainant very vile names in the house of a Mrs. Barrow, naming a man named Hoe in connection with her.

Hoe was called and the complainant was called, and they both denied that any impropriety had ever taken place between them. Johanna Connolly was called by the defendant. She said it was nothing "in the world o' goodness but a jingle amongst women." The bench ordered the defendant to find two sureties of £5 each for six months.

THE FIGHTING FEMALE SHOP KEEPERS

Marine stores were a common type of junk shop in the 19th century. They often sold items of interest to sailors, hence their name – but they really sold anything, with much of it second-hand stuff, such as clothing.

On May 18th 1872, the St Helens Newspaper delightfully described how two rival shopkeepers from Liverpool Road had fought over a boy customer leading to an appearance in court:

Catherine Aspen, proprietress of a repository for rags and bones, professionally called a "marine store," was summoned by Bridget Mary Hayes, who rejoices in the ownership of a similar museum of curiosities, for an assault. The object of the proceedings was to have Mrs. Aspen bound over to keep the peace to all citizens in general, and to Mrs. Hayes in particular. The complainant, when she was sworn, made a statement to the effect that on the previous Tuesday her youthful daughter found a customer in the shape of a small lad who had a bag of rags to sell. Now the defendant had a habit, as Mrs. Hayes expressed it, of trying to "involve" all such people to her own store, and on this occasion she was as watchful and as energetic as ever. As soon as the boy and the bag were observed in companionship with the young Miss Hayes, the defendant attempted to capture what she considered a lawful prize by seizing it much as a policeman seizes an unruly law breaker.

Mrs. Hayes was attracted by the noise, being generally alive to her business, and she went outside immediately, although burdened with a child in her arms. She seized the bag boldly, and held on to it tenaciously. Her opponent became very wroth, and then dangerous, declared she would have the bag or a life, and intimated that as she did not intend to commit suicide, Mrs. Hayes would hardly be under any misapprehension as to whose life was in jeopardy. She struck out and the blow, being unfortunately ill-directed, fell upon the cheek of the innocent baby Mrs. Hayes was nursing. The infant acknowledged the undeserved assault by a succession of screams, and the mother got frightened and drew off, leaving her triumphant opponent to carry off boy, bag, rags, and bones, to her own premises.

In opening the defence, Mr. Marsh [solicitor] grew indignant that such a "palterly" case should be brought before the court, and asked the bench to dismiss it. He called several persons to show that Mrs. Hayes was the individual who had provoked the disturbance. The defendant's statement was that the boy who carried the bones of contention in his bag was one of her customers, and in the habit of contributing to her museum for trifling considerations. Mrs Hayes's daughter had blandished him on this occasion, and she thought she was justified in resisting such a proceeding. Of course she never committed an assault at all, but had her arm scratched by Mrs. Hayes until the blood came. The magistrates ordered her to find two more burgesses to guarantee for her peacefulness during the ensuing month.

In other words Catherine Aspen (or Aspin) had to find two more persons prepared to pay £5 sureties to guarantee her good behaviour for a month – having only recently been bound over for another row and forced to find sureties.

The Weird & Wonderful Things
St Helens Folk Have Said...

This chapter is devoted to a compilation of quotations from St Helens people that have appeared in local newspapers.

...**ABOUT THE MOTOR CAR** – At the 28th annual dinner of the St Helens Cyclists' Club in February 1904, the then mayor Joseph Massey praised the cycle as the *"most marvellous machine existing today"*. Comparing the bike with the motor car, Alderman Massey was quoted in Cycling magazine of March 2nd 1904 as declaring:

Joseph Massey

The motorcar is a fool of a thing. Some people may like it; I do not. The other day I was out riding on a motorcar, when it ran into a wall and I found myself on my back.

LIVE LETTERS
CONDUCTED BY THE OLD CODGERS

"MOTHER OF FOUR," writes from Parr, St. Helens, Lancs:

DO people who decry family allowances really want to turn the clock back ! What is the point of progress if the younger generation are not to benefit from it !
People have been bemoaning their lot since

An island

...**ABOUT THE SHAWL SOLUTION** – The Daily Mirror's "Old Codgers" was the letters column that the fictional pair hosted between 1935 and 1990 under the banner "Live Letters". During that 55-year period, many St Helens' residents had their queries answered, gave advice, demonstrated St Helens' wit and expressed their thoughts on issues of the day. Some contributors penned their full name or adopted a pseudonym to identify themselves – but most used initials. On February 26th 1972, "Mrs E. K. from St Helens" won the accolade of "Live Letter of The Week" with her shawl solution to dealing with children:

> No doubt there's a lot to be said for the modern generation, and some of their capabilities amaze us old 'uns. But I still prefer our way of loving children. We used to wrap a huge shawl around ourselves and our child, who would snuggle closer to enjoy the feeling of security and love. These days a child has no sooner found its feet than it is being dragged from shop to shop. The child cries because it gets tired, and then the smacking starts. One sees this routine every day in town and it makes me wish the shawl was still in use. I know I'm old-fashioned, but that's the way I like it – and I'm sure today's children would, too.

...ABOUT THE QUEEN'S BLOODY CURTAINS! – Then on April 21st 1972, "J. D., St. Helens, Lancs." wrote this letter to the Mirror:

> I took my mother to London earlier this week as a special treat. She's sixty-five and had never been to London before. I took her to see Buckingham Palace and she stood there staring at the residence of the Queen. Then she turned to me and said in disbelief, "She hasn't got a bit of bloody curtain up!"

...ABOUT KISSING YOUR WIFE – "Mrs. E. McM., St. Helens, Lancs" was the name attached to this missive published in the Old Codgers' column on March 31st 1958:

> Every week my husband gives me my house keeping money on the day after pay-day. He stands with his back to the fire dressed in overcoat and cap, ready to go to his work. He then puts his hand in his right-hand trouser pocket, hands

me the notes which are always folded into four, says "Ta" and walks out without another word. Once I hinted that some husbands kiss their wives before they go to work. He just looked at me and said: "What for?"

...ABOUT BAREFOOT NEWS BOYS – On July 31st 1970, the St Helens Reporter described how Richard Eden, of wholesale newsagents Abel Heywood & Sons of Haydock Street, was celebrating 50 years in the newspaper trade. The brief piece provided a first-hand account of the widespread poverty in the town during the 1920s, with shoe-less newsboys selling their papers on the streets of St Helens:

I've been in the business so long I must have handled millions of newspapers. Looking back, don't let anyone kid you they were the good old days. They were the bad old days and I hope they never return. I remember the barefoot boys queuing up in all weathers, hail, rain, and snow so that they could be first in the line for their papers. They were bad days. People were poverty stricken.

...ABOUT GOSSIPY SUTTON WOMEN – An anonymous letter written to the St Helens Reporter in September 1915 said:

My advice to anyone thinking of coming to live at Sutton is: "Don't you come unless you can lock yourself and your character up in a suit of chain armour, otherwise the 'poison bombs' manufactured by the women's tongues will blast you and your character to smithereens."

...ABOUT MOLESTING GIRLS – On January 23rd 1899, a young man called Henry Eaves of Oxford Street in St Helens was charged in court with assaulting a girl called Alice Lockhart. The 14-year-old had been returning to her home in Cooper Street after undertaking a shopping errand when Eaves grabbed hold of her shawl, causing Alice to scream and run away. Upon learning that the young man was drunk and had been staggering about the pavement, the prosecuting counsel Henry Riley told the Bench:

I am rather glad of that, as it is notorious how women and girls are assailed by the tongues and hands of idlers in our thoroughfares, and particularly at the corners of them. If the defendant had been sober I would have been compelled to ask the bench to make a striking example of him.

...ABOUT CHANGING TIMES – Mr A. Sharrock in the St Helens Star of August 23rd 1985 wrote:

Sutton before the war was a lovely place, a small community with church-goers in bowler hats and smart suits although some wore cloth caps. But all were friendly. Non-existent today. Pity that everything has gone.

...ABOUT EMIGRATION – Joining in a debate in the Daily Herald on May 3rd 1949 on the pros and cons of emigrating to another country, Percival Nicholson of 342 Fleet Lane in Parr wrote:

My advice is stay here. If you can't earn your living and be happy in this, the sweetest, land on earth, you can't do it anywhere.

...ABOUT THE H-BOMB – 69-year-old Lily Smith from Bramwell Street in Parr had this brief letter published in the Herald on December 10th 1958:

We have had only two summers that have been worth the name since 1950. I blame all the H-bomb tests. Scientists say this cannot be proved. I say stop the testing for two or three years and see what sort of weather we have.

...ABOUT INFANT MORTALITY – The O'Keefe family of doctors and councillors were a fixture in Parr and Sutton during the first half of the 20th century. At times controversial and outspoken, they were also seemingly much loved by their patients. In 1904 Dr Patrick O'Keefe claimed to have discovered why St Helens had an abnormally high infant mortality rate. Addressing the council's Health Committee, Dr O'Keefe said:

Mothers place their children in cradles too near the floor, and they thus lie in the draught from under the door, which sets up pulmonary troubles. If cradles are placed upon a chair the cold air will whistle harmless underneath.

...ABOUT MODERN GIRLS – This was what Dr Patrick's son, Dr Tom O'Keefe, had to say about modern girls in 1939:

I find and deplore that girls today are far less domesticated than they were twenty years ago. From a health point of view I feel this to be most unsatisfactory because these girls are the wives of tomorrow and this lack of domestication ill equips them for the really difficult task of maintaining in sound health, a family, probably on a meagre income. The schools might do more in this direction to make up for training which is lost at home.

...ABOUT CHIVALROUS MALE DRIVERS – What the St Helens Reporter called the *"worst winter in living memory"* took place at the end of 1939 and during early 1940. Their edition of February 2nd 1940 described children building Hitler snowmen, frozen water pipes, deliveries by sledge, the suspension of public transport and the effect of the blizzard cutting St Helens off from the rest of the world. They also quoted an unnamed young woman from Haydock:

Will you please allow me, a very ordinary girl, to say how very much I and a companion appreciate the kindly help given to us by certain motor drivers who have passed us as we tried to trudge our way to work? It meant a lot to us – the loss of wages if we did not turn up at our jobs, no matter what the cause. So we made up our minds to walk to town from our homes at Haydock. It was very hard going; but thanks to a lorry driver and in another case to the driver of a Government vehicle, we got to our jobs in time. The drivers were most kind and chivalrous, with none of that 'nonsense' which some of us have been taught to guard against, if ever we were invited to have a ride with strange drivers. We were nearly as lucky on our return journey. It was the driver of a private motor car who then gave us a lift, and he added to his kindness by giving us a big drink from a flask of hot cocoa, with which he had provided himself.

...ABOUT THE DIRTY QUEEN VIC – In 1968 St Helens celebrated its centenary since becoming a borough. In June of that year this letter written under the pseudonyms "Disgusted Females" was published in the St Helens Reporter:

Up to now in our centenary celebrations, we have noticed that the Town Hall has been decorated with streamers and window boxes of daffodils, the bus shelters have been given a face-lift but yet Queen Victoria's statue – which occupies the most prominent position in Victoria Square – remains disgustingly filthy. Is it any wonder the Queen did not come to St Helens on her recent visit to the North-West when we cannot even manage to give her ancestor a wash?

...ABOUT ROTTEN PEARS (And Rotten Buses!) – Another correspondent to the Reporter during that month was Ann Wilson of Newton Road in Parr. She criticised the state of the town's bus service (caused by staff shortages) and the fruit in local shops:

I have just arrived home from town, after waiting for buses, to find I have bought three rotten pears for 1s. 5d. I used to feel sorry for the shopkeepers in town thinking that the infrequency of the buses had stopped people from shopping there. Had I shopped locally I could have taken them back without having to pay 1s. 2d. bus fare. But they ARE going back. They must think we housewives are barmy to accept such rubbish.

...ABOUT TRAMS – On January 11th 1918 in St Helens Police Court, Chief Constable Ellerington told the Bench that when a police officer had told Harry Daglish that wartime legislation required him to travel by tram instead of by motor car in order to save petrol, the boss of the St Helens Foundry replied:

Do you expect me to ride in a dirty, draughty, inconvenient tramcar with dirty, verminous people, some of whom sit on your knee?

...ABOUT EPIDEMICS – A public meeting was held at St Helens Town Hall in January 1921 to approve St Helens Corporation's proposals for new legislation. The plans included stronger powers to close local schools during epidemics. One man called Ghee was reported as saying:

Closing schools to prevent the spread of infection is quite useless. It is put forward by the medical profession and the medical officer to instil fear into the minds of the people, just as children are frightened by tales of ghosts. It is an idea used simply for the aggrandisement of the officials of the health department.

The man argued his case so persuasively that the meeting voted against the enhanced powers.

...ABOUT BEAT GROUPS – In February 1964, Pilkington Brothers announced a ban on pop music at the St Helens Theatre Royal, which the glass firm had taken over and extensively refurbished. A spokesman told the local Press:

No one is taking a dead set against beat groups, but there could be risk of damage to the new theatre. You know what beat group followers are like when they get worked up by strong beat music. There are the hysterics, the stamping, the shrieking and the general over-excited behaviour. This is the last thing the firm wants in a theatre which cost £100,000 to renovate. These things can so easily get out of hand.

...ABOUT CORPORAL PUNISHMENT – On September 12th 1918, eight boys and one girl from Silkstone Street were charged in St Helens Police Court with stealing produce from an allotment in Knowsley Road belonging to John Anders. The Chairman of the Bench – Ald. Alfred Foote – said that nowadays parents did not look after their children, as they ought to. The 72-year-old retired general merchant said:

Ald. Alfred Foote

...they let them run about and do as they liked. If the parents thought the children deserved thrashing they ought to thrash them. What is the good of people spending time on plots if children can go and rob them and do damage?

...ABOUT GERMAN SOLDIERS – In 1916 Nathaniel Houghton had stood at the bar of the Fleece Hotel in Church Street in St Helens while recruiting for WW1 was taking place outside and said:

Only the scum of the Earth join the English Army. If the Germans landed here and came to St. Helens, I would be the first to meet them at the station, shake hands with them, and show them up the main street.

Strange how Houghton thought that German invaders would come by train! On February 17th the engineer from Bickerstaffe Street was sent to prison for 6 months with hard labour for "making statements likely to prejudice the recruiting, training, and discipline of his Majesty's forces."

...ABOUT AMERICAN SOLDIERS – The listed Nutgrove Hall in Nutgrove Road was known to many St Helens folk as "St Aggie's" – or the home for "fallen women". Over the years its official name changed from St Agnes Maternity Home & Crèche to the St Agnes Home for Moral Welfare and later St Agnes Approved School. At its annual meeting in 1944, the home's superintendent Margaret Bathe revealed that the Americans stationed at the Burtonwood air base were creating problems:

> Most of the girls we deal with are about fifteen. A soldier aged twenty-nine came inquiring after one of them but was not allowed to see her. Girls become infatuated with the American soldiers; they like their romantic American accents. They think that because they are addressed as sweetheart and such endearing terms that these soldiers mean it.

A Mrs Dirley told the same meeting that clothes were presenting a difficulty for young girls as they sought to impress boys:

> She runs through her [ration] coupons buying shoddy, cheap, unserviceable clothes. Girls of fifteen are frequently women of the world, smoking, drinking, and using lipstick and rouge. It is the work of Agnes moral welfare to alter these things.

...ABOUT THE TREATMENT OF BROKEN SOLDIERS – An ex-soldier adopting the pseudonym "A True Briton, Sutton" had this remarkable letter published in the St Helens Reporter in May 1919 in which he contrasted two events five years apart:

August, 1914 – "Your King and Country need you" Town Hall Square, St. Helens:- Hundreds of men, trying to get their names enrolled as England's bodyguard, loitering all over the place, to await their call for enrolment, to be sent to Warrington [army depot] in chars-a-banc, to be made fit and ready to meet their country's foes. No charge is made against them for obstruction or loitering. Old men giving years below their legal age to meet the foe, young, strong healthy men, ready to be trained in the hard school of discipline, who feared no foe, and later, proved their prowess against centuries-old disciplined, yet barbarous and cruel enemies, the Huns. And the Huns had to get out or get under. Our brave soldiers, our heroes, saved this Empire.

May 28th, 1919 – Town Hall Square:- The same heroes, crippled, broken, gassed, and maimed. The same Town Hall Square, but not the same spirit that sent these men to be crippled, broken, gassed, and maimed. They form up in an orderly queue, to ask and receive the miserable pittance that is meted out to them for their glorious work of saving this Empire. To-day they are loitering, causing an obstruction, moved on by the police as though they were felons, loitering with intent. This town must understand it is a free town, and its freedom was won by these men who were called "Patriots" in 1914. What is the difference? Are these men, broken in their country's cause, not entitled to justice? This is not Bolshevism. It is pure British thinking, and thinking of this kind has made England what she is to-day. Never forget, England was saved by these broken men, St. Helens men included! God save our King!

...ABOUT THE IRISH – On February 15th 1862, Bernard Dromgoole, the editor and owner of the St Helens Weekly News *(the forerunner of the St Helens Newspaper)* wrote these comments about the large Irish contingent in the town:

We think the Irish have much both in the past and present to complain of, but they must learn to deal with these matters in a more practical way, and by uniting and persevering for the obtaining of possible reforms. If the Irishmen of this town were united for good, instead of week after week wasting their hard earned wages in drinking and rioting; how much better it would be for their friends and families.

...ABOUT VANDALISM – Complaining about teenage vandalism to his premises in November 1966, George Boardman, a grocer from Robins Lane in Sutton, was quoted in the St Helens Newspaper as saying:

I'm losing £8 a week alone through these young hoodlums fouling my cigarette machines. They jam it with silver paper and chewing gum. I've had two large plate windows smashed. The wall at the back has been worked loose and overhanging bricks are dangerous. If they were my kids I'd disown them. These girls and boys have orgies. They are a gang of filthy, stinking kids. And if I catch any of them doing anything I'll clobber them.

...ABOUT THE DERIORATION OF CARR MILL DAM – On May 4th 1973, a woman using the pen-named "Distressed" told the St Helens Reporter how she had cried upon seeing how her beloved Carr Mill Dam had been allowed to deteriorate:

From 1944 to 1949, I lived in Clock Face near St. Helens with my eldest son whose father was in the Army serving abroad. Our happiest days were spent at Carr Mill dam, where we went sailing and fishing or sometimes just for a picnic. There was an atmosphere of peace there, I never found anyone else. Carr Mill dam was destined to become a bustling little place, ringing with the sound of happy children, who rode on the little locomotive that appeared later on. It travelled round, to the end of the lake and back, for a few pennies a ride. A good day's outing could be had, for a few shillings. A café which was built did a roaring trade in snacks, or you could take your own food. Later on a sand pit and paddling pool, were made specially for the tots with a little helter-skelter and rocking animals. At one side a skating rink and swings were built for the older children.

Although I am a native of Adlington, I left a bit of my heart in St. Helens and I've watched Carr Mill dam slowly being torn to pieces. It hurts, when I think how lovely a place it used to be. You couldn't wish to go to a bonnier place on a Summer's day. I hadn't been for a number of years, until Easter Sunday. And I sat in the car on the road, heart-broken at what I saw. I hadn't even the heart to get out and look further. I'd seen enough. Tears filled my eyes and I wept. Who had done this to my Carr Mill dam, and who had allowed it to be done? Empty, desolate buildings with broken staring eyes of windows; burnt-out railway station; glass strewn floors; an empty, barren lake. Whoever has done this thing should be made to visit Carr Mill dam, with me, weep and be ashamed.

...ABOUT SPEEDBOATS ON CARR MILL DAM – The Reporter asked its readers for their thoughts on the Dam. Someone calling themselves *"Deaf From the Damn Dam"* wrote on May 25th 1973:

You ask has Carr Mill got any future? Well, yes, it has – as an instrument of torture, one that the residents for miles around will live to regret unless some thing is done soon. I am already dreading the summer with the agony it will bring with the power boats which are getting worse every year, roaring away from morning till late at night. The noise from these monsters is so bad that if Concorde were to circle low over Carr Mill Dam for an hour, no one would notice it. Not so long ago, you could walk round Carr Mill Dam. It was peaceful and quiet – just a few rowing boats and a small band of Morris dancers enjoying themselves. Now, with the erosion of the banks caused by these power boats, it is worse than any assault course in the country and, in some places, very dangerous.

An illustration of Newton Races held on Newton Common

...ABOUT NEWTON RACES – The annual Newton Races was renowned for drunken behaviour and a magnet for pickpockets and other criminals. Horse racing had taken place on Newton Common from at least 1678 and continued until 1899 when Lord Newton accepted an offer from a syndicate to rent land in Haydock to establish a new course that we know today as Haydock Park.

Huge numbers of St Helens folk would attend Newton Races, often taking advantage of special train services. In February 1835, the vicar of St Helens, the Rev. Thomas Pigot, commented on what he saw as the sinful behaviour that accompanied the horse racing:

I have always cautioned those committed to my care against the sad excesses of Newton race week, and I always will, because I know full well the accompanying demoralization.

Very many poor sinners have confessed to me on their death beds that they commenced their wicked career at Newton races.

...ABOUT MESSED UP HOTEL ROOMS – The Chalon Court Hotel in St Helens opened its doors in October 1992. Weeks earlier the hotel's head housekeeper Nicola Roberts from Windle had described her intensive cleaning regime to the Liverpool Echo:

I've got my own views on what makes a perfect hotel room. I really hate dirt, and I find cleaning itself very therapeutic. It's very rewarding to walk into a messed-up hotel room and leave it looking immaculate. People get up to all sorts of dreadful things in hotel rooms. Mind you, I wouldn't dare tell you about anything I've seen. But I will say that businessmen are the best guests; their rooms are usually left clean and tidy. And newlyweds are among the worst. The last thing they're interested in is tidying up after themselves!

ST. HELENS ⅋ DISTRICT
REPORTER

No. 5,612.   FRIDAY, JUNE 11, 1943,   PRICE 2d.

...ON THE FILTHY LANGUAGE OF WOMEN WAR WORKERS – St Helens women did a sterling job in both world wars working in factories while many of the male employees were on military service. However, a letter published in the St Helens Reporter on June 11th 1943 by someone adopting the pseudonym "Husband" claimed that the women war workers were adopting some of the males' bad habits – in particular, swearing:

I would like to open my heart to you about the language used by many women in works and factories, in the dual

99

hope that (1) someone with more influence than I have can do something to stem it, and (2) that those who are degrading themselves and polluting others with their foulness may see this letter and be shamed into decency. My wife has for some time been on "directed" work in a St. Helens factory. She has a reasonable code of conduct and speech, and in many ways is quite broad-minded. But she complains bitterly to me of the behaviour and particularly of the speech of many of the women among whom she works, which she says, makes her blush with shame and causes her much more pain and suffering than the unaccustomed heavy work in which she is now engaged.

She complains, not so much of the strong language used by women when things go wrong but shudders at the all too-frequent use of what I can only call "sexual swear words," and words with sexual implications, which comes from the lips of mere strips of girls as frequently as they gush from the lips of older women, many of them married. Perhaps a psychologist could explain why women normally correct in their behaviour and clean in their thoughts and speech, fall from grace as soon as they work with their fellows in large numbers on unaccustomed jobs; but, frankly, I cannot.

...ON WHERE THERE'S MUCK – Speaking at a Licensed Victuallers dinner dance and whist drive at St Helens Town Hall on December 12th 1957, the Mayor, Cllr. John Henebery, said:

St. Helens is not a pretty town, though we have our beauty spots, but the town is a living proof of the old North country maxim, "where there's muck, there's money".

...ON AN ENVELOPE – And finally, the Liverpool Mercury of May 21st 1863 wrote how someone corresponding with Thomas Park of the Sutton Rolling Mills, had decided to put some style into his letter, writing Park's address on the envelope as a poem:

Please, postman, come thou near, and hark!
Give this to Mr. Thomas Park.
You'll find him (listen where to go)
Employed by Newton, Keats, and Co.
Away ! away ! o'er dales and hills,
To Sutton Copper Rolling Mills,
Near St. Helens, Lancashire.

The Teenage Parading
On The Streets Of St Helens

*"The yells that come from these "clickers" is astonishing.
Their love-call sounds something like woo-woo."*

The Sunday evening parading of young people was a longstanding custom in certain parts of St Helens – and, seemingly, in many other towns in the country. Writing about the subject in the St Helens Reporter on April 23rd 1926, one correspondent wrote:

It is a matter of common knowledge to those who have travelled that similar parades take place in every town and city in Great Britain and that the problem has baffled the intellect of social reformers for at least a hundred years.

Why anyone would be baffled by youngsters wanting to meet up in groups and walk and talk together – and, perhaps, form relationships with the opposite sex – baffles me! The "problem" as far as the authorities was concerned was that usually unthinking boys or girls would obstruct other pedestrians and force them off the footpath into the road.

The tradition was largely restricted to Church Street, Duke Street and what was known as the "Long Wall" on the perimeter of Sherdley Park. Sometimes called "monkey walks", Frank Bamber *(b. 1910)* described the weekly Sutton parade in his 1987 memoirs:

When the Sunday evenings darkened the "Long Wall" was the habitual meeting place for the teenagers from the surrounding districts to "Parade", groups of boys and groups of girls walking continually up and down the path alongside the wall and usually there was a friendly policeman slowly walking up and down to prevent these groups from joining up and causing an obstruction on the path, it was all done in a cheerful way and the police were given the respect to which was their due, so different from the present day. The older boys and girls who wanted to dally made their way around the 'Score' where all was quiet, and there, no one interfered, it was a favourite place for courting couples.

The Score was the public footpath that ran through the then private Sherdley Park. Although Frank believed that the Sutton parade caused no problems for the public or police, it was a different story in St Helens town centre.

THE CAMPAIGN AGAINST OBSTRUCTIONISTS

A picture postcard of Church Street in St Helens c.1910

In October 1918 the St Helens police began a campaign against the boys and girls accused of causing a nuisance in Church Street. *"They are blocking up the street from end to end"*, the town's Chief Constable, Arthur Ellerington, told St Helens Police Court. After receiving several complaints of unruly behaviour on the footpaths, the police went on a Sunday night stake out. As a result of their undercover operation, five summonses were issued against three lads from College Street and two girls from Ramford and Tickle Streets. PC Reynolds told the magistrates that he'd watched the five standing in front of a jeweller's shop at 9:15pm on a Sunday evening, forcing a number of people – including wounded soldiers on crutches – into the road.

None of the defendants turned up to the court hearing but the mother of one did. She accused the police of telling untruths – saying she believed her boy's denial of doing anything wrong. The youngsters were each fined 11 shillings in their absence.

> The days when men and women, girls and youths were able to gather together on the footpath and indulge in horseplay seems to be over in St. Helens, and the probability is that those who try to engage in it in future will find themselves in unpleasant places.

So wrote the St Helens Reporter on February 11th 1919 as they celebrated another successful police "raid" on Church Street as the campaign against Sunday night "obstructionists" moved up a gear. The Reporter's article described how twenty young males and females had been caught "red-handed", with some of the walkers having forced pedestrians off the pavement into the roadway.

A couple of the obstructionists had refused to give their names to the police but relented after receiving a threat to "run them in". When the group appeared in the St Helens Police Court – the aforementioned unpleasant place – most of them received 10-shilling fines.

A fortnight later Ernest Litherland, Henry Foster and Thomas Purcill (all of Albert Street, off North Road), Edward Phillips from Morley Street, Francis Anderson from York Place and a lad called Canington appearing in the Police Court.

They were charged with "obstructing the free passage of the footpath" opposite the Meadow Dairy in Church Street. From half-past seven until eight o'clock, PCs Reynolds and O'Hare had watched the lads "interfering" with passers-by, including pulling girls by their arms and clothing and bumping into people.

However, the youths claimed mistaken identity, with one saying: *"Some of the girls don't want any bumping into; they can do it themselves, and can whistle as well to anybody."* Superintendent Dunn told the Bench that a lot of jostling did take place on Sunday nights and the girls were as bad as the boys. The youngsters, he said, flocked to Church Street from as far away as Haydock and Thatto Heath.

The Chairman of the magistrates described the Church Street goings-on as *"quite a pandemonium"* and told the five lads that they would be fined ten shillings each, adding: *"If you want a bit of fun you must get out of Church Street"*. Just where they were supposed to go was not stated – unlike in another case of obstructionism on March 21st 1919 when the Bench felt a country walk was a suitable substitute.

That hearing concerned Christopher Howard from Speakman Road and Joseph Bibby from Abbey Road in St Helens. PC Hall stated that on the previous Sunday evening he had watched the 16-year-olds acting the goat in Church Street. He said they were both *"very rough, pulling one another about"* and their activities caused people to leave the pavement and go onto the road. The Chairman of the Bench said he'd seen for himself this *"disgraceful conduct"* and then future mayor Peter Phythian told the boys:

> You lads could get better enjoyment I should think by taking a walk in the country. You must find fresh places to go and enjoy yourselves and not be rowdy in Church Street.

They were both fined ten shillings, although sadly I can't tell you whether they took the Chairman's advice and went for country walks on Sunday nights! If they did they were on their own, as a week later a police constable gave a damning assessment of Church Street on the Sabbath. PC McHale told magistrates:

> Church-street at the present time has become unbearable, and respectable people cannot walk down as there are thousands of people standing on the footpath on a Sunday night.

The officer had been in plain clothes and seen Thomas Foster from Crowther Street *(near Boundary Road)*, William Atherton from Friar Street *(near Victoria Park)* and another man from Atherton Street in Dentons Green blocking the pavement. PC McHale claimed that many people had been forced to go into the road to get round them. All three were fined the usual ten bob with the Chairman of the Bench remarking that this kind of thing must be stopped.

Three more Church Street "rowdies" were in court on March 4th. Collier Samuel Helsby from Graham Street in St Helens, cleaner Thomas Lyon from Friar Street and miner Thomas Hightown from Ramford Street were charged with obstructing the footpath.

PC Manser and PC Taylor had been in plain clothes on the previous Sunday on the lookout for "obstructionists". The pair gave evidence of observing the threesome *"intercepting young women"* at the corner of Church Street and Hardshaw Street. The lads were accused of making such remarks to girls that forced them to walk into the road. All three denied committing the offence but the magistrates found them guilty and fined them ten shillings.

Another batch of "Church Street obstructionists" appeared in St Helens Police Court on June 27th 1919. PCs Pugh and Shepherd had observed John Chadwick from Juddfield Street, George Greenall from West End Road, James Littler from Clipsley Lane and Jack Traverse from Vicarage Road having too much fun. The police accused the four Haydock lads of:

> ...staging and shouting in the street at the top of their voices. They were singing and shouting and jostling about, turning everybody off the footpath.

Superintendent Dunn also told the court that such youths were coming in regularly from Haydock on Sunday nights and causing a nuisance – although, as usual, there was no suggestion of alcohol being involved. The Chairman of the Bench said they were determined to put this kind of conduct down, telling the lads:

> You come in from Haydock, and you think you can act as you like. However, this is a first offence, and you will be fined 5 shillings each.

Although the Haydock obstructionists in Church Street were older boys and sometimes girls, the younger ones had other means of having fun. On July 25th James Greenall from West End Road appeared in St Helens Police Court charged with discharging fireworks in the street. The boy and his mates had been amusing themselves by chucking crackers under the long dresses that ladies then wore! James was fined 7s 6d.

Playing "tig" *(we'd call it "tag")* was another Sunday evening activity by lads in Church Street. The police had kept Arthur Rigby from Lyon Street, Alfred Leyland from Halefield Street and Joseph James from Chapel Street under observation for an hour to gather evidence of them playing tig prior to intervening. The magistrates fined them between 7s 6d and 10 shillings for causing a nuisance.

When William Nolan and Henry Lewis appeared in court on January 16th 1920, PC Alsopp said the pair had been standing outside the Church Street Post Office. The lads were aged about sixteen and, along with some other boys, had pushed passers-by, pulled girls' hair and grabbed hold of their clothing.

Three girls were also knocked into a doorway. Quite often the defendants in such cases claimed mistaken identity in the busy street and that was William and Henry's defence. However, they were still fined 5 shillings each.

THE DUKE STREET CLICKERS

By the later years of the 1920s, it seems that the parading "nuisance" had largely departed Church Street and relocated to Duke Street. It was also taking place on other nights, as well as Sundays. The St Helens Reporter on April 23rd 1926 wrote:

Complaints continue to reach us of obstruction caused in Duke-street nightly by boys and girls, who obstruct the paths and otherwise make themselves a nuisance in their efforts (as the protestants put it) to "click."

There are a couple of George Formby songs that refer to the practice of "clicking" with girls on the street. In later years other slang terms – such as "pulling" or "getting off" – have been similarly used to describe the meeting and pairing off of young people.

TUESDAY. APRIL 13. 1926.

TRYING TO "CLICK" IN DUKE STREET.

"UNEDUCATED PROGENY OF HOBOS."

BOYS' GIGGLING AND GUFFAWING.

Duke-street comes in for severe criticism at the hands of a "Reporter" correspon

It was a letter from Edward Egerton that started the ball rolling when the 27-year-old complained in the St Helens Reporter of April 13th 1926 about a nuisance called "Clicking":

Allow me to register what I honestly think is a really justifiable protest against the practice of obstructing the parapet in Duke-street. Several times of late I have passed through this thoroughfare with strangers who have agreed that Duke-street is badly in need of a police patrol or some other deterrent to this stupid and ignorant practice. There are a good many irresponsible individuals ranging from fourteen to eighteen who resort to novel forms of hilarity, such as giggling and guffawing and screeching in dulcetto tones, in the vain hope (in the slang term) of trying to "click." Both girls and boys of tender years. These people imagine they may hold a complete monopoly of the pathway, but they are so ignorant as to be absolute strangers to even the most rudimentary ethics of courtesy and grammar. You will hear phrases like "It was her, it wasn't me," or "It's them, not us," in explanation of the obstructing practices. This is the uneducated progeny of hobos. It is deplorable in the extreme. Obstruction of the type I refer to is carried on wholesale from 7 p.m. to 10 15 p.m. every evening.

THE DUKE STREET "CLICKERS.".

THE GRADUATES FROM "CHICKEN ROW." | LIGHTER SIDE OF A SERIOUS NUISANCE.

Then on April 23rd the St Helens Reporter published a collection of correspondence about the subject – with some feeling that Mr Egerton was making far too much out of a minor problem. However, most letter-writers agreed with him, including a correspondent who called himself "D.J.":

Almost any time after the shops have closed, you will find knots of boys and girls standing just off the path, in the channel, projecting a couple of feet or a yard into the roadway. Perhaps that is their idea of escaping police attention for obstructing the pavement. It is full of danger. If a motorist has to pass another vehicle approaching him, he has of necessity to draw in as far on his left side as possible, and when he finds his progress blocked by these gossiping youngsters there is danger for all parties. It is hardly any use sounding your horn. I have sounded mine until I must have made myself an unmitigated nuisance; but believe me, I have known young fellows, in the presence of their fair charmers, actually to defy me to come on.

Another correspondent adopting the pseudonym "Anti-Clicker" told the Reporter that the clicking practice went on in other St Helens streets, as well as Duke Street. And the "mating" call of the participants was "woo-woo"!

If anyone travels down Higher Parr-street, Fingerpost, after the shops are closed, especially on a Sunday night, he will find that this street can hold its own with the giggling boys and girls of Duke-street. Here there are a number of shop doorways which these "clickers" delight in. Quite recently I saw a number of these raw-breeds come rushing out of a doorway and bump into a perambulator and upset it, causing the mother and the child to speak very angrily. The yells that come from these "clickers" is astonishing. Their love-call sounds something like "Woo-woo." If the other party returns the call, they stop and promptly monopolise the pavement – that is, if there is not a shop doorway vacant; many iron gates at these doorways are bent through people using them for camping purposes. These young people are aged from fourteen to sixteen, and they are looked upon as the chickens who frequent "Chicken Run," as this area is known. After they have served their apprenticeship in the "Chicken Run", they graduate to Church-street, Baldwin-street, and Duke-street; and anyone who stands for a time at any street corner en route will see the same old faces bobbing up and down with the regularity of a clock ticking, from seven o'clock till turning out time of the pubs. If they fail to "click," they take a walk down Shaw-street, Corporation-street, and Cotham-street, back to the street where many young people have, alas, met their Waterloo.

A picture postcard of Duke Street in St Helens

Then another correspondent – unprepared to reveal their identity but calling themselves "Fair Play" – felt prosecution was not the answer. Instead, he felt that all the youngsters needed was some chummy advice:

> Suppose the police were to prosecute wholesale? Suppose they were to place the stigma of a Police Court conviction on hundreds of irresponsible lads and lasses what useful purpose would be served? It would almost certainly clear Duke-street at night, I quite agree, but the parade would simply shift to another part of the town, as it always does. A little chummy advice from parents, and a little more guidance from the pulpits, is an infinitely more sensible way to deal with the trouble. After all, you know, you cannot abolish young people even, if they are a bit of a nuisance at times.

Fair Play was not wrong. You certainly can't abolish teenagers!

The Obsessed Dad Who Shot His Daughter In A Hospital

""You shall never marry him," he declared, and drew from a pocket a six-chambered service revolver."

This gloomy looking building is the former Chiswick and Ealing Isolation Hospital pictured around 1932. That was the year when an obsessed father from St Helens walked into the West London infirmary and shot dead his daughter – before turning the gun upon himself. The hospital matron was also wounded while attempting to protect her young nurse from John Armstrong's weapon.

The so-called Major Jack Armstrong had been a very well-known figure in St Helens. A tailor living in Doulton Street, he and his cello-playing daughter were members of the St Helens Orchestral Society, under its esteemed conductor George Groves. When informed by the St Helens Reporter of the double shooting in

London, all that the shocked and "stupefied" orchestra leader could utter were the words "I am not surprised". Shocked by the terrible news – but not surprised, it seems, that Armstrong would undertake some dreadful act.

He did have a reputation as an enigma; a man who could be pleasant and convivial but had developed a dark side through his often thwarted desire to always be in control. Perhaps that came from serving in the army in India – although even Armstrong's wife, Maggie, confessed to knowing little of her husband's supposed military past.

The native of Belfast would even threaten his family at gunpoint to force their compliance with his demands, often after heavy drinking. In January 1924, Armstrong had appeared before the magistrates in St Helens Police Court charged with committing a breach of the peace.

A constable gave evidence of hearing a whistle being blown and finding the former army officer fighting with his sons. It certainly sounds like John Jnr. and Cecil *(aged about 20 and 18, respectively)* had endured quite enough of their drunken, domineering dad, who in court blamed the disturbance entirely upon them. The Liverpool Echo wrote:

> Defendant complained to the magistrates of having been very much ill-used. He said his sons stayed out late, and when he remonstrated they began to beat him. He blew the whistle in order to secure police protection, and while he was blowing it he was struck in the mouth and his teeth and the whistle were knocked down his throat. The magistrates bound him over to keep the peace for six months, and told him if he would avoid drink his life would be very peaceful. Defendant asked for protection against his sons, and the police court missionary [probation officer] was requested to interview the family and make peace.

The fact that John Armstrong Snr was the only one of the three combatants summoned to court, suggests that the police had not been taken in by the man's protestations of innocence.

At that time his daughter Annette Sybil *(known to her friends as Aggie and to others as Sybil)* was only 14 or 15 and had little choice but to obey her father's orders. But as she grew into a young woman, Sybil sought an independent life away from the strictures of the home and aspired to become a nurse.

Armstrong's two sons wanted nothing more to do with their domineering dad. Both moved away from the family home, leading to their father doting even more on his daughter. At one point she developed a friendship with a young man in St Helens – but that relationship was ended when her father threatened to shoot him.

An unnamed friend told the St Helens Reporter that Sybil's father had created "fearful scenes" whenever his daughter had been seen in the town with a young man. "He seemed madly jealous of anybody who spoke to her," she added.

Sybil knew she had to leave home if ever she was to have a life of her own and early in 1932 obtained a probationary nursing position in Battersea. However, Armstrong employed his usual revolver diplomacy to force Sybil to leave London and return to St Helens.

That was after the domineering dad had discovered that his daughter planned to marry William John Henry Bambrick *(known as Will but referred to as John in newspaper reports)*.

Three months before the tragedy the 25-year-old welder from Pimlico had injured his hand and been treated by Sybil in the hospital.

"We took to each other at once", Will later remarked, adding that when Armstrong had travelled to London to take back his daughter, he'd said that he would rather see his daughter in the grave than married to him.

Speaking to the St Helens Reporter, Will provided a fuller account of Armstrong's interventions:

> Very curiously, I met Sybil through an accident to my right hand. I had to go to hospital at Battersea. She attended to me, and we fell in love. She remained there for some weeks, till her father learned of our attachment. He was opposed to it right from the outset, and ordered her back home. She went, but she wrote every day declaring her love for me. She came back to London, and lived in a flat of her own in Winchester-street near to me, intending to stay there until we could get married. She had not been there long when her father came and again ordered her back home.
>
> I was not at the interview but heard from the landing how vexed he was at the idea of her being in love with me. Again she went back to St. Helens but she was not there long before she returned to London. This time she told her mother, not her father, that she had secured a post as probationer nurse at the Chiswick and Ealing Isolation Hospital. How her father got to know of her whereabouts I cannot say. Sybil had told me that her father had threatened two or three times to shoot her if she persisted in marrying me. Five weeks ago he went to her flat, pulled out a revolver and said: "You will never marry him. This will stop you."

But Sybil continued her romance with Will Bambrick. Their marriage was set for August 4th and only hours before her death, the 22-year-old had bought her wedding dress.

After eventually learning where his daughter was employed, probably through his wife, Armstrong was determined to bring Sybil back to St Helens once again. However, this time the young woman refused to return home with her father – with tragic consequences.

Issued

NURSE SHOT
DEAD IN HOSPITAL BY FATHER

TWO KILLED IN DRAMA OF BANNED WEDDING

A PRETTY, auburn - haired nurse's decision to marry

SYBIL ARMSTRONG

How the Daily Herald reported the story on its front page

On July 13th 1932, the Daily Mirror described the tragic events that had unfolded in London in an article bearing the headline *"Two Dead in Hospital Drama of Love"*:

> A father's objection to his daughter marrying – the ceremony had been planned for three weeks hence – is said to be the reason why he shot her dead in a West London hospital yesterday and afterwards turned the revolver on himself. The bullet that killed the girl passed through a photograph of her sweetheart. The matron, in an heroic attempt to avert the tragedy, threw herself between father and daughter, and was wounded in the arm by a bullet which ricochetted [sic] off a wall....The dead girl had been on the staff of the Chiswick and Ealing Isolation Hospital for five weeks when, yesterday afternoon, her father asked to see her. He had come from his home in Doulton-street, St. Helens,

116

Lancashire. Miss Armstrong was surprised at the visit; she had entered the hospital unknown to her father, who had previously taken her away from another London hospital.

She was terrified at the thought of seeing him alone, and the hospital matron, Miss Gregory, arranged that the interview should take place in her own private room, she herself being present. Father and daughter had been talking only a few minutes when a quarrel broke out. A stormy scene followed, during which the father accused his daughter of callousness to her parents. "You shall never marry him," he declared, and drew from a pocket a six-chambered Service revolver. Two shots were fired at his daughter, who was dressed to go out, and the girl fell forward on the floor. Major Armstrong then put the revolver to his own head and fired...News that there had been a shooting at the hospital caused great alarm in the neighbourhood, and dozens of mothers hurried to the hospital gates anxious about the safety of their children, patients in the wards. There were pathetic scenes of relief as the women were reassured.

AFFECTION THAT WAS PERSECUTION

SAYS SHE WENT IN FEAR OF HER LIFE

SECRET ROMANCE THAT LED TO TRAGEDY

FATAL BULLET THROUGH SWEET-HEART'S PICTURE

A PAINFUL sensation was created in St. Helens on Tuesday evening,

The St Helens Reporter's headlines on July 15th 1932

The St Helens Reporter's account described how a "painful sensation" had been created in the town once news of the double shooting had spread and the paper had broken the news to Sybil's brother. Cecil Armstrong of Dearnley Avenue in Blackbrook said that since his marriage six years earlier, he'd had little association with his father, with whom he'd found it "difficult to live in harmony".

One Reporter journalist knew John Armstrong personally and only a week before the shooting, the amateur musician had complained to him about his family: "My sons never come to see me and now my daughter has left. I will sell up all the [musical] instruments in the house and give it all up."

The newspaper described Armstrong's "intense affection" for Sybil as amounting to "a form of parental jealousy that led to persecution" and his constant surveillance had made his daughter's life a misery.

The Hospital Shots Drama

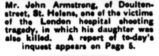

Mr. John Armstrong, of Doulton-street, St. Helens, one of the victims of the London hospital shooting tragedy, in which his daughter was also killed. A report of to-day's inquest appears on Page 5.

John Armstrong and Will Bambrick in the Liverpool Echo of July 14th 1932

The inquest on Sybil and her father was opened on July 14th at Ealing. The Daily Express wrote that: "Mrs. Armstrong, the girl's mother, attended the inquest, and shook hands warmly with Mr. John Bambrick, the young man who was engaged to her daughter."

During the brief hearing, Maggie Armstrong described how her husband had been a very heavy drinker and, when drunk, would behave "like a madman". On several occasions she had been forced to "fly" for her life when he had picked up a gun. Mrs Armstrong also explained that her husband had been very angry about their daughter's engagement to Bembrick.

MRS. ARMSTRONG (left), wife of the man who shot their daughter Annette and then himself at the Chiswick and Ealing Isolation Hospital, after visiting the hospital yesterday. The dead girl's fiancé, Mr. John Bambrick, is on right.

Daily Herald picture & caption July 14th 1932

Since WW1 and stricter firearms legislation, St Helens police had acted more stringently over the possession of weapons. However, Armstrong had used his guns legitimately to shoot game. He was also a former army officer and so appears to have been fully licensed and so experienced no problems with the police.

The only witness to the shooting had been the hospital matron, Ida Gregory, who was still recovering from her ordeal – and so the inquest was adjourned for two weeks. However, the coroner said it was clearly a case of wilful murder and suicide and that Armstrong's objection to his daughter's engagement had amounted to an obsession.

The inquest resumed on July 29th with the wounded hospital matron as the key witness. Miss Gregory told the coroner that three weeks prior to the tragedy, she had received a letter from Sybil's father. Armstrong wrote how his daughter had departed from his home in St Helens without his knowledge and he'd subsequently heard she was working at the hospital. Miss Gregory said she was asked to confirm if that was true and, if so, let Mr Armstrong know if his daughter was happy. Then on July 7th, Sybil surprised the matron by handing in her resignation, explaining that she was going to be married. Miss Gregory told the hearing:

> I talked to her and asked her if she had thought about it seriously and if her parents knew about it. She said they did not know, but she was going home to be married. I tried to give her a little advice and asked her to think about it for a time. In view of her father's letter, I sent a note [to Armstrong] saying she had resigned. I had a letter from him saying he was coming, and asking me not to let her know until he arrived.

In answer to a question from the coroner, Miss Gregory said she had not been aware at the time that Sybil was afraid of her father. The matron then described the dreadful events that occurred on July 12th:

> Mr. Armstrong arrived about 12.30. He began by telling me how very fond he was of her. He was very upset that she would not stay. He said he had found out that she intended to marry and I gathered he did not approve. I said I would fetch nurse along. I got her from the ward, and told her [her] father was there, and asked her not to make a fuss. I took her to the room where he was. He tried to be very affectionate with her, and she would not have anything to do with him. He asked her if she was prepared to go home with him, and she said, "No," she hated him. I asked her to go very quietly with him and not say unkind things to her father. Then he asked her for the last time if she would go, and she said "No." Then he turned to his overcoat, which was on a

chair. I asked her to go away without making any fuss. I turned round and he had a revolver in his hand. He put up his hand to fire, and I appealed to him to come to his senses. I tried to get hold of his wrist, and I got the first shot. I was pulling his hand down and the revolver just went off. I tried to get to the office door and call for help. He fired three shots in quick succession.

The first two bullets struck down Sybil and the third, final shot hit the gunman in his own head. The Coroner said that the jury could come to no other possible conclusion than it was a case of murder and suicide.

By today's standards and data protection laws, a matron communicating private information to a 22-year-old nurse's father would probably be in breach of the law. However, this was the 1930s; times were very different and Miss Gregory thought she was doing what was best and could never have imagined such a terrible outcome. The coroner certainly had no criticism of her, telling the jury:

The matron should be highly commended for her conduct. She showed very great pluck. Instead of running away and getting frightened, as a lot of people would have done, she tried to tackle the man and do everything she could. It is for you to say the state of his [Armstrong's] mind. There was a half bottle of brandy found on him, and he had obviously had drinks. You will remember that his wife said that when he had had drink he was like a madman. He seemed, in a way, to have been fond of his daughter but to have been doing all he could to prevent her marrying this man. You will have to say whether it was a case of unsound mind or felo de se [suicide]. He had this extraordinary obsession against this marriage. I ought to say in fairness to the young man that he seems to have acted quite properly.

After retiring for four minutes, the jury returned a verdict that Armstrong murdered his daughter and then committed suicide while of unsound mind. "We should like to add our commendation of the matron", the foreman added." In October 1932 the Carnegie Hero Fund made a bravery award to Ida Gregory.

In the wartime census known as the 1939 Register, Mary Armstrong, the widow of John Armstrong, is shown living at Kingsway at Prescot with her son John Jnr. Will Bambrick does not appear to have ever married and died in 1961 in Hitchin at the age of 53.

I conclude this chapter with this thoughtful appraisal of Jack Armstrong that was published in the St Helens Reporter on July 15th 1932. It was written by *"One who knew him"*, who I expect was the aforementioned journalist / friend of the family:

"Jack" Armstrong was a human enigma. His acquaintances numbered thousands; his friends scarcely one. It is doubtful whether anyone beyond his immediate relatives really understood him. One wonders whether he understood himself. In some things he had a touch of genius; in others he displayed an eccentricity that marked and set him apart from his fellows. Whatever may have been his shortcomings in some directions, he could never be accused of meanness. He always appeared to have plenty of money and he spent it lavishly and impulsively. Once I saw him give half-a-crown to a tramp to help him on his way, and, in the days when his sons and daughters resided with him at Doulton-street, he often invited the neighbours in to supper and to a musical evening. No charitable appeal was made to him in vain, and often in days gone by he took concert parties and orchestras to Eccleston Hall Sanatorium to give entertainment to the patients and staff. His love for music amounted almost to a passion, and he encouraged his children and helped them in every way to realise their musical ambitions. On the darker side, his service in the sweltering heat of India may have had some bearing on his conduct of more recent days. Thousands commiserate with the physically afflicted. The unthinking jibe or grin at those afflicted in mind. Perhaps "Jack" Armstrong was deserving more of pity than of blame. His skill as a tailor was outstanding, and for many years many of the Beau Brummels of the town sort him out and gave him commissions. Armstrong was always well dressed and his suits were of the best material. He was a picturesque figure. He had a proud way of holding his head erect, a trait he had no doubt acquired in his Army service days, and he boldly looked the world in the face. Of late years he had greatly favoured suits with plus four trousers, and he was somewhat inclined to embonpoint.

He loved a day's sport in the country and was often seen making his way to the railway station with his sports gun. When in company he was ever ready to debate any topic under the sun – and usually he ranged himself on the side opposite the first speaker. He was, perhaps, a little more dogmatic than diplomatic in debate, but whenever he took up the cudgels on behalf of any cause, the discussion never lacked piquancy. Fishing, shooting, music, debating, and the keeping of strange pets were among his hobbies. He once tamed an owl which he kept in his parlour to do all manner of strange things. In the cool of a summer's evening he would open the front door and liberate the bird for several hours, but it never strayed far away, and always responded to his call to come indoors at bed time. A curious mixture of human foibles and good qualities was Jack Armstrong. His was a bizarre personality. He had many good points, and one cannot help feeling a tinge of pity that a life possessed of such potentialities should have ended in such stark tragedy, taking with him a daughter, gifted and beautiful, who might have lived out her life in peace and happiness with her husband-to-be.

"Dear Sir" – A Collection Of Curious Correspondence

This chapter is devoted to a wide range of letters that were sent to the St Helens' newspapers during the 19th century – or correspondence that townsfolk had published in other papers. Usually signed with a pseudonym, these can be amusing, revealing, disturbing and provide more insights into the social life of St Helens at that specific period than newspapers' own reports.

THE DIRTIEST STREETS IN LANCASHIRE

On November 19th 1870, this letter was published in the St Helens Newspaper from an individual calling himself "A. Traveller" who did not think much of the town's streets:

> To the Editor of the St. Helens Newspaper. – Sir, In the course of business I visit nearly every town in Lancashire and the neighbouring counties, but of all the towns St. Helens has the proud pre-eminence of having the dirtiest roads and streets of any town in Lancashire and the adjoining counties. I would recommend your town council to wipe off the dirty disgrace by putting a little more activity into the scavenging department. – Yours &c., **A TRAVELLER**. Raven Hotel, St. Helens.

THE CRYING EVIL OF THE INFANTRY BRIGADE

The Mechanics Institute was an organisation that met at St Helens Town Hall and held some public events. Before the days of amplification, it seems that peripheral sounds from the audience – such as coughing or the crying of babies – could prove more irritating for attendees than today. One correspondent to the St Helens Newspaper on November 29th 1862, was so upset by what he dubbed the "crying evil" of the "infantry brigade", that he complained about their racket in this letter:

Sir, – Whilst admitting the general excellence of the entertainments given by our Mechanics' Institute, I would beg leave to call the attention of the committee to a crying evil that ought to be remedied, if the general comfort of their audience is worth consideration. I allude to the combination of anything but sweet sounds, that we are invariably treated to by the Infantry Brigade. If the Committee would prevent the entrance of children in arms, they would remove a great source of annoyance to those who frequent these otherwise well conducted meetings. – I remain, Sir, for Self and Fellow Sufferers, **A REGULAR ATTENDER**.

TWO HEARTS BOUND WITH A CHAIN OF LOVE

This letter was published in the Prescot Reporter on March 26th 1870, much, I expect, to the embarrassment of its author. It was a private love letter that had been found near Rainhill National School and handed into the paper. The Reporter redacted all the names but otherwise the missive is as originally composed:

My dearest _____ Excuse me taking the liberty of addressing you, but I don't know how to make your acquaintance. I will be at Church on Sunday morning, I will wear a Black cloth coat, And will have my handkerchief a little out of my pocket, so that you will know me, If you wish to speak to me, I shall be happy for you to do so as I am coming out of Church. As you cannot think how I long to make your acquaintance, I cannot express my feelings, and the love I have for you. If you do not speak to me I don't know how I shall pass the day as I am deeply in love with you Ever since the first time I saw you. You cannot think how my Heart warms when I see your sweet face, O how I long for Sunday morning, so that we can have a chat. I would very much like to have a walk with you under the beautyfull canapey of Heaven were no one can over hear our conversation with two hearts bound with a chain of love.

O my darling _____ be shure and do not dissippoint me in being at Church on Sunday morning. Or I am shure I shall go mad as the love I have is so great I am shure it will turn my brains. But it is very well I am near the Asylum if in case anything happens to me that you don't speak. Would you oblidge me with putting your handkerchief a little out of your pocket so that I shall know whether my letter answer is the purpose or not. Please to come out of this gate nearest to the station, then I will accopupany you if it will be accepted which I hope it will. So no more at present, hopeing this will find you well so I must conclude with my kindest love. – Yours real admirer. _____ Rainhill.

I wonder if the woman spoke to the author after church? Although, the fact the love letter was found dumped on the street does not sound promising. And I don't think the man's dodgy spelling would have helped his case!

VIOLENCE AT RAINHILL LUNATIC ASYLUM

The Rainhill County Asylum tended to do well when inspected. However, those making such visits were mainly individuals from institutions like Whiston Workhouse or the administrative area known as the West Derby hundred – and their pre-announced inspections were cursory. And anyway, who would believe an inmate in a lunatic asylum if they did complain of ill-treatment?

There had to be strong corroborative evidence, such as on September 15th 1873 when Frederick Bellamy appeared in St Helens Petty Sessions charged with brutally assaulting a patient. A witness called the attendant "the greatest rascal on the face of the earth" and a doctor reported a black eye and cuts on the victim. Bellamy denied the accusation but was fined £2.

Two weeks later the St Helens Newspaper published this letter from an inmate called James Draper. His home was in Milk Street in St Helens but he said he had been incarcerated at Rainhill for four years:

Sir, – Will you for the sake of humanity insert this letter in your valuable paper. I have been a patient in this wrong-called County Asylum, Rainhill, which is at Sutton, about four years and three months, and should have not been kept five months. Superintendents have too much power. If an Act of Parliament was passed appointing Government inspectors the patients would then be protected. I have been beaten with brushes, sticks, fists, kicked and thrown down to the floor in a cruel manner by the attendants. When in No. 6 Ward, having had porridge and dry bread about 7 a. m., I cried for food before dinner time, and was asked if I wanted a sugar butty: it is true; and, I do not care how soon there is an enquiry. I am, dear sir, yours truly, **JAMES DRAPER**, 14, Milk street, St. Helens, 16th Sept., 1873

RELIEVING POVERTY

The office of the St Helens Relieving Officer was located in Tontine Street. The man did not completely relieve destitution and poverty, as such, but gave those in dire need subsistence payments *(usually as food coupons)* to keep them out of the workhouse.

It was far cheaper if the poor lived in their own homes than be kept at Whiston. The assistance was minimal and its amount fluctuated week by week. During one seven-day period in 1869, £64 9 shillings was spent on the poor within the St Helens district helping 1,119 such people. According to my calculations, that averages a little over one shilling each. However, during the previous week,

£102 had been spent on a similar number. Many did not qualify for such relief and had to rely on begging or other forms of charity, as this letter published in the Newspaper in June 1864 makes clear:

SIR, – I beg leave to intrude upon your valuable space for a small portion, to insert therein an instance of a deplorable nature to which I have been an eye witness, and, being a ratepayer, I wish to lay it before the public. On Monday, June 27th, I happened to be in the street opposite the relieving officer's door. I saw there six poor persons, who seemed to be in a state of abject poverty; they were in two parties – a man and wife and two children, one eighteen months, the other two months, composed one party; and a woman and child, six months old, composed the other; they were all together. At the time that I saw them it was nine o'clock at night. Now, seeing them placed in such a wretched position, at such a late hour (until half-past ten o'clock), they not having a fraction to pay for their lodgings, I consequently went to a police-constable to see if anything could be done for them. He came with me, but said that he could do nothing for them, as the relieving officer could not assist them. Then, seeing that they were likely to be lost, I went from house to house to get as much as would pay for the unfortunate people's lodgings. I got a few generous subscriptions, the total of which paid their way for the night. – I am, sir, yours respectfully, **A RATEPAYER**.

THE TOWN HALL BIGOTRY

"WANTED" classified adverts for domestic help in the 19th and early 20th century newspapers often specified that female applicants had to be "respectable", "strong" and "willing". A Protestant religion could also be a prerequisite for employment – which might be seen as code for "no Irish". Such blatant discrimination in the home was tolerated – as that was seen as a matter of personal choice. But when in a Liverpool Echo recruitment advert in December 1890, it was stipulated that job applicants for a position at St Helens Town Hall had to be Protestant – in a town with a high level of Catholics – that requirement caused a bit of a backlash.

WANTED. Girl about 20 years of age for the Town Hall. Good wages given. Protestant. Good character. Apply Hallkeeper, Town Hall, St. Helens.

WANTED, good General Servant; small family —

James Drake was assumed to have been the person responsible for inserting the job advertisement in the Echo. The 34-year-old was the curator / hall-keeper – we would call him caretaker – of the Town Hall in Corporation Street and he is referenced in this letter that was published in the St Helens Lantern newspaper on December 12th 1890:

WANTED, – Girl about 20 years of age, for the Town Hall. Good wages given. Protestant. Good character. Apply, Hall-keeper, Town Hall, St. Helens. – Liverpool Echo, Dec. 4th, 1890. – SIR, – The above is a revelation of the spirit of bigotry prevailing in municipal matters at St. Helens. Who is responsible for this fresh manifestation. Can it be the new Town Clerk? He will probably plead ignorance of the whole affair, but I cannot imagine Drake, the curator, making such an announcement on his own responsibility. Surely a Catholic could shake the mats and "polish up the handle of the big front door" as well as a Protestant. Drake is allowed [paid] for his assistants by our corporation, and there should be no religious disability about even a menial appointment. As a member of a body forming about one third of our population, I strongly protest against this municipal intolerance. – I remain, yours etc.

A CATHOLIC. St. Helens, December 9th, 1890.

THE PERFECT BEDLAM OF BUZZERS!

During the 19th century as St Helens became more industrialised, so the town became a noisier place to live. As many lived near to their work, the larger firms used loud sounds to summon employees to their shift and announce breaks. The ringing of bells was the simplest, traditional means of so doing – but the age of steam changed that.

In February 1869 a letter writer in the St Helens Newspaper, calling themselves "Promptitude", called for more works to replace their bells with steam whistles *(a.k.a. buzzers or hooters)*. That recommendation did not go down well with someone adopting the pseudonym "Anti-Humbug", who had this response published in the paper on February 13th:

> To the Editor of the St. Helens Newspaper. – Sir – I hope the humane employers of labour in St. Helens will never adopt the insane recommendation of your correspondent "Promptitude," by substituting the obnoxious whistle, or "buzz," in lieu of the bell usually used at the various works in the town. Just fancy what a perfect bedlam our town would resemble, supposing all the works (50 or 60) used the "Buzz". I have, during this winter, been often startled from my slumbers at 20 minutes to 6 in the morning by the hideous din of that infernal "buzz". Why, sir, if we had 50 more roaring at the same time, I feel sure I should start from my bed, and spring through the ceiling of my chamber, some dark morning. In fact, should the buzz be adopted at all the works, Rainhill Asylum would soon require to be again enlarged, for, depend upon it, the nervous systems of our good townsfolk could not stand the effect. It would be intolerable. We may endure one "buzz," but 50 more would be nothing short of a public nuisance."

> – I am, yours, &c., **ANTI-HUMBUG**

DISPENSING JUSTICE WHILE EATING DINNER

During the 1870s, the St Helens Newspaper campaigned for paid, stipendiary magistrates to sit on the St Helens Bench – rather than the lay magistrates who were mainly councillors and industrialists. Sometimes none turned up for a sitting or were very late, causing considerable inconvenience to many.

It was an inconsistency in the system that a professional judge or recorder would deal with a huge number of civil cases every Tuesday in the St Helens County Court in East Street. However, amateurs, guided by their law clerk, were expected to administer the more important criminal cases in the town's Petty Sessions.

On July 12th 1873, the St Helens Newspaper published this letter from someone calling themselves "Manners" who was far from impressed by the magistrates' behaviour in court:

To The Editor. Sir – About halfpast eleven to day (Monday,) one of the two representatives of the administrators of the law of this country, was observed sitting on the Bench with his wig on – not a white one, but a black one, something like what is usually worn by English gentlemen when walking the streets, or something like the Shah's hat, plus a rim but minus the brilliants. Not a voice was raised – Hats off, or white Wigs on. Last Monday, the representatives of the administration of the law, were observed getting their dinners, whilst sitting on the bench trying a few poor wretches, who were in the hands of the police. Your correspondent observed a little boy and a little girl, who were prisoners for stealing some paltry thing. It was hard to see the wistful looks of that poor boy and girl, as they directed their little faces towards the Bench, and saw the two administrators of the law, so called, eating sandwiches and drinking what appeared to be water, laughing and talking to each other, whilst a case was going on, and yet that poor boy and girl no doubt were very hungry through having skilly [thin broth] for their breakfast, but could not have their dinner until they had been tried. Who ever saw a judge at the assize[s], a county court judge, or anyone but a lay magistrate, keep his hat on in court, or get his dinner whilst on the bench? Oh, do have manners, ye magistrates, although you have only poor people to deal with. Query, who paid for the sandwiches? – **MANNERS**, St. Helens 1873.

Persons criticised in the newspapers by correspondents rarely responded. And so there was no follow-up letter from the magistrates in a future edition of the paper defending their behaviour. That was pretty much the case with all the letters in this chapter – it was as if doing so would be beneath their dignity.

THE LOTTERIES THAT CAUSED HUNGER, STARVATION AND MISERY

Lotteries used to be illegal and St Helens police regularly carried out undercover operations against shop-owners for selling tickets. During the 19th century, the so-called "Connolly's" tickets were the most popular type of lottery in

A Connolly's ticket from 1889

St Helens. They cost one shilling and were linked to horse racing with prizes typically ranging from 5 shillings to £10.

It was said that at times as many as 15,000 tickets were in circulation in Lancashire, earning the organisers up to £400 per week. As well as buying lottery tickets, the punters purchased lists costing halfpenny to see if they'd won. On February 6th 1869 this letter was published in the St Helens Newspaper which claimed that more illegal lottery tickets were sold in St Helens than in any other town in England:

Sir, – Yourself and readers must be aware that for some years an extensive number of tickets have been sold in this town, by whom I will not mention, but the police and our superintendent, I dare say, could put their hands upon them if required, and I dare say you have seen a crowd of both young and old, of both sexes, on a Monday evening, between seven and eight o'clock (with what is called a "correct list" of the winning numbers), not far from _____ street and in other streets. These tickets are sent into this town by those who have been before the court at Liverpool, and I think that if the seller of such tickets, for the getting up of such monster drawings as these are, is liable to imprisonment, those who aid in the disposal of such are as guilty as the issuer himself.

I am sure it is quite time these drawings were put a stop to, for I know myself several instances where working men, instead of clothing their children and filling their bellies, have gone and spent seven, eight, and ten shillings to try their luck. I can assure you there are more tickets sold here of one sort and another, than in any town in England. What is the result? Hunger, starvation, and misery must attend it. And even if they do get a prize, who gets the best share but the [pub] landlords, for there is sure to be some one at hand to help the man to spend it when he goes to draw it. I think our worthy and highly esteemed superintendent of the police cannot do better than follow up the suit, and insist that this unwholesome swindle, if I may so call it, shall exist no longer. – I am, Sir, yours &c., **WORKING MAN**.

Presumably the Newspaper censored the name of the St Helens street where the winning lottery number lists were circulated on Monday evenings to prevent their readers from being encouraged to pay a visit.

THE SUNDAY PANDEMONIUM IN GREENBANK

In April 1957 a public inquiry was held into council plans to demolish 167 houses in the Greenbank district of St Helens. Clearance began later in the year and it was the beginning of the end for the mainly Irish district around Liverpool Road, which for a century had been bedevilled by poverty and *(mainly minor)* crime.

In the St Helens Newspaper of March 23rd 1872, this letter was published decrying the state of Greenbank *(with John Barleycorn being a reference to a folk song about alcohol):*

SUNDAY IN GREENBANK – Sir – About ten o'clock on Sunday morning the desecration of the Sabbath really commences; all the juveniles of this populous district are on the streets. As the day advances, the elder portions of the community are on the alert; and the grievances that have taken place on the night previous, consequent upon too great a familiarity with John Barleycorn, are settled either by the tongue or the fist, as the necessities of the case may demand. In the afternoon the children may be seen playing at shuttlecock, skipping-rope, chasing each other from street to street, and uttering phrases which cannot be found in any prayer book.

Compulsory education in this benighted neighbourhood would be the greatest boon under the canopy of heaven. As twilight puts on her mantle, the whole place teems with life, where ignorance and impudence hold high carnival; and I have no hesitation in saying that it would be rather dangerous for a decent person to pass through the locality. And yet in this highly privileged Christian (?) locality the minister of religion is never seen, the emissary of the law seldom. Instead of expending so much money annually to evangelise the heathen, it would be well if the ministers appointed over these unenlightened districts would look after these poor souls entrusted to their care, and show that Christianity is not a name but a reality. The name of Greenbank suggests to the mind something pastoral – something of rustic simplicity and child-like innocence. But what's in a name! If a truly Christian man spent one Sabbath here he would imagine he was near the gates of pandemonium. Hoping these few remarks may have a salutary effect in this portion of the populous town of St. Helens, – I am, yours, &c., **RECTITUDE**."

THE POISONOUS PRESCOT GAS

You know how some people when they see a sign marked "Wet Paint" feel the need to stick their paws on the freshly painted object to see if it really is wet? Well, in 1869 a man in Prescot decided to do something similar – but with his domestic gas supply! He lived to tell the tale – but only just.

Adopting (appropriately) the persona of "Blue Peter", the chap was responding to a letter in the Prescot Reporter from someone called "Blue Billy" who'd complained that the gas supply in Prescot was dangerous. So "Blue Peter" decided to check if it was – with almost fatal consequences. His extraordinary letter was published on March 6th under the headline "Impurity of Prescot Gas":

Sirs, I read the remarks of your correspondent "Blue Billy", with considerable interest, but some doubt. The doubt I determined to satisfy, and it occurred to me that I could do so very easily. Instead of lighting my chandelier at the usual time, I simply turned the gas on, and sat down determined to judge for myself whether the gas really was poisonous. I had not been sat down more than two or three minutes when I found the air in the room had become most polluted. I continued the experiment, however, determined that the trial should be a fair one, until I could only breathe with the greatest difficulty. Already the sensations I experienced were most painful. My head felt like "splitting", and it was only with very great difficulty that I managed to walk to the door to open it. As soon as I could manage to get to the chandelier, I discontinued the experiment, fully satisfied that all Blue Billy says about the poisonous character of the gas is quite correct. I quite agree with him that the gas is poisonous, and if any one doubts the fact after hearing of my experiment, let him try it for himself as I did, and he will require no further argument. – Yours, etc., **BLUE PETER**, Prescot, March 3, 1869.

He would require no further argument, as he would probably be dead! Perhaps the brainless Blue Peter's next experiment was to set himself alight to see whether fire really was dangerous? Although to be fair to Blue Peter, the supply of gas to homes and industry was in its infancy in 1869 and clearly consumers needed some education on its dangers if not handled properly.

THE EARLY CLOSING OF SHOPS

On November 21st 1855, the Rev. Edward Carr chaired a public meeting in St Helens Town Hall. The Vicar of St Helens was leading a campaign to improve the "social, moral, intellectual, and religious well-being" of the townsfolk. Rev. Carr claimed that incessant labour made men "bilious and ill-tempered" and called for shops to close earlier so staff could have more leisure time.

Although the work of shop assistants was not as strenuous or dangerous as those employed in coalmines and industry, the men were expected to labour for very long hours and receive low pay. Rev. Carr suggested that on weekdays shops should shut at 7 or 8pm, with 10pm the limit on Saturdays.

The vicar's campaign had some success – although a letter published in the St Helens Newspaper on March 13th 1869 suggested that the reduction in working hours had mainly benefited shop workers in winter, when the town's poorly-lit streets and worse weather reduced footfall:

Sir – Will you kindly insert the following appeal to the public on behalf of the assistants employed in the various business houses of our town. During the winter months we have been able, through the sympathy of the public and the kindness of our masters, to procure the seven o'clock closing system; and I believe I am speaking the truth when I say that the public have not been in the least inconvenienced, nor have masters suffered through lack of business. But the benefit conferred has been immeasurably great to the recipients; and I firmly believe that the time has not been lost; insomuch that the majority of those so employed are truth-loving and knowledge-seeking young men.

But alas! we look forward to summer, with its expectant beauty and enchantments, with fear; for the precious hour which we have had allotted to us is to be recklessly and thoughtlessly taken from us, during which time we are confined within the narrow limits of brick and mortar, gazing with envy at the passers to an fro in the streets, whilst all nature besides seems blithe and gay. Unless we can gain a reprieve from the sources before referred to, then let me ask you men of business and the public of St. Helens, is it to be, or not to be? Happiness or misery? – that is the question. – I am, &c., on behalf of the community in question, **J. B.**

PAINTED SPARROWS

The avian version of the animal con trick known as the "pig in a poke" was apparently the painting of a live sparrow in order to pass the bird off as a canary. On October 26th 1864 this letter on the subject appeared in the Newspaper from one who claimed to have been conned by an unscrupulous dealer:

> Sir, – Allow me a space in your valuable journal to expose a fraud and trick played on me by a noted bird merchant, residing at Gerard's Bridge. I bought two birds from him (canaries, as I thought), and took them home, when, on close examination, I found them to be painted sparrows, beautifully coloured, so as to deceive the sharpest eye. Hoping, sir, you will give publicity to this, in order that it may be a warning to others, you will oblige your humble servant, **THOMAS DOHERTY**, St. Helens, Oct. 23rd, 1864.

LET THE DEAD BURY THE DEAD

This was the main entrance to the St Helens Borough Cemetery in which a Burial Board provided basic funerals for the very poor. Under the headline *"Let The Dead Bury The Dead"*, this witty letter criticising silent members on the board was published in the St Helens Newspaper on September 17th 1870:

138

Sir, I suppose that the members of the Burial Board, having for a length of time very kindly seen to the interment of the dead of the parish, sundry members of the board have had the same kind office performed for them in return; at least, that is the conclusion I come to from reading the reports of the late meetings. It is true I have very little to judge from, and the little I have is of a very negative character, but, negative as it is, it is of a very conclusive character. Generally speaking, if a man cannot speak he is supposed to be either dumb or dead. I have not heard of any of the members being struck dumb, and I think I should have heard of it if it had happened. I am therefore driven to the conclusion that a number of the members are dead, as they never appear to open their mouths at the board meetings.

Perhaps some one will say that "a still tongue shows a wise head." I am quite willing to admit this may be the case in some instances, but who would venture to say that the members of the St. Helens Burial Board have wise heads? It would be a libel upon a very motherly set of anti-painstaking pantalooned "shemales," who meet at the burial board when they have nothing else to do. – **I. C. U.**

The underlying purpose of the letter was to criticise the Vicar of St Helens' alleged appropriation of the cemetery's lodge and the Burial Board's inaction on the matter. Researching the 19th century meaning of the word "shemale", it could be used to describe a man dressed as a female – but in this context I think the author was simply labelling the board members a bunch of old women!

Flying Saucers Over St Helens

"I am convinced this was the real thing. There are seven people besides myself who saw this terrifying thing."

At the time of writing this book it was stated that the Americans had decided to reclassify UFOs as UAPs – standing for Unidentified Aerial Phenomena. That is apparently because not everything that's strange in the sky flies. Presumably, that was also the principle behind why flying saucers became known as unidentified flying objects, as not all celestial spectacles look like saucers.

This chapter is devoted to the period between the end of WW2 and the late 1970s when the quaint term "flying saucer" was very much in vogue. Such sightings within the St Helens district go back many years, with some easily explained – but most not.

On November 29th 1947 the Liverpool Echo published a report of a flying saucer having been spotted over Merseyside earlier that day. Dockworkers reported witnessing a cone-shaped object travelling through the sky at a speed they felt was far too fast for a jet plane. "It looked very much like a saucer," said one. "It was noiseless and a red flame was issuing from it."

That report led to follow-up accounts by Echo readers – including this one from Richard Formby of Manchester Road in Prescot:

I saw the spectacle at Prescot. It appeared to come from the Widnes direction, travelling very fast and fading out over Liverpool. Its brilliance seemed to increase several times during its flight. I also saw one on Wednesday, November 26, about 5.30 a.m. I was then in the Haresfinch district of St. Helens. This one appeared from over Bootle area and, travelling in the same manner, faded out the other side of St. Helens, thus travelling West to East. They made no noise.

140

KHRUSHCHEV IS AT IT AGAIN!

During the evening of June 15th 1960, what the St Helens Reporter described as a "strange cylindrical shaped object, without wings and emitting a dazzling aura of fluorescent light" was spotted flying over Victoria Square.

A Reporter employee was among the many people that were patiently waiting for buses who were intrigued by the strange manifestation some 2,000 feet above them.

At the time Soviet premier Nikita Khrushchev was promoting his space programme and the American U-2 spy plane was making headlines, after one had been shot down over the Soviet Union while conducting photographic aerial reconnaissance.

These were referenced as members of the puzzled bus queue speculated on explanations for the mysterious object that was hovering over their heads. *"Khrushchev is at it again"*, said one, *"Perhaps it's a U-2"*, commented another and *"It's a cigar version of a flying saucer"*, declared a third.

Five months later on November 16th 1960, the St Helens Newspaper's column called *"Let's Look Around With Paul Newsman"* wrote:

> **A FLYING SAUCER?** – We are reminded that flying saucers are still in the news, by this letter from 12-years-old Sandra Leach, 52, Hillbrae Avenue, Moss Bank. She writes to say: "Last Thursday my friend and I were walking through Clinkham Wood. We were looking at the sky and suddenly saw something come into view. It looked like a flying saucer. The colour of it was like a light bulb. It began to come lower and lower, but then began to ascend slowly. Eventually it just disappeared, but it did look like a flying saucer, I am sure."

FLYING SAUCERS IN FORMATION

It took William and Josephine Cassidy sixteen years to go public over their 1962 sighting of five flying saucers hovering in formation. That was after feeling fobbed off by the authorities who told them the mysterious objects they'd studied from their home in Parr were simply weather balloons.

The couple lived on the second floor of a three-storey block of flats in Cherry Tree Drive that had an unobstructed view over wasteland towards Haydock and Billinge Hill. William Cassidy described the couple's strange experience in the St Helens Reporter in 1978:

It was 12.30 p.m. and I was getting ready to go on duty at Winwick Hospital where I worked as a staff nurse. I looked out of the window and to my utter amazement I saw a formation of flying saucers. I called my wife and we both observed them from the back window. They would hover and then move on, hover and move on alternatively. Moving very slowly their altitude would be not much more than 1,000 feet. As they passed out of sight round the side of the flats we went to the front window and on the way I grabbed a hand telescope. When they came into view I looked at them through the telescope.

No portholes or doors were visible, just what appeared to be continuous metal all the way round. We watched them until they passed out of view over the tops of the houses. They were five in number, one large like a mother ship and four small ones. In colour they were silver. They travelled from Haydock over towards Burtonwood airbase. They were low down and lots of people must have seen them. We contacted the Air Ministry, who said the objects were weather balloons released each day at noon from Preston. They were certainly not balloons.

THE SPACE VISITOR TO PARR!

FRIGHTENED BOYS TELL OF 'VISITOR FROM SPACE'

The drawing of the Flying Saucer by William Holland.

This drawing of a flying saucer was made by William Holland and published in the St Helens Reporter on July 27th 1963. The 12-year-old was amongst a group of lads who insisted they'd witnessed such an alien craft performing manoeuvres in Parr.

Being boys some probably did not take their claim that seriously. Particularly as in the days before their sighting, some unusual craters had been discovered in other parts of the country. These gave rise to theories about extra-terrestrial crashes – and so might have been seen as providing a stimulus for the lads' imagination.

But, as you can read from the Reporter's front-page article, the threesome were adamant they had witnessed a flying saucer – and at least William's parents had accepted his claim.

The report was published under the headline *"Frightened Boys Tell Of 'Visitor From Space'"*:

Mysterious craters which appeared in fields in Dorset and Scotland last weekend gave rise this week to theories about Flying Saucers crashing and visitors from outer space. The crater in Dorset, however, was caused by a small meteorite and the others have not yet been excavated. If a hole had suddenly appeared in waste land opposite Redgate Drive, Parr, on Monday, however, at least three local boys would not have been surprised – they claim they saw a Flying Saucer over the tip. The boys, twelve-years-old William Holland, 42, Redgate Drive, and two friends, Paul Lightfoot and Keith Kerfoot, were playing on the tip about 8:30 p.m. when they noticed a shining object in the sky.

Master Holland takes up the story: "We saw this thing very high up at first, then it came down very fast. It stopped in the air about 70ft. high. It had a red flashing light on top of it and flashed like those on police cars. It was spinning when it first came down but then it stopped and the flashing light went out. We were all watching it when something slid back underneath it and what looked like a periscope came out. It swivelled round and pointed at us. Then it went back in and the machine went up very fast into a cloud. We saw it again about five seconds later, then it vanished."

William told the Reporter that the machine was silver and shining brightly and he and his companions insisted they'd never previously seen photographs or drawings of flying saucers. His parents told the paper they'd been sceptical of their son's story at first but he had been very frightened when he ran into the house. "The colour had gone from his face," Margaret Holland explained.

And William Holland Snr. said: "He and his friends are obviously in earnest. He was told that the joke would be on him if he was pulling our legs, but he insisted he was not and that he, Paul and Keith, saw this thing."

EGG-SHAPED AT A TERRIFIC SPEED

It took a Mrs Jones from Kiln Lane in Dentons Green fourteen years to publicly admit to her flying saucer sighting in March 1964 – although she did make a report to a UFO organisation at the time. In 1978 Mrs Jones described her experience in this letter that she sent to the St Helens Reporter:

> I was taking the washing in off the line at our Kiln Lane home when I heard this high whine. I looked up and saw this egg-shaped thing, silver in colour, travelling at a terrific speed. I ran inside and told my husband but he could not see it. The object then stopped dead as though it had hit a brick wall and hovered over the Recreation Park for a couple of seconds. It then went straight up at a fast speed until it went out of sight. It was amazing and I still can't get over the way it shot straight up into the sky.

THE BOBBY THAT SAW 6 FLYING SAUCERS!

A surprising number of Lancashire policemen have publicly admitted to seeing flying saucers. However, PC Donald Cameron probably holds the record for seeing the most at any one time. The Liverpool Echo of May 17th 1966 told his story under the headline *"Saw Six 'Saucers', Says P.C."*:

> Policeman Donald Cameron is keeping his camera ready hoping for a recurrence of an incident that has left him and his wife, June, shaken, startled and unbelieving. For Donald, aged 22, and June, aged 20, saw not one, not two, not three or four or five – but SIX flying saucers. The "invasion" took place at St. Helens on a dull, grey morning, when Donald, off duty sick, looked out of his back window at 25 Chiltern Road. Hovering in the sky above were six glowing white objects. Said Donald: "One was obviously the mother ship as it was

bigger than the rest. The smaller ones were oval shaped, but the large one had a cup-shaped dome. I shouted to my wife and she watched them with me for half a minute before they disappeared at a great speed towards Manchester. No one else on the estate that I know of saw them, but it [was] early in the morning and our house is the only one that faces in this particular direction. I did not believe in flying saucers before this, but when two of us see it..." Said June: "Now we are keeping our camera ready – just in case they should ever return."

THE TERRIFYING THING OVER POCKET NOOK

A month later Bob Marsh reported seeing a flying saucer in Pocket Nook. The 62-year-old from Scholes Lane in Thatto Heath had been with his colleague Harold Sadler and six workmen when they spotted a rugby-ball shaped object flying 150 ft. above Forsters glassworks.

Then employed in the security industry, Bob had formerly worked as a military policeman and in the war had served as an aircraft tracker. During his military career handling radar, he said he'd dealt with dozens of eyewitness accounts of unidentified flying objects. And so throughout the fifteen minutes while the mysterious object was hovering over Pocket Nook, Bob made a detailed log of times and bearings and later took his findings to the Liverpool radar headquarters for analysis. This is what Mr Marsh told the St Helens Reporter on June 10th 1967:

It was 12:20 a.m. when Mr. Sadler and myself were on a tour of duty near the workshop at the Merton Bank section. I looked towards Pilkington's and saw a phosphorus light about 150ft. from the ground. We took a bearing and while we were watching, a small object dropped from the bottom of the shape. The smaller object had a light on it and it circled round and then disappeared into the top of the bigger

146

object. I dashed into one of the shops and called out as many people as I could. Later, we all saw it. It seemed to be just above St. Mark's Church in North Road. It was like looking straight into the sun. As we looked the glowing light went out. It began going up in jerks. There's nothing at all in this world that could keep up with that thing at the speed it was travelling. I am convinced this was the real thing. It was certainly not an aeroplane or a hallucination. There are seven people besides myself who saw this terrifying thing.

The Reporter contacted St Helens Police and a spokesman said that during the previous few months they had received a series of reports of flying saucers in the district's skies, although mainly from people living in the Billinge area.

THE RUSKIN DRIVE MYSTERY

On December 10th 1971, the St Helens Reporter described how a mysterious object that had been slowly traversing the night sky had interrupted a game of football being played at Ruskin Drive's recreation ground. The piece was published under the headline *"Flying Saucer Holds Up Game"*:

A shot across the sky halted a soccer match, this week. One by one, players stopped to stare as a brightly-lit object moved slowly across the night sky over St. Helens. As it vanished, the game started again on the Ruskin Drive pitch. But minutes later, the UFO returned – travelling in the opposite direction. Pilkington player Jim Walker, 25, of Bryn, said after the sighting on Tuesday: "It wasn't a satellite or a star. And it was moving too slowly for a plane. I'm certain it was a flying saucer, or some other kind of UFO." Team-mate Johnny Parker, 29, of Wycliffe Road, said: "I'd never seen anything like it. It was definitely something very unusual."

STRANGE LIGHTS OVER ST HELENS

On October 29th 1973, the Liverpool Echo published this letter from a man adopting the pseudonym "Puzzled, Bootle":

Sir. – A few weeks ago I was in St. Helens, when I saw what I thought was a bright planet. It was completely stationary. I pointed it out to two of my friends who also agreed it was bright. We forgot it for a moment, then I looked up and noticed it was moving. While we were looking at it, it appeared to blink out, and vanish. Another of my friends has seen strange lights in the sky in a similar area. We are all aware of the shape of aircraft at night, being keen aircraft enthusiasts, but none of us can identify these lights. – Puzzled, Bootle

THE BOLD POWER STATION MYSTERY

By the late 1970s, the term "UFO" had largely replaced "flying saucer" in newspaper accounts of mysterious celestial sightings. For one thing, those claiming to have witnessed such objects rarely said they had been saucer-like. In fact their shapes as described were often quite bizarre!

Pictured here is the St Helens Reporter's simple sketch of the object that two police officers claimed buzzed Bold Power Station in 1978. Although this case is fairly well known, I'm including this strange story as the newspaper's front-page report triggered many other accounts of similar sightings.

This was the Reporter's initial article from January 20th 1978:

A clear sighting of an unidentified flying object has been made over Bold . . . by two traffic cops. Peter Lowe and Gareth Roberts were hurtling along the M62 when they saw a brilliant white object hovering in the sky. "It was large and shaped like a three-pronged star," said Police Constable Lowe, aged 44. "Neither of us believed in UFO's, but after this we are firm believers. It was very bright and seemed to be pulsating. The object was brighter at [the] bottom than the top and was surrounded by a throbbing glow." Police Constable Lowe, of Knotty Ash and 38-year-old Police Constable Roberts of Penketh, radioed their Prescot headquarters. Air traffic control at Speke and Ringway were contacted but no aircraft were in the area at the time of the sighting. "It hovered for about five seconds before taking off at a terrific speed towards Warrington," said Police Constable Roberts. "The object stopped again and then went straight up into the sky at an alarming speed. It was in view for about 15 seconds."

The two experienced officers made their sighting at 4:45 p.m. last Wednesday. They later learned that two members of the public also reported seeing the same three-pronged object on the Wednesday. Police Constable Lowe described the UFO as a "pure white light" and added: "It was right in front of us and there is no way it could have been an aircraft or simply a star. The thing hovered over Bold and moved horizontally before taking a vertical path out of sight. I am convinced it was a UFO." Police Constable Roberts said: "The object was something which could not be picked up on the airport radar scanners and I am now convinced UFO's exist. I did not on Tuesday but I do now. The sighting makes me curious about the possibility of there being another world and we will both be keeping our eyes open for UFO's from now on."

LIKE A BLAZING WHITE DIAMOND

The publication of the sketch proved a shock to Eileen Callery. Almost a year to the day before the Bold sighting, the 57-year-old had opened the front door of her terraced home in Crag Grove in Clinkham Wood and seen the same star-shaped object.

"It gave me such a fright when I saw the sketch in last week's Reporter," Mrs Callery said. "It was exactly the same as the shape I saw last year. It was shining like a blazing white diamond. Lights were throbbing all around it and I was numbed and could not move."

Eileen Callery's account was published in the paper on January 27th 1978, alongside an interview with local UFO expert Brian Fishwick. The 25-year-old fireman from Chamberlain Street in St Helens told journalist Phil Wolsey that a dozen credible sightings of UFOs had been made in the town during the previous two years.

And he reckoned to have witnessed twelve himself since his first sighting of an orange object over St Helens Cemetery in 1966. That had "hovered for three or four minutes before shooting off at a terrific speed".

The article claimed that St Helens could be a "cosmic Spaghetti Junction in the Interplanetary world of UFO's" – essentially because some considered the town to be on the aliens' global flight-path. Mr Fishwick explained:

Over the last couple of years St. Helens has been one of the top areas for UFO sightings. There must be many more sightings which people have not bothered to report and there could be hundreds which go undetected.

Although the term "flying saucer" was used once in the piece, it was stated that the appearances of the many objects varied wildly.

That led to the Reporter publishing a graphic of some of the more common shapes that had been reported.

Did you spot any of these?

This graphic was published in the St Helens Reporter on January 27th 1978

In the following week's edition of the paper, four persons claimed to have witnessed flying saucers and other mysterious objects in the skies over St Helens. Janet Clark from Moss Lane said in May 1977 she'd seen a "dark, alien blob" that she described as having been "long and cigar-shaped".

And then on February 10th more extracts from letters were published. 21-year-old John Smith from Albion Street in St Helens claimed to have made numerous sightings over the past 10 years with one notable encounter having taken place near Earlestown in which a boomerang-shaped object had manifested itself. John wrote:

Reporter artist's impression of John Smith's sighting

151

One night my brother William and I were cycling along Sankey Valley near the nine arches bridge when we saw a boomerang shaped object, glowing white, hovering in the sky. We took it to be a star but then it moved slowly, picked up speed and then shot out of sight at a tremendous velocity. I am, I suppose, what is commonly known as a flying saucer freak. I am a keen observer and can tell the difference between balloons, clouds, planes or a speck of dust in my eyes.

TRAIL OF FIRE

It can be a bit disappointing when rational explanations are provided for flying saucer / UFO sightings. On January 5th 1979, Jacqueline Jackson-Dalton of Lickers Lane in Prescot told the Echo of a strange object that she had seen in the evening sky. However, the orange light with a "trail of fire" behind it bore the hallmarks of a meteorite or shooting star falling to earth.

In 1991 a light show that was part of Blackpool illuminations sparked a scare of an alien invasion as many concerned persons up to seventy miles distant from the resort contacted the police. However, one of the strangest natural explanations for a saucer sighting was made in St Helens in 1957. On January 5th of that year the Reporter wrote:

A disc-shaped object, roughly two yards wide, was seen in the Mill Lane, Sutton, area at about 3:30 p.m. on Tuesday afternoon, by 10 people. The people claim that the object was travelling at a high altitude in a Northerly direction and was in view for one minute. Among the witnesses were Messrs. G. Thompson, G. A. Langsdale, J. Lart, A. Hunter, A. Jadwatt, M. P. Pattel, the Misses A. and J. Rhodes and Mrs. G. Rhodes, at whose home they were having their photographs taken.

However, a week later the Reporter revealed that the craft that had mystified ten persons in Mill Lane had only been Peter Barker's model plane! The 15-year-old from Leach Lane had been flying what seemed to have been a Christmas gift on fields off Hawthorn Road. The paper explained:

Peter launched his 39 in. span powered model into an East wind and it flew at a height of roughly 150ft. for three minutes. It made a very wide arc towards Mill Lane. The people who saw the object last week described it as disc-shaped and flying at a high altitude, an impression which could be explained away by the fact that it was a dull day.

And I will conclude this chapter with another quote from John Smith. In the St Helens Reporter in 1978 the self-confessed "flying saucer freak" offered a curious – if, perhaps, tongue-in-cheek – theory as why spaceships were seemingly visiting Earth:

We have all seen the travel agent in the high street. Well, suppose that in the solar system there are numerous agents giving cut-price sightseeing tours of good old terra firma?

At the time of writing this book, billionaires are paying for seats on short duration space flights. So, could the flying saucer / UFO manifestations prove a similar, extra-terrestrial tourist trip of our planet? I'm not so sure it would be cut-price though!

A Collection Of Bizarre Rainford Stories

Having been born and brought up in Rainford, I do have a particular affinity with the village. Rainford stories do leap out at me from the old newspapers and here are a few of my favourites.

1) THE "TERROR OF RAINFORD'S" MURDEROUS ASSAULT ON THE POLICE

"It appears the prisoner has for some time been a terror to the peaceful inhabitants of Rainford, and for some time been committing offences with impunity, the persons fearing the desperate character of the man."

This is Richard Rothwell pictured in his prison uniform in 1874. This gentle-looking grandfather from Maggots Nook in Rainford was then serving a long sentence at Parkhurst prison after being convicted of stabbing and nearly killing a policeman – just 50 yards away from Rainford police station.

Rothwell had been born in Bickerstaffe c.1803 and had moved to Hydes Brow / Maggots Nook in Rainford around 1840 with his wife Alice – and the couple had eight children. Persons in Victorian times were on average 4 to 5 inches shorter than we are today and it was rare for anyone to reach 6 ft. And so standing at nearly 6 feet 1 inch, Rothwell was very tall for the time and probably used to getting his own way with his neighbours. Upon his arrival at prison the records describe Rothwell as being stout and bearing a fresh complexion. The picture suggests that after eleven years of incarceration in a harsh Victorian gaol, both of those features were long gone.

Rothwell had been in trouble with the law before his attack on the police. The coal miner had served a month in prison in 1849 for stealing potatoes and a further fourteen days in 1852 after being caught poaching. However, the charge made against him in 1863 was much more serious.

It was a curious policy of the time for the police not to routinely search suspects on the street. I am not certain of the reasons why, but suspect that the bobbies preferred examinations to be made in a well-lit police station with witnesses, rather than on a dark street. That dangerous policy could lead to attacks on police and the attempted disposal of evidence while suspects were being marched to the station.

SATURDAY, JULY 4, 1863.

Capture, and Desperate Attempt at Escape, of a Robber, at Rainford.

A POLICEMAN STABBED.

For some months past there have been carried on a series of robberies in Rainford and neighbourhood. The perpetrator of them has all along been suspected

The St Helens Newspaper's initial report of Rothwell's arrest

The non-searching practice almost cost the life of PC James Shaw, as he and PC Rigby escorted Richard Rothwell to Rainford Police Station from his place of arrest at Victoria Colliery. The station was then located in the stretch of Church Road from Pasture Lane to the Derby Arms that was known as School Brow and the coal mine was situated in Old Lane, where a tar works would later be sited.

This is the St Helens Newspaper's initial report from July 4th 1863 into what had occurred on that fateful night:

For some months past there have been carried on a series of robberies in Rainford and neighbourhood. The perpetrator of them has all along been suspected but his well known daring character has in some measure aided his successful attempts to elude the vigilance of the police. Matters however came to such a pass, that strict orders were given to the policemen to keep a most wary eye upon the suspected person, and to capture him if possible. Accordingly police-constables Shaw and Rigby have been particularly watchful of this person's proceedings for the past few days, and on Wednesday night they were dogging him at various places.

Early on Thursday morning, about one o'clock, they were in a barn, and followed him to the Rainford colliery. Shaw left behind his cape, and when they returned to the barn the man they had been watching had walked off with it. Soon after they saw him stealing some timber from the Rainford colliery, and took him into custody. The man's name is Richard Rothwell, and he is tall and robust, and somewhat advanced in years. He allowed himself to be taken quietly, but asked not to have both his hands fastened. They acceded to his request.

Shaw put the handcuff on the prisoner's left hand and held him by the right. As they were going along, the prisoner made a sudden dash to escape, and lifted up his right hand and stabbed Shaw on the ribs; he then made another determined stab at Rigby, but only succeeded in cutting through his clothes on one of the arms and slightly grazing his lip. Rigby immediately got his staff out and belaboured the prisoner right well, and although Shaw was hardly sensible he used a brush that he had in his hand against the prisoner, who never succeeded in getting loose from Shaw's grasp. The man was firmly secured and brought to St. Helens on Thursday afternoon. Shaw, it was ascertained, had received a very dangerous wound, and is confined to his bed.

He will be unable to appear to give evidence for some days. The knife was afterwards found near the spot covered with blood, and one of its blades, the smaller one, was fairly bent double, such had been the force of the blow. The weapon was a pocket knife containing two blades, about five inches and four inches respectively. The smaller blade was used. On searching the prisoner's house a pig cote was discovered, nicely whitewashed; above it was a false roof, and under the floor was also found to be equally false. Both places were stored with the produce of his many robberies.

The Liverpool Mercury in their account described the 60-year-old Rothwell as a *"powerful-looking man"* and said he had committed a *"murderous assault"* on the two bobbies, adding:

It appears that the prisoner has for some time been a terror to the peaceful inhabitants of Rainford", they added, "and he had for some time been committing offences of various kinds with impunity, the persons aggrieved fearing the desperate character of the man.

Court proceedings had to be delayed for a few days until the condition of PC James Shaw had improved. By July 9th the 37-year-old officer was deemed fit enough to give evidence but still unfit to leave home. So the courtroom was moved from New Market Place in St Helens to Shaw's police house in Rainford's

School Brow and the constable gave his testimony to magistrate William Pilkington from his bed.

The longwinded charge that Richard Rothwell faced was of "feloniously wounding Police-constable James Shaw, with intent, in so doing, then and thereby feloniously, wilfully, and of his malice aforethought, to kill and murder the said James Shaw". This is part of the injured officer's court statement:

> I reside at the Rainford Police-station, and have received information of many robberies in and about Rainford, and from time to time I have reported them to Mr Superintendent Jervis. I have called at the places where the robberies have been committed, but the people have refused to tell me what they knew. On the 1st June, Mr Jervis instructed me to watch for the prisoner, who is a tall, powerful man, and a terror to the inhabitants. He is a labourer, but for some time has not followed any employment. Late on Wednesday night, the 1st instant, I went to Alice Birchall's farm, in company with P.C. Rigby.

> We went into the barn and remained there some time; we then left the barn, where I left my cape, and proceeded to the Victoria Colliery, a short distance off. About half-past two o'clock in the morning I saw a man going from the direction of the colliery premises, carrying something. I directed Rigby to meet him, whilst I went behind; the man had not proceeded many yards before he saw Rigby coming, and he immediately threw down the three boards produced and ran back, when I met him and stopped him; he tried to pull from his pockets the ropes I now produce. The moment we got hold of him and attempted to handcuff him, he commenced struggling and fighting to get away, but I succeeded in getting the handcuffs on his left wrist and then we prevailed on him to go quietly, and he promised to do so.

158

I went on with him holding the handcuffs, and he had his right hand at liberty and occasionally put it in his pocket; [PC] Rigby followed behind with the timber. We went for about a mile, and had got within 50 or 60 yards from the station, when the prisoner suddenly turned round upon me and struck me a violent blow on my left jaw, and I could feel something cut across; then he struck me on my left side over my heart; I thought my ribs were broken and it made me bend double; I still held the handcuffs fast to his left wrist, and I then struck him with a brush I had taken out of his pocket. He was striking at me again when Rigby got up and the prisoner turned on him and knocked him backwards, and then Rigby knocked him down with his staff.

He then said he would go quietly, but as soon as he got up he turned on me again and struck at my left arm and kicked my left leg. I was bleeding fast and fell two or three times from exhaustion in the struggle, but we got him in at last. It was then about three o'clock. Dr. Shepherd was called in to me, and has attended me up to the present time. I have kept my bed ever since. I have known the prisoner for some time, and about three o'clock on the morning but one before this took place, I met the prisoner on the road carrying a basket. He said "I understand you are in search of me." I said I am only in search of people that are doing wrong. He then told me to look out, he would do for me yet. I don't know how he opened his knife except he did it in his pocket as we were walking along. These are the clothes I had on on the morning in question, and they are saturated with blood; the cuts were not in them before I struggled with the prisoner.

PC James Rigby told the hearing how Rothwell had also struck out at him. The 26-year-old constable added that once the prisoner was locked up, he and James Shaw's 13-year-old son Charles had gone in search of the knife. The boy found it in a potato field 12 yards from the scene of the struggle, with the blade being bent and having blood on it.

The doctor, Thomas Shepherd, also gave evidence but Rothwell denied stabbing the two policemen and even claimed they had attacked him first! The unusual court hearing concluded with the 60-year-old "terror" committed to the South Lancashire Assizes.

Rothwell's trial in front of a judge and jury was held six weeks later and largely contained the same evidence as given at Rainford. Although PC Shaw did add that when he apprehended Rothwell leaving Victoria Colliery, he'd said to him "I have caught you at last". To that Rothwell replied, "Oh dear, let me go; I am out of my mind." The constable's injuries had been so serious that he'd been confined to bed for a fortnight and had still not returned to work.

Dr Shepherd stated in his evidence that but for the blade of the knife bending by contact with the injured man's ribs, the wound would have proved fatal. The jury found the prisoner guilty and Rothwell was sentenced to penal servitude for twenty years.

Rothwell's prison record at Millbank Prison in Westminster and later at Parkhurst suggests he was a cantankerous old man – constantly being reported for minor offences, such as being abusive to warders and refusing to obey their instructions. After reading this article you will probably not be surprised by that!

The terror of Rainford was released from prison in 1876 after serving two-thirds of his term, a year after his long-suffering wife Alice had died.

Rothwell's release on licence at the age of 73 was upon him agreeing to a few conditions. One was that he must not "habitually associate with notoriously bad characters, such as reputed thieves and prostitutes" – which sounds like it was all right for him to see such folk from time to time but not to make a habit of it! Richard Rothwell died in 1879.

31, 0 2 6

ORDER of LICENCE to a CONVICT
made under the Statutes 16 and 17
Vict., c. 99, s. 9, and 27 and 28 Vict.,
c. 47, s. 4.

WHITEHALL,

14 day of *December* 187 *6*.

HER MAJESTY is graciously pleased to grant to

Richard Rothwell

convicted of *bounding with intent to do grievous bodily harm* who was
at the *Assize holden*
for the *County of Lancaster at Liverpool* on
the *5th* day of *August 1863* and was then and there
sentenced to be kept in Penal Servitude for the term of

twenty years

and is now confined in the
Parkhurst Prison

The *"licence to be at large"* that Queen Victoria granted to Richard Rothwell

2) THE RAINFORD CHURCH STEAM AND LIGHTNING ACCELERATOR MACHINE

"The music will be of the most dismal and horrible description, and includes a choice selection of pandemonium melodies."

This is the old Rainford Parish Church, which in 1878 was replaced by the present building. In 1870 worshippers had the added attraction of the "Royal Patent Steam and Lightning Accelerator Machine" at the Sunday morning service – at least that's what handbills claimed. During the 19th

century, the promotion of events was more likely to be in the form of handbills or posters *(often called placards)* – rather than adverts in newspapers. Whether churches regularly distributed bills to advertise their services I cannot say. However, Rainford Church's service held on June 26th 1870 was certainly promoted in that way – but not by its minister! This is how the bizarre handbill read:

GRAND AND STUPENDOUS SACRED MORNING PERFORMANCES. On and after next Sunday, until further notice, will be performed weekly in the RAINFORD CHURCH by the Royal Patent Steam and Lightning Accelerator Machine. The whole of the Morning Service including Sermons and Hymns. By means of this latest and astounding mechanical invention, the entire service is guaranteed not to exceed 74 minutes and 59¾ seconds. The music will be of the most dismal and horrible description, and includes a choice selection of pandemonium melodies. Carriages and in most cases, dinners may be ordered for 11:45 a.m.

The St Helens Newspaper reproduced the poster and explained that there'd been criticism of the form and duration of services in the church – and consequently attendances had dropped off. So some joker had chosen to spoof the services – but at the same time convey the message they were machine-like, too short and featured dodgy music.

As a result of the handbill's appearance, several Rainford residents had their views on the subject published in the Newspaper. One referred to the spoof advert as a *"clever placard"* that had *"for days being the delight and the talk of the Rainford people"*.

However, two other correspondents supported the church, calling it a *"horrid hand-bill"* and a *"nasty placard"*. But my favourite missive was from someone calling themselves "A Church Goer" whose letter was very much in support of the handbill, writing:

Sir, I'm no scholar but will yolse give me a word or two about the Rainford Services. If there was another Church within a mile of Rainford I am sure I should go to it for the Services at Rainford seem so cold and dull that I cant get any good from them and the singin I cant abear. Oh! that Ministers had more energy and not be so frightened of themselves. Why Sir – there are houses of churchmen in Rainford as had not had a Minister in them for years and what are Ministers paid for – I am Sir, yours respectfully, **A CHURCH GOER**, Rainford, June 28th, 1870.

3) BOY MEETS GIRL – 1860s STYLE!

"On the officer taking him into custody he seemed drunk and stupid but when taken outside he appeared rather sober and afterwards admitted he went there to see 'for the girl'."

Over the years there have been many ways in which boys and girls could get acquainted – taking into account the social standards of the time. My chapter "The Teenage Parading On The Streets Of St Helens " demonstrates one means.

Breaking into the bedroom of a girl and hiding under her bed is another method for a boy to get to know a prospective girlfriend – but probably least likely to result in a positive outcome! But that is what dopey George Shuttleworth did in 1862.

The incident took place in the Brewers Arms in May Pole Brow in Rainford, which was in Higher Lane, near the top of Cross Pit Lane. There was no suggestion made in Shuttleworth's court case that a sexual assault of any kind had been intended – although clearly alcohol had played some role in the affair. The St Helens Weekly News published details of the resulting court case on April 2nd 1862, under the headline *"Going A Courting Without Leave"*:

In this case it appeared that George Shuttleworth, aged 17 years, (who was now brought up in custody) had been drinking in the house of Mr. Hugh Penketh, Rainford, on Saturday night last, and of course was turned out at the usual closing time; on the daughter's (about 14 years of age) going to bed, she found that he was under it, and immediately went and told her father, who came and pulled him from under, he either being asleep or "shamming" at the time. A constable was fetched and the boy given in charge [arrested]. It was found that he must have got in by the window, as a pane of glass was broke and the curtains turned aside; there was also a rain-tub outside, by which he would be enabled to reach the window.

On the officer taking him into custody he seemed drunk and stupid, and said he didn't know what he was there for; but when taken outside he appeared rather sober and afterwards admitted he went there to see "for the girl". The boy was the son of a neighbour and nothing was known against him [had no prior convictions]. Mr. Marsh appeared to defend. After a short consultation the magistrates thought it would be better for the parties to make it up; and Mr. Marsh said the father was quite willing to pay any compensation that might be required; the case was therefore settled amicably.

The 1861 census tells us that publican Hugh Penketh was also a wheelwright; his 14-year-old daughter was called Sarah and her 17-year-old suitor, George Shuttleworth, was a colliery labourer.

One document I have not been able to locate is a record of marriage between Sarah and George. Clearly, hiding under your intended's bed is not a recommended method of courting!

4) THE SHAMEFUL SHADOW DANCE AND NUDES IN RAINFORD VILLAGE HALL

"It was simply shameful. The band was curtained off and the room was in semi-darkness. It was simply disgraceful."

Rainford Village Hall has witnessed countless events since it opened in 1907 – and sometimes these have caused offence. Of course, breaching the highly conservative moral code of the past could easily be achieved.

In 1920 a man was banned from holding dances at the Village Hall because of previously promoting a *"Shadow Dance"*. That was a popular dance during that decade which involved the hall lights being turned off and a beam of light then flashed onto dancers – an early version of the disco mirror / glitter ball.

However, when lights are off couples could potentially get up to all sorts of shenanigans. At least that is what official minds thought and led to the council's ban.

The St Helens Reporter of February 20th 1920 – under the headline *"Rainford Councillor Alarmed – Condemns 'The Shadow Dance'"* – takes up the story:

At Monday evening's meeting of the Rainford Urban District Council, held at the Council Offices, an application was read for permission to hire the Village Hall. It was explained that in all probability it would be used for a dance. Coun. J. Evans – "The last time these people had a dance they had what is called the 'shadow dance'. It was simply shameful. The band was curtained off and the room was in semi-darkness. I do not think it is a thing we ought to have in Rainford; it was simply disgraceful." It was resolved not to let the hall to the applicant.

Then the conversation turned to a different dance that had been held on the previous Saturday in which the hall caretaker had been threatened:

Councillor Huyton said he had heard that thirty men were drunk and that when the police were sent for they would not attend. "It is quite time this sort of thing was stopped", he added. The Clerk to the council advised the councillors to take some action as otherwise, he said, the Village Hall would become a "Bedlam Hall". Cllr Eden added that if it was not possible to conduct the Village Hall without the aid of the police then it was time to close it down. It was ultimately decided to ask those that had threatened the caretaker to apologise and if they refused, legal proceedings would be taken against them.

There had been no suggestion that anything untoward had actually taken place during the shadow dance but its promoter had still received a ban – unlike the organiser of the drunken event.

Fast-forward 46 years and it was the council itself that was promoting an event that got the local vicar hot under his dog collar. Under the headline *"Protest Over Nudes in the Village Hall"*, the Liverpool Echo on August 6th 1966 wrote:

The Rev. Harry Bellis, (Vicar) and some of the 6,000 villagers at Rainford, are registering strong objections to an art exhibition to be staged by the North Western Museum Art Gallery Services, in Rainford Village Hall on August 24, 25 and 26. The exhibition is being sponsored by Rainford U.D.C. [Urban District Council] and will include some 25 nude paintings, but there will also be local paintings, sculpture exhibits and pottery.

Said Mr. Bellis: "I don't see any need for an exhibition of this sort in a place the size of Rainford. I object because I think it could have an adverse affect on the morals of young people in the community." Disagreeing with a suggestion by County Councillor Mrs. Sarah Heyes, a member of Rainford Council, that the exhibition would be educational, Mr. Bellis said the only people to benefit would be art students, who take lessons on nude art as part of their curriculum.

The exhibition is being advertised on posters carrying a pen drawing of the rear view of a buxom nude, but a local resident commented: "With all the publicity given to the objections, it will not need advertising." County Councillor Mrs. Heyes of Mossborough Hall Farm, Rainford, replying to the vicar of Rainford, said: "Young people do not need to see this sort of thing to have their morals affected. Television does that already." Stating that the Council could not be the censor of the public morals, Mrs. Heyes said: "I cannot say that I admire this sort of thing, but I am not against anyone who does."

The story made its way into the Sunday People, which quoted Rev. Bellis as suggesting that Rainford citizens were not sophisticated enough to view such paintings. This is the brief article, which was published under the headline "Vicar Protests Over Nude Show":

A row over 25 nude paintings has flared in the sleepy Lancashire village of Rainford. The council plans to exhibit them in the village hall, and to advertise the show with posters showing the rear view of a buxom nude. But the town's vicar, the Rev. Harry Bellis, said yesterday: "These nudes will be grossly out of place in a village such as ours. They may be all right in a city where the public is likely to be more sophisticated than we are here. I feel the paintings will offend many people and perhaps impress our youngsters the wrong way."

Protest over nudes in the village hall

The Rev. Harry Bellis, (Vicar) and some of the 6,000 villagers at Rainford, are registering strong objections to an art exhibition to be staged by the North Western Museum Art Gallery Services. in Rainford Village Hall on August 24, 25 and 26.

would be educational. Mr. Bellis said the only people to benefit would be art students. who take lessons on nude art as part of their curriculum.

The exhibition is being advertised on posters carrying a pen drawing of the rear view of a buxom nude. but a local resident

The Liverpool Echo August 6th 1966

5) THE RAINFORD RAGING INFERNO

"Such a season of terror has never been known in the neighbourhood."

Present-day Rainford place names – such as Thickwood Moss, Moss Nook, Moss Brow, Moss Lane, Mossborough Road and Holiday Moss – are reminders of the village's past landscape. In those past times, winters were very wet, marshy swamps abounded and during very dry summers, wild fires would rage.

On October 28th 1921, James Hoult wrote an article in the St Helens Reporter titled *"Rainford and Mossborough"*, which began:

A river in miniature, which runs the length of the township from north-west to south-east gives [its] name to Rainford. This brook empties itself into the Mersey. Moss lands were plentiful until the last century as place names indicate. Its position among the bogs and mosses caused its early history to be little known to the outside world.

Five decades earlier, on August 11th 1869, Lord Stanley of Knowsley Hall recalled a time not long passed when a *"very large proportion"* of Rainford and other nearby villages had been *"occupied by those unsightly and uncomfortable swamps which people hereabouts called marshes."*

Lord Stanley of Knowsley Hall

The former Foreign Secretary remembered how after wet weather, the land had been unsafe to walk over and useless for cultivation. Although some of the marshes still remained, Lord Stanley said most had been reclaimed and consequently many hundreds of acres of land could now be cultivated.

Seventeen years earlier – at the end of April 1852, before St Helens newspapers began – the Liverpool Albion newspaper published this account of how a drought had led to several miles of the Rainford district becoming a raging inferno:

For several days fires have been raging on Rainford Heath, about ten miles from Liverpool, and in various other districts in that direction, extending for miles round. In that locality large tracts of land are kept as game preserves, and are in places covered with a kind of moss of considerable depth, and which, owing to the long drought, had become very dry. The keepers and stewards of the Earl of Derby, knowing the danger of firing the heath, had given strict orders to the tenantry not to burn anything upon it; but in the middle of the week a farmer named Swift unwisely set fire to some rank grass. He quickly discovered the error he had made. There was a strong westwardly wind, and the fire was driven along until it obtained a communication with the thick beds of furze [type of bush], which blazed as though they were impregnated with an inflammable liquid. Trenches were dug and sods placed down in the hope that they would act as barriers to the progress of the fire, but still the flames sped on, leaping over trenches, creeping through the long grass and furze, and stretching over places where the soil was exposed, and across high roads and by roads, to spots where traces of their ravages might be left.

The supply of water in the locality was small, and messengers were despatched to the nearest place, where such a vehicle could be found, for a water cart. But the attempt to extinguish the flames by that means proved abortive; for still the fire extended until the nearest plantation was reached. A scene of fearful grandeur ensued. The trees, dry as firewood, gave fuel to the flames, which shot high up into the air. Like a giant refreshed, the fire then extended still further, and destroyed another plantation on Rainford Heath. The screams of hares and rabbits, and the cries of pheasants and partridges, as they were being roasted alive, were quite distressing.

Numbers of partridges were seen to rise from the burning heath, ascend a little distance, and then, some from suffocation, and others, because of their scorched pinions failing them, tumbled down into the fire. On Friday the fire, or, rather, fires, were at their greatest height. One had been burning several days, in that part of the parish of Bickerstaff through which the East Lancashire Railway passes. It had commenced, apparently, by the side of the line, and was caused, it is supposed, by a hot cinder from an engine falling upon the dry grass. The only dwelling on the line, called "The Level Crossing-house," is a lodge placed as a protection to the Earl of Derby's private carriage-road.

The occupant, Thomas Shacklady, a hale old man, and his son were obliged to exert themselves most strenuously on the nights of Thursday and Friday to prevent the flames extending to their home and destroying it. They describe the scene, on Friday morning, at eleven o'clock, as one of a fearful nature. Such a season of terror has never been known in the neighbourhood. An aged man, whose years numbered more than a hundred, says he has frequently known the moss to be on fire, but never to such an extent as on the present occasion.

The poor old man at the gate-house, when questioned on the subject by our reporter, appeared quite bewildered, and unable to give the slightest account of the matter:- "I've known note about how it got agate, nor how far it goes; there be fires all round, for miles round," he said; and afterwards, in alluding to the great exertions he and his son had used, he observed, "I've never had such another job in my life; we've been hard at it all day, and ha' been obliged to sit up two nights, and shall again to-night. There's no depending how soon the flames may break out again." On its being suggested to him that the most providential thing would be a good shower of rain, he exclaimed, "Aye, dear, what a good thing that would be; it would be worth anything if it would come a good shower of rain. Aye, how thankful we should be, to be sure."

The Pioneer Record
Retailers Of St Helens

"I happily remember ballad singers – fellows selling a popular song at a copper or two for each printed sheet of words and music, and singing the song to prospective customers."

a) INTRODUCTION

A chronicle of record retailers might seem little more than a listing of shops, dates and locations – a worthy undertaking, but, perhaps, a little dull. However, a deep dive through local newspapers reveals a number of remarkable stories behind those engaged in the retailing of music in St Helens.

There was the pioneering businesswoman who turned the tables on her violent husband and ran her Hall Street shop for 50 years. Then there's the Duke Street war hero who did not let the fact he had only one arm hinder his business. And the hysteria in Ormskirk Street when Frankie Vaughan opened Rothery Recordings and a huge mob of teenage girls screamed, swooned and clawed at the crooner.

This chapter is not intended as a comprehensive list of record retailers within the St Helens district. Over the years many dealers have sold discs – including my own father Tom Wainwright in Rainford, traders on St Helens market and in the town's department stores. My intention is instead to describe how record retailing developed in the town – and reveal some of the remarkable background stories of those who were involved.

b) THE BALLAD SINGER SALESMEN

Do you remember the booths in record shops that allowed prospective purchasers to preview discs before purchasing them?

Music lovers in the 19th century also liked to hear their song sheets demonstrated prior to coughing up their cash and so salesmen vocalists paraded the streets. It was a simple sales pitch and the practice continued into the 20th century, as Thomas Owen *(b. 1899)* remembered in an article published in the St Helens Reporter in May 1970:

> I also happily remember ballad singers – fellows selling a popular song at a copper or two for each printed sheet of words and music, and singing the song in the street to prospective customers. I bought "Mother Machree" and "When Irish Eyes are Smiling" that way.

However, the singers had to be careful that their lyrics did not offend the police. On May 12th 1873 a crooner called Patrick Hayes found himself in St Helens Petty Sessions, charged with singing what the St Helens Newspaper called "filthy street songs", although in reality the lyrics were little more than suggestive. The Newspaper wrote:

> Patrick Hayes was charged with singing and vending obscene songs in Shaw street and other parts of the town, on Saturday evening. The prisoner denied the obscenity. Several of the songs were submitted to the bench, and while they contained no sentence which was absolutely obscene, the words were yet so arranged as to suggest obscenity. It was proved that he had been cautioned once, and afterwards tried to follow his offensive occupation and at the same time keep clear of the police. The prisoner appealed to the bench to let him off, promising to leave the town at once if released. He was fined £2 and costs, with a month's imprisonment in default of payment.

Other newspapers stated that Hayes was unable to pay the fine. And so for simply singing suggestive songs, the man had to serve the alternative prison term.

c) THE PHONOGRAPH AT ST HELENS

Just when the people of St Helens were given their first opportunity to hear recorded music, I cannot be certain – but it may have been 1889. Then the phonograph was demonstrated at the Town Hall to a rather apathetic public. The St Helens Reporter described its poor reception on December 21st of that year:

> On Friday and Saturday evenings last week the people of St. Helens had the opportunity of seeing and hearing Mr. Edison's new invention, the phonograph, brought to St. Helens through Mr. G. W. Whitfield. The wonderful instrument was on view at the Town Hall, but St. Helens, as usual, showed its indifference to scientific subjects, as there was a very sparse attendance of the public on both evenings. The principle of the phonograph was first explained by Professor Archibald, M.A. (Oxon), by the aid of diagrams thrown on the screen by a lantern. The sound is produced by the instrument on the same principle as sound is conveyed by the human ear. Dealing first with loud records, the machine gave a repetition of cornet solos, brass bands, coach horns, and other sounds, which it had captured. Afterwards low tone records were given, six persons at a time with tubes in their ears being able to hear them on the platform. The low tone records included a rendition of "Tit Willow," given with the perfect quality of a male voice.

However, it's possible that the phonograph may have been demonstrated in St Helens well before 1889, as the device had been exhibited in Liverpool eleven years before. On July 23rd 1878 the Liverpool Mercury wrote:

> The phonograph is like the small, but precocious brother of a young lady. It will repeat everything said in its presence without any regard for blushes.

On October 25th of that year the Mercury published an advert for a fundraising event in aid of St Silas's Church in Toxteth in which a "phonograph or talking machine" was one of the attractions. Admission was sixpence, although for one shilling extra punters could have their voice recorded on a phonograph.

Not that the customers would have been able to play the disc at home, of course, as they would not have had a machine. However the phonograph disc would have been played back on the stall, creating great amusement, no doubt, for those with a bob to spare.

The first reference that I can find to the machine being used as a novelty fundraiser in St Helens was in 1894 when a Catholic Fancy Fair was held in Dentons Green. This was in aid of the re-roofing of Holy Cross Church and the many attractions included a phonograph exhibition.

d) MARY PETERS OF HALL STREET

Mary Peters was probably the first retailer of phonographs and gramophones in St Helens. Her Hall Street music shop – selling

machines and discs, musical instruments and sheet music –
opened its doors in 1902 and lasted for over fifty years. A
remarkable woman, Mary suffered brutality in her marriage,
obtained a rare divorce and sought revenge on her former spouse
by keeping the business that he had founded.

Born of Irish parents in Liscard on July 28th 1875, Mary Josephine
Noblett married James Peters at Toxteth Park in 1898 and the
couple had three children. The family moved from Liverpool to St
Helens about 1902 and opened their music shop in Hall Street on
September 11th of that year. The first newspaper reference to the
Peters' shop that I can find was published in the Bolton Evening
News on December 2nd of 1905:

> Mrs M. J. Peters, a musical instrument dealer of St. Helens,
> was summoned in that town, on Friday, for causing street
> obstruction through playing phonographs and gramophones,
> causing large crowds to assemble outside her shop. For the
> defence it was stated that the matter was an important one
> for music-dealers generally, as if they were prevented from
> trying their instruments and gramophone records in the shop
> there was an end to their business. Councillor Hatton, who
> was in the shop at the time purchasing a record, said he
> would not buy one without first trying it. Upon the defendant
> undertaking that the records should not be played except
> when customers were in the shop the case was dismissed.

The newspaper article is interesting on two counts. The large
crowds demonstrate that machines that were able to reproduce
music from a disc were still very much a novelty. And Mary is
identified as a musical instrument dealer – rather than a purveyor
of phonograph records.

As the business developed, so its focus shifted increasingly
towards musical recordings – but the retailing of musical
instruments and song sheets helped to keep it afloat.

Mary clearly had a very difficult time with her husband and she took the brave and highly unusual step of getting a divorce, as described in the Evesham Standard on October 23rd 1909:

Mrs. Mary Josephine Peters petitioned the president, Sir John Bigham, for a divorce on the ground of the cruelty and misconduct of her husband Mr. James Peters, music and musical instrument dealer of St. Helens Lancashire. There was no defence. Mr. Newton Crane, who appeared for the petitioner, stated that the respondent was a man of ungovernable tamper, and from the time of the marriage, which took place in Liverpool in 1898, he had used great violence towards his wife. In addition to this he had an assistant named Maggie Glover, compromising letters from whom were intercepted by the petitioner. His lordship, having heard all the evidence as to cruelty and misconduct, granted a decree nisi with costs.

That was a reasonable summary of the case – but the St Helens Reporter provided a far more detailed account. As well as the Hall Street shop, James Peters ran a book and music stall in the marketplace and Maggie Glover had been his assistant.

After the young woman went into domestic service in Knotty Ash, Peters became a twice-weekly visitor to her employer's house and had got the girl pregnant.

The Reporter wrote that Maggie's employer in Knotty Ash had discovered incriminating letters from Peters inside the girl's bedroom. At the divorce hearing, Mary's barrister told the judge that they were of "...such a revolting and disgusting character that I cannot read them in open Court."

Mary gave evidence of numerous acts of violence committed by her husband. These included one time when she alleged that James had injured his finger through hitting her so hard. That blow led to Mary losing a tooth and another becoming loose. On a further occasion he had attacked her for simply wanting to go to church on a Sunday morning. Mary even claimed that James had given her a black eye after the initiation of divorce proceedings.

Two weeks after getting her divorce, James Peters paid Mary a visit, as the Liverpool Daily Post of November 17th 1909 described:

> James Peters, musical instrument dealer, of the Market Hall, was charged on warrant at St. Helens yesterday with threatening his wife, from whom he was divorced. Mr. W. Webster prosecuted for Mr. Hutchen [solicitor], and said that Peters was last month divorced on the petition of his wife. Prior to the proceedings in the High Court he had been violent to his wife, and just before the final hearing he knocked her insensible in the shop. Mr. Webster said that after business hours on Saturday, Mrs. Peters was in her shop making up her cash when she saw accused looking over the window in the door.
>
> He came inside, and said, "Don't think you have got rid of me yet. You have robbed me of this shop. It is mine by moral right. I will knife you before the week is out." His attitude was so threatening that she anticipated immediate violence, and her two assistants, hearing his voice, rushed into the shop and prevented any violence. He had also written her saying that he was desperate, and although the court had given the woman the custody of the children he had tried to get them away from her, and had made allegations against their mother. Complainant was in fear of the accused, and asked for him to be bound over in substantial bail....The bench ordered Peters to find surety in £10 and two of £5 each.

James had opened the Hall Street shop with his money – but then put the business into his wife's name after getting into financial difficulties. But after her violent treatment from her husband and the ensuing divorce, Mary had refused to give it back.

Peters then took legal action against his ex-wife to try and reclaim the shop and in the end a settlement was made between the warring parties. Mary agreed to pay James a total of £156 in three instalments, including a down payment of £50 and two subsequent payments of £50.

Although these were then considerable sums of money, Mary must have felt the payments to be worth it, as she obtained numerous conditions, which, if obeyed, would give her freedom from her violent ex-husband.

The terms included James agreeing "...that the Hall-street shop should belong to Mrs. Peters, not to interfere with her in the conduct and management of the business, and not to enter the shop or frequent the outside thereof; and not to molest or hold any communication with her or her children."

St Helens Newspaper headline from April 28th 1911

However, James quickly broke the agreement and so Mary refused to pay the instalments. That led to a hearing in St Helens County Court in East Street on April 26th 1911. Mary told the judge that her ex-husband had broken the terms by frequently visiting the shop and waylaying her and their children on the streets. She even

179

claimed that he had written to her parents in Ireland and made the "most vile accusations" against her.

After hearing the evidence, Judge Shand ruled that James Peters had interfered with and molested his ex-wife and children contrary to the agreement and so had forfeited his rights to the remaining payments. From then on the business thrived.

In December 1912 the M. J. Peters Music Warehouse at 4 Hall Street was advising customers in its newspaper advertisements to "Look For The Dog", with His Master's Voice gramophones and records touted as the only ones that were genuine. Despite now being a single woman, Mary continued to describe herself as Mrs M. J. Peters, due, no doubt, to the stigma of being a divorced woman at that time.

LOOK FOR THE "DOG."

A SEASONABLE :: PRESENT. ::

"His Master's Voice"

GRAMOPHONE & RECORDS.

NONE OTHER GENUINE   "   ASK FOR CATALOGUES.

Mrs. M. J. PETERS, Music Warehouse,

4, HALL STREET, ST. HELENS.

"Look For The Dog" advert from M. J. Peters Music Warehouse in1912

At Christmas 1917, the shop was advertising gramophones from £3 15 shillings, with "the largest and most up-to-date selection of records in town, including all the latest dances, songs etc." Mrs Peters was also selling violins, mandolins and bound books of music with "everything suitable for Xmas presents".

Shortly after the declaration of the armistice in 1918, Mary Peters had a large advert published in the St Helens Reporter under the heading "The Boys Will Soon Be Home". She invited her customers to: "Get ready to give them the welcome they deserve". This, Mrs Peter felt, families could do by buying from her Hall Street shop "all the latest patriotic songs and dances for the piano".

The price of gramophones appears to have risen as they now cost from £6 10s to 15 guineas, either with horn or hornless. "Also thousands of new Zonophone records. All the latest songs, dances, &c.", declared the advert.

At Christmas 1919, Mary Peters was offering six free records with every purchase of the Apollo, Dulcephone or the Commonwealth wind-up gramophones. All the latest dance records "in strict time for dancing" were available, with hundreds to choose from. A year later her advert said: "Make This Xmas a Zonophone Xmas – The greatest singers, musicians and entertainers in the world enter your home with the coming of your Zonophone instrument." Then at Christmas 1921, Mary Peters was advertising:

M. J. PETERS

Is now showing this Season's Models of "His Master's Voice" and "Columbia" Gramophones; also "His Master's Voice" and "Columbia Celebrity" Records.

OUR WINDOWS THIS WEEK.

Gramophones and records for Xmas. Mrs. Peters has the best selection in town. Cabinets, table grands, hornless and horn models, from £3 0s 0d. "Celebrity" records by all the great artistes; also the latest dances and songs on "His Master's Voice," "Zonophone," "Columbia," "Regal," etc.

Two St Helens newspaper advertisements from 1925 and the St Helens Reporter obituary on Mary Peters from September 28th 1954

On September 11th 1954 – exactly 52 years to the day after her music shop had opened – Mary Peters gave up her business because of ill-health. A week later at the age of 79, she died at the home of her youngest daughter in Moss Bank Road and was cremated in Anfield.

e) HOLDINGS RECORDS IN DUKE STREET

Like the M. J. Peters Music Warehouse in Hall Street, the record shop at 39 Duke Street was an institution in St Helens during the 20th century – but traded under several different names. Siblings Albert and Maud Holding had founded their business in the early 1920s, selling records, sheet music and musical instruments.

Albert who never married had lost his right arm while serving in the Royal Army Medical Corps in WW1. However, being single-handed did not stop him from being able to insert records into bags and securely tie them up.

My late father, Tom Wainwright, was a regular visitor to the shop in the 1940s. He recalled Albert inserting string into the hole in the centre of the disc and then through another hole in the bag. He would then tie the string up at the open end of the bag so that the disc would not fall out – all accomplished using just one hand.

The siblings decided to retire in the late 1940s and sold their shop, which became known as 'The Record Lounge'. In August 1969, Albert Holding died at the age of 74 at his home in Standring Gardens in St Helens.

f) THE HYSTERIA AT THE OPENING OF ROTHERY RECORDINGS

When Frankie Vaughan came to St Helens on December 8th 1956 to open Rothery Records (or Rothery Recordings as they then preferred to be called), the 28-year-old was a huge star. The Liverpool-born crooner was then residing at number 3 in the British singles charts with 'The Green Door' and would later be voted Showbusiness Personality of the Year.

Rothery Radio was also doing very nicely, having established themselves as arguably the leading electrical retailer in St Helens – with their main premises situated in Baldwin Street. The phenomenon of teenagers spending their cash on pop discs was still in its infancy – and there were few specialist retailers that did not also sell musical instruments and / or sheet music. Modern facilities like listening booths were also not routinely available.

In 1956 Rothery's eyed an opportunity to expand into the burgeoning record market in St Helens – which then included the new 45 rpm singles, as well as 78 rpm discs and albums. The firm wanted to create a northern version of HMV's store in London's Oxford Street and open the "finest record shop in the north of England". Rothery Recordings' pre-launch advertising campaign in St Helens newspapers offered some freebies and the chance for punters to meet a star on its opening day:

50 RECORDS FREE – To the first 50 customers who buy a long-playing record we will give a FREE 78 r.p.m. record of their own choice! Hear your L.P. records as they should be heard; on our wonderful high-fidelity sound system, and take advantage of this fabulous free offer.

Frankie Vaughan

Rothery's claimed their Hi-Fi equipment and listening booths in the "North's Most Modern Record Shop" had been designed on the same lines as HMV's "wonderful showrooms" in London, adding: "Make your choice – 'Pop,' 'Rock,' 'Jazz' and 'Classic' – from a vast selection. Frankie Vaughan will autograph every one of his records bought during the afternoon."

And Rothery Recordings must have shifted some stock on their opening day – as Frankie spent over six hours signing discs! Under the headline *"Hysteria Sweeps At Singer's Visit"*, the St Helens Reporter's Tuesday edition of December 11th 1956 wrote:

Hysteria, brought on by the visit to St. Helens of Frankie Vaughan, idol of the teenagers, swept a crowd of 1,500 outside Rothery Radio's new record shop in Ormskirk Street, on Saturday. One hour before Frankie's visit, a large crowd gathered in Baldwin Street and Ormskirk Street. Excited youngsters, unlucky to have arrived late, climbed on shop window ledges and on projections of the Parochial Hall opposite the new shop. A score of policemen, and several policewomen formed a "chain" to keep over-excited youngsters from rushing the shop. Frankie had decided to leave his car a distance from the shop and walk the rest of the way. As this happened, the crowd went wild. Young girls swooned, policemen were swept off their feet and tiny children screamed as the crowds crushed them. The police were eventually forced to use strong measures, and by sheer brute force Frankie, with a six-man police escort, eventually reached the shop. With coat half-torn from his back, tie disarranged and red-faced, he was ushered inside. A record broken over the shop door handle was originally to have officially opened the project. However, the crowd's wildness forced the record to be tossed to them.

Then Frankie retreated inside the shop and behind the counter, to begin a marathon record and photograph-autographing session. While the shop's huge plate glass frontage bulged ominously inwards, Frankie blew kisses, smiled and winked at his adoring fans outside. Six hours later he was still there, catering to the fans. Later, he left for Liverpool, his mother's home – and peace. After the teenage kingdom's idol had departed, work began on clearing the street outside the shop of ear-rings, gloves, handkerchiefs and other trinkets, ripped, grabbed and torn off in the melee.

The adverting slogan of Rothery Recordings would soon become "The Rendezvous of the Stars", as within two years of Frankie

Vaughan's opening of their shop, there had also been visits by Lonnie Donegan, Marvin Rainwater and Edmund Hockridge.

St Helens Reporter May 31st 1958

Then on February 26th 1964, Ken Dodd autographed copies of his latest single 'Eight By Ten' at Rothery's. Frankie Vaughan made a return visit to Rothery's on February 16th 1965 to sign autographs. But the beat group explosion of the early '60s had by then considerably diminished his fame – and so there were no more reports of hysterical fans.

St Helens Reporter December 7th 1957

When St Helens Was Called
The Worst Town In England

"St. Helens is nothing but blasphemy written large in brick and stone. I have never witnessed so much dirt, squalor, and wretchedness."

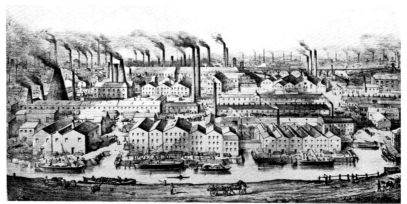

In 1870 it was stated that St Helens had 345 large furnace chimneys

When you walk through the streets and parks of St Helens today, it's hard to imagine that it used to be considered a dirty, stinking town. The renowned poet and writer Matthew Arnold even went so far as to label St Helens a "hell-hole" and newspapers throughout Britain queued up to rubbish the town – describing it as "grimy", "repugnant" and "dreary".

The many factories in the borough – particularly the dozen or so chemical works – were the cause of many of the problems. On June 15th 1872, the St Helens Newspaper published this damning editorial on the smoke nuisance:

For some time great complaints have been made in St. Helens and the neighbourhood, of the smoke and vapours which are continually being poured out of the chimneys of our glass, iron, chemical, and copper works; and although the latter have had to bear the brunt of all the blame for nearly all the damage that is done to growing crops, and all the unpleasantness that is experienced by the inhabitants, still there can be little doubt that much of the annoyance, and no little of the injury, may fairly be attributed to the other works, and notably to our glass works.

Our chemical works are said to be under inspection, and we are expected to believe that little or no damage or nuisance is caused by them; but yet Tontine street, Bridge street and the whole centre of the town, is at times enveloped in so dense and disagreeable a fog that many persons are constrained to believe that virtually there is no restraining inspection connected with some of our chemical works. Our copper processes admittedly defy control. We are told, however, that our copper smelters are very anxious to prevent the escape of these deleterious vapours, but that hitherto science has been completely beaten in every attempt. All we can say is that science ought to be ashamed of itself, and should be compelled to haul down its flag of high pretence, if, with all the appliances at its command, it cannot devise some method of carrying on a profitable business without devastating the surrounding country.

In 1896 a magazine article on the chemical industries of St Helens and Widnes described how foul gases "belched forth night and day". Undercover journalist Robert Sherard claimed in his piece – which he called *"The White Slaves of England"* – that pollution killed trees and grass for miles around.

That was probably an exaggeration, as new parks were being opened in St Helens. Plus the geographical spread of the town meant pollution would likely have been in patches and dependent upon wind direction. However, three years later the Coventry Evening Telegraph described St Helens as that "far from salubrious town where they manufacture chemicals and provide odours innumerable. It is a busy place, St. Helens, but distance lends attraction to the view – and the scents."

In May of 1899 a massive explosion at the Kurtz alkali works *(where the St Helens Retail Park is now)* killed five men and decimated parts of Peasley Cross. It also caused more damage to the reputation of St Helens. The Glasgow Herald claimed that on the day after the disaster, rain had exaggerated the "normal squalor of the district".

Months later a Worcester paper said St Helens was "the town for pills and explosions", as if factories blew up as often as Beechams made a pill! Then the Pall Mall Gazette had a pop at St Helens, describing its "unloveliness" and "dreary, monotonous streets", adding that six parishes couldn't get curates because of the explosion's bad publicity.

The rapid expansion of St Helens during the 19th century was the root cause of the pollution. Between 1801 and 1891, the town's population had grown 10-fold, as more workers were needed by the expanding number of factories and pits. That led to dozens more industrial chimneys dotting the St Helens skyline and belching out an increasing amount of filth.

Dreadful smells often hung over the town and were especially bad on still or foggy days. Plus the growing workforce needed more houses, leading to more smoky coal fires that boosted pollution. Regulators struggled to keep up, although by the 1890s the town had made some strides in cleaning up its act.

Efforts had first begun during the 1840s when an Improvement Commission was created and they were boosted when the town was made a borough in 1868 and granted more powers. These were badly needed as four years earlier it had been reported that most of the agricultural land in the outlying areas of Parr, Sutton,

Burtonwood and Bold was fast becoming unproductive because of the vapours that were being emitted.

St Helens--Work and Rest

This picture postcard from the turn of the 20th century had a clear meaning

The link between air pollution and health was better understood towards the end of the 19th century. During the 1880s, Dr Robert McNicoll, the St Helens Medical Officer for Health, campaigned for improved air quality and was especially critical of the heaps of chemical waste. Not only did they emit toxic gases but they also drained into the town's brooks where they met acid waste.

Progress was slow as the prevailing view was that some pollution of the air was only to be expected in a manufacturing town like St Helens. However, a five-minute black smoke limit for works' chimneys was introduced and a government inspector investigated the worst smells. These and other measures, such as improved sanitation, helped to make life better for the town's citizens.

However its reputation took much longer to heal as the mud had stuck. Matthew Arnold's "hellhole" jibe from 1880 was often repeated by British newspapers when mentioning St Helens, despite the fact that he was actually referring to a perceived lack of social manners amongst its people.

Milk Street in St Helens captured on a murky day with the women having a difficult job to keep their washing white

In 1908 an article in a Manchester newspaper advised on cycling routes through Lancashire. The author defended the county's dreary reputation, although he described St Helens as an "unlovely" place. Cyclists were, however, assured that they would soon pass through it! By 1914 the smoke nuisance in St Helens was on the decline and the Liverpool Echo advised its readers that:

> What was once a repugnant desert of mere bricks, mortar, and waste heaps is now beginning to blossom as the rose.

The growth of parks, recreation grounds and bowling greens were definitely helping to boost the town's reputation. Although it did need a lot more improving as a 1915 article in the Echo explained. The author argued that the town had been so rubbished in the past that it would need much advertising for the "really intrinsic beauty of its character" to be readily accepted. In the article entitled *"A Maligned Town – St Helens as a Holiday Resort"*, the author listed the town's many attractions, concluding that St Helens was a "wonderful place".

Although there had been many improvements there was still much to do. In 1925 the government's Atmospheric Pollution Committee listed St Helens as the 7th sootiest place in Britain, with Newcastle and Liverpool the worst offenders.

THE WORST TOWN I HAVE EVER SEEN

Then in 1929 Arthur Jalland – a barrister, Liberal Party politician and future judge – put the cat amongst the pigeons when he made this damning comment in a speech at the Manchester Liberal Club:

> It was my misfortune to pay a visit to St. Helens. It is the worst town I have ever seen. I am bound to say that St. Helens is nothing but blasphemy written large in brick and stone. I cannot conceive that hell has any terrors for a person born or brought up in St. Helens. I have never witnessed so much dirt, squalor, and wretchedness. There is not a tree or a blade of grass to be seen, and the conditions under which the people lived are appalling. The depression of spirits which such a condition of affairs produced was deepened by the sight of a queue of hopeless men and women outside the Labour Exchange.

Arthur Jalland was then a prospective Liberal candidate and his views carried some weight. So it was important that prominent people in St Helens rejected his slurs and one that rapidly responded was the Rev. Canon Childs.

The Vicar of St Helens had travelled throughout the world and served as a missionary in China and had much experience of other places in England. He told the Liverpool Echo:

I certainly do not agree with him. There are other places much more squalid than St. Helens. We have many bright spots. He must have missed the trees in Victoria-square, and other parts of the town. Of course, they are not in leaf just now. I think, perhaps, we are suffering from lack of vision in the past, but we try to make up for it in the present, and I don't think we are any worse than most of the other industrial towns. People coming in by train get a wrong idea of the town and they never dream that there are such places as St. Anns on the Prescot-road, Denton's-green, and the Windlehurst Estate. It will probably be an eye-opener to tell him that people come in from Liverpool during the summer to see our Taylor Park.

Alderman Richard Waring was the deputy Mayor of St Helens and chairman of the Housing Committee and he furiously denounced Jalland's comments as "simply outrageous".

BRITAIN'S POOREST TOWN

PREPARING FOR CHRISTMAS IN BRITAIN'S "POOREST TOWN"
No Bob Cratchit Air About St Helens

From our Special Correspondent

ST HELENS, WEDNESDAY. | cakes at from 6s to 12s 6d each and
This week the Thatto Heath Old | taking orders for "a dozen of mince

The (Manchester) Guardian of December 21st 1950

There was more bad publicity for St Helens in 1950 when the town was declared the poorest in the country with income levels 13% below average. Of course, how you define the best and worst in any category depends on the set criteria – which those at the top of the pile think is fair, but those languishing at the bottom consider most unfair! And St Helens certainly did not like the fact that the Marketing Survey of the UK had calculated its prosperity index by including such factors as rateable values and car ownership. The Manchester Guardian *(as it was then known)* decided to see if things were really that bad in the town and on December 21st 1950 published a lengthy account of their findings. These are some extracts from its report:

This week the Thatto Heath Old Men's Benevolent Fund provided its annual Christmas treat for 400 pensioners. "Cheery words were exchanged and Christian names freely used"; further, every man received a pound note and a small bottle of brandy. The brandy would have been a gallant touch anywhere. In a town which, according to the new edition of the Marketing Survey of the United Kingdom, is the poorest in Britain, it has a really superb panache. The hosts were still full of just pride over the occasion when they woke up to learn from one or other of their two thriving local papers that their income level, based on rateable values, vital statistics, and such factors as the ownership of cars and telephones, was 13 per cent below the average for the 145 largest centres of population outside London. "I'd never have guessed if I hadn't read about it that this was the poorest place in Christendom," said one of them to-day.

St Helens, it seems, is doomed to be unlucky in its publicity. It handicaps itself heavily, to start with, by arousing starry expectations. The home of the world's largest glass factory should surely be a crystal city, glittering like the New Jerusalem. But the county directory declares the town's aspect to be "uninviting." There is a stern passage about "a forest of tall chimneys, shafts, and other weird erections," and "fumes of acid and smoke of furnaces" which make the atmosphere "almost unendurable to the stranger," and to-day's reality, with a sky like sodden blotting paper low over streets two inches deep in slush, did little to discredit it. The crowds plodding through them, predominantly women with loaded shopping bags, most of them noticeably, well shod against the wet, were little concerned with the endurance of strangers. The town, not, perhaps, with ebullience but with steady determination, is preparing for its own Christmas celebrations, and why not? Of St. Helens's 105,689 people fifty thousand are in work; eighteen thousand of them in the glass industry, which takes in six hundred juveniles a year, eight thousand in the collieries, the rest in breweries, the sewing trades, the copper rolling mills, and a variety of miscellaneous jobs.

Unemployment is described as "negligible," there is a rising birth rate (infantile mortality, though, is another story), a death rate little, if any, above the national average, and a child population claimed to be proportionately the largest in the country. "If this is the worst-off town in Britain, then some of the best must be doing very nicely indeed," is the reaction of a visitor after a glance round the shopping quarter, which is ready to repair your false teeth within the day or sell you (for eighteen guineas) a double-curb albert with gold sovereign pendant and ten-year gold-filled fifteen-jewel hunter watch. The butchers proclaim "Poultry for all" over their windows heaped with turkeys with their heads in bags; the bakers are handing out iced Christmas cakes at from 6s to 12s 6d each and taking orders for "a dozen of mince pies for Saturday."

The toyshops find it worth while to stock fleets of red and blue children's tricycles at £7 5s, dolls' prams at £4 17s 6d and dolls to fill them at prices ranging from £2 to £8. There are smart florists with cactus and carnations in their windows, and a pet shop offering tartan collars or "overcoats" (these at 35s each) as a Christmas gift for Fido. Outdoors, the council has put up Christmas trees here and there in the town; indoors, life at St Helens, from now until the new year (which the local Young Conservatives are seeing in with a dance which starts at 12 30 a.m. on January 1 and goes on till 5 30 a.m.) seems to he a whirl of gaiety. Only at Thatto Heath are they on the brandy standard, but elsewhere there is an impressive number of old folks' teas, with boiled ham and trifle, fancy cakes, paper hats, false noses, and all. All the big firms have Christmas parties for the children of employees, with the traditional toys and fruits and sweets to take home, and the local Territorials provided a fifteen-foot Christmas tree for their children's party.

TRANSFORMATION

On March 20th 1959 Robert Buckley wrote a lengthy article in the Liverpool Echo on the transformation of St Helens. Although there was still much to do in improving the town centre and demolishing what some would call slum housing, St Helens was going green and Mr Buckley was highly impressed:

A legacy of smoke, grime and cramped living space has made St. Helens of to-day one of the most parks-conscious towns in the North-West. The townsman who spends his working day by the side of a stifling hot tank of molten glass or minding machines in a dusty engineering shop turns naturally to nature for his relaxation. He likes to see garden features dotted about his town; to smell the sweet scent of cut grass, although it may be surrounded by a cluster of smoky chimneys instead of trees. St. Helens Parks and Cemetery Committee have long been aware of this need. Besides continually developing their eight parks and numerous recreation grounds, they are now beautifying even the industrial areas with a string of garden features. Ugly derelict sites are being transformed almost overnight. Although a count has never been taken, it is now estimated that there are about 250 small features dotted about the town. And this number is increasing daily.

The article revealed that the Parks Department employed 104 gardeners and grew plants in over 20,000 sq. ft. of greenhouse space, often for special events at venues like the Town Hall. The article concluded with these comments:

> St. Helens, the town of grime and smoke, will soon be
> ablaze with the colour of a million flowers.

WHAT THE AMERICANS THOUGHT OF ST HELENS

Although some criticism of St Helens in the past has been justified – there has also clearly been exaggeration, caused, perhaps, by critics making too fleeting a visit. In 1960 when a party of eleven American females came to stay in St Helens, they spent six weeks in the town, allowing ample time for a considered study of the place and its people.

They were representatives of 'The Experiment In International Living', which had been founded in 1932 and, at the time of writing this book, still exists. The organisation provides intercultural exchange trips for young students and its logo bears the strapline *"A Program Of World Learning"*.

Before arriving in the town, the group, with an average age of twenty, had heard how St Helens was a pretty grim place. However, during their four-week stay the young women were surprised to discover that was far from being the case – as Ann Zimmerman told the St Helens Reporter on July 23rd 1960:

> When coming over, we read in an encyclopaedia that St.
> Helens was an unpleasant industrial town. We were agreeably
> surprised to see the small gardens in front of houses and the
> scenery around the town. We were told to bring with us only
> our more sombre clothes and expected to see the girls

dressed in quiet shades. You can imagine our surprise when we saw the bright and colourful dresses your girls wear.

The Reporter described two more aspects of St Helens life that the young women found fascinating – the local dialect and Lancashire chimney pots, which were described as rare in central-heated America. The paper added that they had all greatly enjoyed their stay with local families and when they returned to the States, the young women would be taking back many happy memories of the people of the town and of St Helens itself.

Another satisfied American visitor was Frank Ziliotti. In November 1960, the 36-year-old left his Californian home with his wife Agnes and two sons to spend six weeks living in St Helens. The former American GI had married an English girl and their family came to stay at the Doulton Street home of Agnes's sister, Jenny Honey.

Frank told the Newspaper that St Helens was a "great little town", although the couple did have a couple of complaints. "It rains nearly every time we want to go out", said Mrs Ziliotti and husband Frank did not like the way English pedestrians behaved. In America, he said, people would be fined for crossing the road when the traffic lights were against them.

THE FOUL AIR PROBLEM

The American visitors had, seemingly, no complaints about the quality of the St Helens air – but concerned father Philip Bond had plenty. In an article entitled *"What, Exactly, Is St. Helens Doing About Foul Air Problem?"*, that was published by the St Helens Reporter on December 15th 1962, Mr Bond, of Hamer Street in St Helens, told the newspaper:

My daughter and other schoolchildren who attend Windle Pilkington school sometimes find the playground covered with a thin layer of soot and grit. In fact, a number of parents have asked the headmaster to allow the children to play

200

inside the school to safeguard their health. It seems little is being done in St. Helens to improve the situation. The town centre is absolutely filthy. It is virtually impossible for washing to be put out to dry and to be brought back in clean.

Doors, window-sills and walls are regularly coated with soot and grit. Like everyone else in the town I am compelled to breathe contaminated air and perhaps more important still, so are the young children at Windle Pilkington school. People in St. Helens are swallowing contaminated air every day. It is time something was done, fast.

The council's Chief Public Health Inspector, Nathanial Birch, was invited to respond and told the Reporter that every day air samples were taken in six parts of the borough for analysis. Since the Clean Air Act of 1956 had come into force, Mr Birch explained how there had been a reduction in the amount of smoke in the centre of St Helens, mainly through improvements made by industrial plants.

Some firms had invested large sums to comply with the law. Mr Birch added that there was still considerable atmospheric pollution from house fires but the council's five-year smokeless zone programme would soon come into operation to ameliorate matters.

However, it took four years to get the badly needed scheme under way. In announcing the clean-air plan in 1965, the St Helens Newspaper wrote how every year nearly 3,000 tons of insoluble grit and dust from chimney smoke fell back on the town. The paper stated that if this pollution were piled up in Victoria Square over an area of 110¼ sq. yards, it would reach the height of the Town Hall clock.

St Helens Newspaper Feb. 16th 1965

The image (on previous page) was mocked up to try and visualise the point.

The paper also quoted Council Leader Ald. Joseph Hughes in stating that St Helens was one of the worst areas in the country for respiratory deaths. In 1963, 111 people had died of bronchitis and, according to Dr Gerald O'Brien, the St Helens Medical Officer of Health, the problem was getting worse.

ST HELENS SHOULD BE ABOLISHED!

How do you abolish a whole town? I have no idea but the Economist in their report on the North West of England that was published on May 14th 1965 thought St Helens should endure that fate, stating:

> St Helens ought to be abolished. It is already disappearing, but too slowly − losing something like a thousand people a year to the suburbs outside its boundaries. At that rate it would take a hundred years for everyone to make his escape. The only thing to do, it seems, is to liquidate this appalling monument to Victorian inconsequentialism and start again from scratch. This is the remedy for the town, but not for its industry, a lot of which is progressive and some of which is comfortably housed. Even so a good many works in St. Helens could do with a touch of the bulldozer....Ugly overcrowded, under-heated back-to-backs still dominate the town and seem likely to go on doing so for years to come.

The report did find a few good points about the town. Not many − but a few! St Helens cemeteries were considered "well laid out" and its parks department was rated good.

Pilkingtons Glass was praised but St Helens Council was slammed as "old-fashioned" and "child-like" in its seeming inability to effect improvements. The St Helens Reporter asked Ald. Joseph

Hughes, the Leader of the Town Council, for his response to the severe criticism and he said:

> This is not the first time someone has tried to write off St. Helens. We know there is a lot to be done but you cannot clean up in a couple of generations the effects of 150 years of industrial development, particularly mining.

Ald. Hughes argued that few towns in the north of England had done as much as St Helens to remove the "ugly, shocking scars" that industry had left behind. He also felt the council should have been given credit for the "tremendous amount of housing development" that was currently taking place.

There clearly was much more that needed doing and over the next twenty-plus years, St Helens was vastly improved in so many ways – including its town centre, market place, housing, air pollution, waterways etc. etc.

At the time of publication there are plans for further re-development of its town centre. And although St Helens has its critics, I don't think there is much call these days for it to be abolished!

Advertising Slogans Of
The Old St Helens Stores

*"All money taken today goes towards a mothers-in-laws
outing. The more we take the further we can send them!"*

This chapter is devoted to recalling the shops and stores of St
Helens from the late 19th century up until the 1970s. Many are
names you will likely have heard of – but others not. In particular I
am focussing on the slogans that they employed in newspaper
adverts and emblazoned on their vehicles and premises.

During the 19th century, few St Helens' businesses utilised slogans
when advertising their wares in newspapers. Extreme politeness
ruled instead and business owners did an awful lot of begging –
that did not result in them being sent to prison!

For example, in one edition of the St Helens Newspaper from
1868, **Miss Catherine Unsworth** of Salisbury Terrace in Church
Street said that she:

> *...begs respectfully to inform her friends and the public that she
> will commence in the tea and coffee business on Saturday
> October 17th. The favour of a trial is respectfully solicited.*

Despite a trade depression in the late 1860s, St Helens was still
expanding and shopkeepers were regularly opening up new stores
or relocating to better trading positions. **Joseph Edmundson**
wrote in the St Helens Newspaper that he:

> *...begs to inform the inhabitants of St. Helens and vicinity
> and the public generally, that he purposes [sic] opening the
> premises No. 2, Liverpool Road, on Saturday, Aug. 21,
> 1869, with a choice selection of Cigars, Tobacco, Fancy*

Tobacco and Snuffs, Tobacco Pipes, Pouches, Cigar Cases, etc, in great variety. J. E. begs to remind the public that at his establishment none but a genuine article will be supplied, and he hopes by keeping a good article, strict attention to business, and civility, to merit a share of public patronage.

There was then the occasional use of what we might call a strapline or slogan in adverts. For example, **George Seddon** – who described himself as a "tailor, draper, hatter" from Liverpool Road in St Helens – used the simple refrain:

To Meet The Times. Cheap, Durable, And Good Fit.

By the 1890s, advertisers in the St Helens newspapers were less gracious and polite and a bit more creative in their promotions. Tailor **Richard Oldbury** kept premises at 77 Church Street, opposite the post office and parish church. In his ads he described his 60-shilling dress suit as a *"wonderful production"*. His shop's slogans included:

From Land's End To John o' Groat's There Is No Better Tailoring Than Oldbury's. – Everybody Beneath "The Union Jack" Should Try Oldbury's Tailoring.

During the painful 1890 coal strike, Richard Oldbury, somewhat dubiously, decided that poetry was appropriate in his ads, writing:

When The Pits Are Opened, The People All Will Sing, That Oldbury Is The Tailor, For Collier, Clerk, Or King!

Of course, clothes need washing and the **St Helens Steam Laundry** in Eccleston Street could do the time-consuming and convoluted chore for you. In fact they would come and collect your dirty clothes and return them nice and clean free of charge.

However, the prices they charged for doing the actual work would have ruled out the vast majority of people in St Helens.

During the 1890s the laundry's slogans were: *"Perfect Sanitation and Ventilation"*, *"Machinery Of The Most Approved Type"* and *"No Chemicals Of Any Kind Used"* as they attempted to persuade a sceptical public of the merits of their operation.

Newsagents were an expanding trade during that decade as levels of literacy rose and the range of periodicals increased. In fact the St Helens district boasted about 45 sellers of newspapers, including a certain **W.H. Smith & Son**, which kept a newspaper and bookstall on the town's main railway station.

None of the newsagents advertised very often. Although an exception was **James Duxbury's Central Newsagency** in George Street and Westfield Street in St Helens. His brief adverts contained the slogan: *"Punctuality In Delivery, Regularity In Supply, And Civility To All."*

Baldwin Street with the Sefton Arms run by John Marsh on the left

The strange slogan employed by the **Sefton Arms** in Baldwin Street in the 1890s was: *"A Good Bath And Every Convenience For Visiting Clubs – Latest Football Telegrams"*. The Sefton was the HQ of St Helens Recs and licensee John Marsh was keen for other sporting clubs to use his facilities and, no doubt, sup his beer. With the telephone yet to make a real impact in St Helens, telegrams had to be despatched for those sports fans and gamblers keen to know the results of matches.

W. G. Dixon had been founded in 1880 in Bickerstaffe Street in St Helens with the firm describing itself as *"Car Proprietor And Undertaker"*. Its slogan was *"Economy In Funerals"*. Dixon's were an early telephone subscriber with their number being 22.

I wonder if anyone ever visited **R. G. Brook's** hardware shop in Wolverhampton House, near the Raven Inn in St Helens, and said: "Can you show me your range of anchors?" That was because Brook boasted that he stocked *"Anything From A Needle To An Anchor"*.

RG Brook's hardware store

Lionel Swift's long-standing bakery in College Street in St Helens

By the early 20th century, there was more inventiveness on show in local adverts. Business owners in St Helens were early adopters of the new motor vehicles – having both the cash and the need for such transport. They also had more space on their motor vans in which their names and products could be promoted. **Lionel Swift's** long-standing Hardshaw bakery in College Street was renowned for its slogan *"Often Buttered, Never Bettered"* which was plastered on his delivery vans.

Of course, advertising comes in many forms, including on the exterior of shops. George Webb liked to call himself a master boot repairer – he was also a master wordsmith! Trading under the name of **G. H. Webb**, his cobblers' shop in Boundary Road carried the slogan: *"Left Boots Made Right"*. A similar play on words was made by **Sam Emery's** rival cobblers shop in Rutland Street, near Victoria Park. This read: *"Hospital For Poor Soles"*!

Pegram's Stores had grocery shops in Liverpool Road, New Market Place and Peter Street in St Helens, as well as in Eccleston Street in Prescot. *"Cheap Lines For Hard Times!"* was the slogan in their Reporter adverts during the 1920s.

"You Know Me", was the simple slogan of **Charles Kinns**, a fruiterer in New Market Place in St Helens from 1898 until 1929. However, locals called him the "Banana King", as the bananas he sold at fourpence per dozen were hung in such quantities outside his shop that they darkened his interior.

During the 1920s the **Peel Café** of Dentons Green Lane was open until 9 pm each evening for the sale of ices and refreshments. In their adverts they said:

Sole makers of the perfect cakes. The only shop
where you may obtain Prima Donna Cake.

Mortons owned the Victoria Bakery in North Road, as well as the Edinburgh Café in Church Street. *"Purchase Dainty Confectionery For Christmas Cheer"*, was their seasonal slogan in 1925.

John Collins delivery van pictured outside St Helens Town Hall

Grocer **John Collins** was based in the Market Hall and his advertising slogans included *"We Sell The Goods – A Trial Order Will Convince You"* and *"We Loop The Loop For Quality In Provisions"*. If you had access to a telephone, you could ask the operator to call 567 and Collins' van would come to you.

Spaven's was a longstanding fishmonger with premises in Barrow Street and Higher Parr Street. In 1939 they opened a wholesale market behind the Nelson Hotel in Bridge Street. *"We Serve Ourselves Best By Serving Others Better"*, was their thoughtful motto, later calling themselves *"The Men For The Best Scotch Fish"*.

Tel.:   ORDERS DELIVERED DAILY   Tel.:

3   3
I   **BEN SPAVEN**   I
4   *for*   4
3   **Best Scotch Fish**   3

Retail—
3 BARROW STREET
121 HIGHER PARR STREET

Wholesale—
TONTINE STREET
Also at **WARRINGTON AND WIDNES**

Alf Critchley was also a fishmonger and operated from the market behind the Savoy cinema. I wonder if anyone ever asked Alf for octopus or shark meat or something similarly bizarre? That was because the firm used the strapline *"If It Swims, Alf's Got It"*.

Fresh Fish Supplies of 22 Bridge Street was a maker of dubious claims, writing in the third person in its 1920 ads:

> *...they have so pleased the housewives of St. Helens that their shop is besieged daily by vast crowds who realize that good fresh fish is an essential part of the family diet and that it means a great saving in the family exchequer.*

Of course, if vast crowds were besieging their fish shop, why did they feel the need to spend a lot of cash on advertising?

Market folk had limited advertising space for the written word and so made up for it with verbal treats and humorous banter. One stallholder was renowned for saying:

> *All money taken today will go towards a mothers-in-laws outing. The more we take the further we can send them!*

Bathroom installers and decorators **W. Swire and Sons** had shops in Duke Street, George Street and Bickerstaffe Street in St Helens – as well as in Church Road in Rainford. *"Swire For Solid Service"* was their slogan during the 1930s and '40s.

I'm not convinced that posh wallpaper could turn a cottage into a mansion – but the **Midland Wallpaper Company** of Church Street in St Helens made that claim:

> *Now Is The Time To Transform Your Home Into A Place Of Beauty For A Few Shillings – Mansion Wallpapers At Cottage Prices.*

Swire's wartime advert

R. S. Slinn's wallpaper shop was a heavy advertiser with premises in Westfield Street, Peter Street and Baldwin Street. Henry Slinn had founded the firm in 1894 and later his son Reginald took it over. *"The Bright and Breezy Shop – Biggest Choice in St. Helens"* was their slogan in later years. **Chenery's** was another longstanding decorating supplies store with premises in Liverpool Road that employed slogans such as *"Chenery Is Here"* and *"Best Quality Paints"*.

Advertising slogans were modified to reflect the season – and hyped up during sales' weeks. The firm known as the **Palatine Arcade** had opened in 1922 with premises in Church Street and during their sales promised *"Bargains Beyond Belief"*. When launched the Palatine called itself *"A Market Within A Shop"*.

Tyrers store in Liverpool Road in St Helens c. 1950

The Palatine, incidentally, had a device for collecting cash that later **Tyrers** would employ. The shop assistant would place the customer's bill and tendered cash into a capsule. This was despatched by an overhead pulley system to the account office in the same building and, within a short time, the customer's receipt and change would return in the same way.

Tyrers began trading from premises in Liverpool Road in 1888 after William Tinsley-Tyer took out a loan of £30. The firm later expanded into Regent House in Church Street, next to the Fleece Hotel, and also opened a branch in Prescot. Then in 1960, their new clothing "superstore" was opened in Bridge Street in St Helens. The firm used a number of different slogans in its adverts.

Tyrers Bridge Street store

During the 1930s, Tyrers called itself *"The Store Value Built"* and employed the straplines *"It Pays To Pay Cash"* and *"Servants Of The Public – Masters Of The Trade"*. Around Easter in the 1960s, customers were advised to *"See Our Windows For A Gay Glimpse of Spring"*.

Berens of Church Street sold "fashionable coats, raincoats and costumes". Their motto at sale time c.1920 was *"Never Mind What It Costs"*. I think what they meant was "Never mind what it used to cost, it's still been reduced" – but that's not quite so snappy!

Stewart's 'The King Tailors' had a branch in Church Street in St Helens and held an annual January sale. The firm insisted they were offering genuine reductions and it was not a *"Cut-The-Price-and-Hang-the-Quality"* sale. In January 1915, their cheapest made-to-measure sale suit cost just 15/3.

Stewart's store in St Helens was renowned for rewarding Saints' players who scored a hat trick of tries with a free, made-to-measure suit or overcoat. In one game Saints' scrum-half Fred

Trenwith scored two tries but was injured and had to be carried off the field of play. Historian Alex Service states that Fred later said:

They took me over the touchline and didn't want me to go back. I said I still needed another try to get the overcoat, and when they weren't looking, I dodged onto the field and managed to score the third just before time.

There was much competition in the motor charabanc market in St Helens in the early 1920s, which organisations could hire for trips to the seaside or countryside. Those looking to serve the higher end of the market were calling their charabancs "coaches" and their drivers "chauffeurs".

Marshall's of Hardshaw Street was one such coach operator and their slogans included:

Marshall's Cream Coaches Convey Customers Comfortably to Charming Country-Resorts on Cosy Cushions with Competent Chauffeurs at Competitive Costs.

Walter Marshall, the former managing director of County Carriers of Boundary Road, had founded the firm. As well as hiring out their "charas" to organisations, Marshalls provided weekend day trips to the seaside for members of the public. In another advert the firm promised a...

Sure, Safe, Speedy Service to the Shining Sea Every Saturday and Sunday to Southport and Blackpool.

Sadly Blackpool does not begin with an "S"! Fares cost 4/6 return to Southport and 8 shillings to Blackpool. Single fares were also available for those wanting to spend a few days at the seaside.

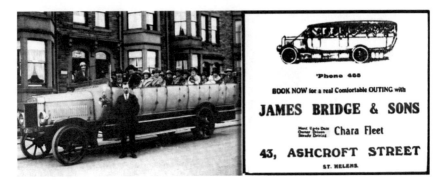

BOOK NOW for a real Comfortable OUTING with

JAMES BRIDGE & SONS

Chara Fleet

43, ASHCROFT STREET

ST. HELENS.

James Bridge of Ashcroft Street in Parr preferred to spell his coaches as "char-a-banc" – *"No party too large"* and *"Book Now For A Real Comfortable Outing"*, were two of his straplines.

Also in the motor transport business was **H. T. Sides** of Knowsley Road who was advertising:

> *Motor Pantechnicons. Any Distance. Reasonable Charges. Personal Supervision.*

Presumably the people of St Helens in the 1920s knew their Greek well and understood that Harry Telford Sides was in the business of hiring out his removal vans.

The town has hosted a huge number of butchers over the years. At Christmastime during the 19th century, the so-called butchers' shambles was the centrepiece of the St Helens Christmas market. In December 1868 the St Helens Newspaper commented how the butchers' stalls had been *"laden to the roof with beef and mutton and the attendants in the whitest of aprons"*, before writing:

> *Most people congregated to feast their eyes not only on blaze and glitter, but on the substantial produce of a holocaust.*

One of the longstanding St Helens butcher's in the 20th century was **Phythian's** whose slogan in the 1920s was *"Don't Live To Eat – Eat To Live!"*. Their adverts encouraged readers to ensure the food they bought was "sound, pure and wholesome" – which John Phythian claimed to sell in his two Liverpool Road shops.

In 1922 **Eastman's Butchers** published adverts with the headline: *"Special Announcement – We Are Giving Pigs Away"*. However, the rest of the Bridge Street butcher's ad simply suggested that their high quality meat was being offered at the lowest price in town – and it seems that customers could not simply walk out of their shop carrying (or even leading) a free pig!

I wonder if anybody showed up demanding one? Knowing St Helens folk, I expect some did. But knowing St Helens butchers, the pigs would have to fly out of their shop before they gave them away!

In later years butcher and former TT motorbike rider, **Brian Ball** from Westfield Street, had one of the snappiest advertising slogans in St Helens in *"Remember, Only The Meat Gets More Attention Than The Customers"*.

The BBC began its first radio broadcasts in November 1922 with station 2ZY opening in Manchester on the 15th. Within weeks, **Cholerton's** of Bridge Street in St Helens (better known for their photography) was advertising wireless receivers using headphones – or "radiophones" as they called them.

"Broadcasting Has Commenced" was the headline to their ads in the local papers. By 1925 there was lots of competition in St Helens for the sale of radios. In a Christmas advertising feature called "Wireless In St Helens" published in the St Helens Newspaper on December 11th of that year, the firm of **A. Sherlock** of Liverpool Road said:

Buy A Loud Speaker And Have A Jolly Christmas.
Dance To The Savoy Bands.

215

Most St Helens' folk with wirelesses during the '20s would have owned headphone-only crystal sets. Even though more than one headset could be plugged in, dancing to the popular BBC bands connected with the Savoy Hotel in London would not have been easy. Ironically, wireless users were then very much wired! So Albert Sherlock's advert freed "listeners in" from that constraint but did have a slight stroppiness about it, writing:

I know he's a clever man who can please everybody, but I am out to do my best for you, and if you don't get Absolute Satisfaction from me, it is your own fault for not speaking.

Storey Bros. of Barrow Street was also advertising in the St Helens Newspaper's feature, saying:

Why Not Buy Your "Sweetie" a Wireless Set? The ideal present for Christmas. It can be used for dancing, entertaining your guests and it will talk, sing and play to you all the year round. A real friend in the home.

Dingsdales was another St Helens business with a lengthy history, which they claimed dated back to around 1890. In the

1930s – under the trading name of George Dingsdale – the firm used several slogans in their advertising. These included *"Dingsdale Defies Competition For Straightforward Dealing, Reliability And Service"* and *"All Roads Lead to Dingsdales"*. Another of their sayings was *"You Can't Afford To Buy Elsewhere"*, often accompanied by a picture of owner George and the slogan *"By George You're Right"*.

In their ads in 1939 Dingsdales added: *"For over half-a-century, thousands of happy cyclists have proved the truth of these statements – over 1,000 models of the world's best cycles are awaiting your inspection."*

At that time Dingsdales were seemingly only selling bikes from premises in Duke Street and Higher Parr Street. However, a shop in Church Road in Haydock was later added and their product range expanded. By the 1970s, Dingsdales was also advertising go-karts, sledges, pedal cars, Triang railways, Scalextric, Lego, dolls' prams, vacuum cleaners and sewing machines.

Frank Waring sold bikes as well as radios from shops in Parr Stocks Road, Westfield Street and Peasley Cross Lane. Their slogans in the 1930s included *"See Frank First"* and *"Frank Waring Gives A Square Deal To Cyclists And A Square Deal In Radio."*

Rothery Radio had premises in Baldwin Street in St Helens and in Prescot and employed many slogans over the years. *"The Best People For All The Best Sets"*, was one from the 1950s.

When BBC1 and ITV began colour broadcasts in November 1969, the headline to Rothery's advert in the Reporter said: *"See Coronation Street in Colour – Only 24/9"*. That was the weekly

THIS CHRISTMAS GIVE A GIFT OF REAL **QUALITY**, BUY A **RADIO**!

Perfection is always desired. The perfect Gift is a RADIO. Their beauty is instantly admired, their enduring quality and practicability always enjoyed and they turn dark days into bright days, banish the black-out blues with music in the home this Christmas.

You have your choice of nationally famous makes—

MURPHY H.M.V.
PYE PHILIPS

Very easy Hire Purchase Terms. Cash Prices from £8.

We Guarantee Deliveries on ALL ORDERS PLACED To-day (Friday) and Saturday.

ROTHERY RADIO Lᵀᴰ

17, BALDWIN STREET, ST. HELENS. Tel. 2950
59 ECCLESTON STREET PRESCOT Tel 6100

Christmas 1939 advert from Rothery Radio

217

equivalent rental of a Ferguson, HMV or Ultra set after a year's deposit had been made.

In October 1970 it was reported that Rothery's employed as many as 35 TV engineers at their Lowe Street repairs depot. They were then on strike, along with four telephone receptionists. The men downed screwdrivers and soldering irons in support of a pay claim – and the women walked out through customers being rude to them because they couldn't get their TV sets fixed!

BRING THE ANNOUNCER HOME!

It is just like having the announcer in your own home to hear him on Rediffusion. All the little familiar intonations of every item come to you as though he were sitting on the other side of the table, quietly telling you of the events of the day, or announcing the next item for your entertainment.

IT'S AS CLEAR AS THAT-BY **REDIFFUSION**

Advert for Rediffusion of Barrow Street in the St Helens Reporter in 1939

After WW2 **Rediffusion** became associated with commercial television franchises and the rental of TV sets from high street stores. However, it began its days as a pioneering cable company with its main shop in Barrow Street. Many St Helens' households unable to obtain good quality reception via their aerials would subscribe to the service. In the 1930s in its radio-only days, Rediffusion adopted the slogan *"Entertainment And News By Private Wire – Direct To Your Home"*, which must have made subscribers feel a bit special. Also *"Bring The Announcer Home"*, which referred to the reception quality being so good that it sounded as if the presenters were sitting in your living room. *"Remember Rediffusion Need Only Cost You 1/6 A Week"* was another thirties' slogan.

Before the name Rothery became associated with radio / TV and record shops in St Helens, it was the moniker belonging to a "high-class" pawnbrokers and jewellers trading in Westfield Street. A very regular advertiser, **Rothery's** used the slogans *"The Old Firm"* and *"Value Every Time"*.

By the late 1920s, sufficient folk in St Helens must have bought cameras of their own for chemist **William Clowes** of Baldwin Street and Thatto Heath to justify paying for adverts on the masthead of the St Helens Reporter. Those promised:

Lovely Glossy Prints. Delightful Postcard Enlargements.

When the Fleece Hotel opened in Church Street in St Helens in 1932, **Bateman's** took one of the shop premises that fronted the new building. *"For Quality and Satisfaction"*, was their slogan alongside a black cat and the text *"Luck In Gem Rings"*.

Rowley & Co. of 84 Church Street posed this question as their slogan during the 1920s: *"Are You Only Seeing Half This Wonderful World?"* As well as standard glasses, the St Helens opticians were also selling the new sunglasses – although that term was not employed in their adverts. Instead, the name of the product recommended to reduce the glare while on your summer hols was "Crookes Glass Spectacles".

She's Bursting with Vitality

Wise Mothers throughout St. Helens & District always include Samuel Mercer & Sons' Bread, Confectionery, Cooked Meats, Pies, etc., in the family diet. They know Samuel Mercer & Sons' Specialities contain only the purest ingredients and vitamins necessary for building health and vitality.

SAMUEL MERCER & SON
(Prop. John Mercer)

Higher Parr St.	Phone	2421
Peter Street.	„	3083
Owen St., Toll Bar.	„	2297

REPORTER ADVERTISING SERVICE

1939 advert from the St Helens Reporter when John Mercer was in charge

Samuel Mercer & Son had several shops in St Helens. The baker and confectioner kept two premises in Higher Parr Street and others in Peter Street and Owen Street. *"Santa Claus Knows A Good Thing When He Sees One!"*, was their Xmas slogan next to a picture of Father Christmas about to tuck into a Mercer's cake.

Pimblett's was a Mercer's spin-off after Samuel's daughter Mary married John Pimblett. The baker's opened as Mercer's in Liverpool Road in 1921 and in 1927 John Pimblett gave up his job as a Pilkington engineer to join his wife. Before long "Pimmies" became a St Helens institution, opening their 7th branch in 1970. *"Fresh Pies Daily"* was one of their slogans, along with *"Make Christmas Complete With Party Foods"*. There was also **Eversons** in Westfield Street who said: *"Fresh cream fancies our speciality"*.

Bardsley's Century Stores was situated in Liverpool Road in Greenbank, St Helens. *"Don't Shiver!"*, was their advice which headlined their ads in the wintertime, adding: *"Wear One of Bardsley's Tip Top Overcoats at 16/11"*.

Woolworths in Church Street used to have the motto *"Nothing Over Sixpence"*. A poem from the 1940s said:

Potatoes and grasses, jugs, bowls and glasses; there's thousands of things of a different kind with wonderful service

– assistants so kind. Try Woolie's whenever you are in a fix,
though its motto is no longer "Nix over six".

Several traders used poetry in their adverts with mixed results. During the flu pandemic at the end of WW1, **Ted Cawley** – who ran the Wellington Hotel in Market Square in St Helens – believed that drinking port could stop you getting influenza. Ted's ads said:

To Avoid The 'Flu And Never Rue, Ted Cawley's
Port Wine Is The Goods For You.

His advert also had a Kitchener-like finger pointed at the reader to emphasise the point. By 1921 Ted's strapline became: *"The Man Who Has The Goods To Sell"*. **William Nicholson** of Bridge Street regularly advertised as "The Practical Hatter" using poetry in his adverts. In 1918 he wrote:

Should you require a neat Cravat,
A Trilby, Shirt, or Bowler Hat,
Call and see the writer, who forsooth
Has traded in these things from early youth.

In the late 1940s, **Jeff Smurfit** of Hardshaw Street in St Helens had what appeared at first glance to be a rather odd slogan for his Christmas advert in the St Helens newspapers:

The Ideal Gift For Her
A FUR COAT
or TIE

We still have Fur Coats at Pre-Budget Prices.
SHOP EARLY FOR CHRISTMAS

Jeff Smurfit, Ltd.
10 HARDSHAW STREET, ST. HELENS

The Ideal Gift For Her.
A Fur Coat Or Tie.

However, two illustrations adjacent to the text explained that the present of a fur coat was for the lady in your life to wear and the tie for her poodle-like dog, which already had a fur coat of its own! Whether Smurfit's actually sold dog leads, was not stated in the ad.

During the warmer months some people swapped their flat cap or bowler for a straw hat. **Balshaw Brothers** of Bridge Street – run by John and Joseph Balshaw – would advertise the *"Newest Shapes"* of straw hats and the *"Latest London Neckwear"*. I wonder how many shapes of straw hats there were – apart from round?

George Marsden founded his shoe shop at 4 Barrow Street. Later branches were added in Parr Street and Cooper Street in St Helens and at Eccleston Street in Prescot. In the 1930s *"Firm For Footwear"*, was his slogan, which later was replaced by *"For All Your Footwear – You Name It We Have It"*.

Clinkards began selling shoes in Westfield Street in 1953, sometimes under the name of its owner W. H. Clinkard. There have been a number of different slogans used over the years, including *"Your Local Family Footwear Specialists"*, *"Boots You'll Love To Wear"* and *"The Good Shoe Specialist"*.

CLINKARDS SHOE SHOP
BETTER THAN EVER
SALE
LADIES' AND GENT'S NOW ON
CHILDREN'S STARTS TUESDAY, 14th
5 Westfield Street : St. Helens

A regular advertiser in the St Helens Reporter's annual 'Back to School' feature, Clinkards claimed in 1969 to keep 1,500 pairs of children's shoes in stock.

Peter Dewar's tobacconist's was founded in 1876 – originally in Tontine Street in St Helens before relocating to Bridge Street and then Church Street – and lasted for a full one hundred years.

The shop was renowned for its figure of a leprechaun called Paddy that used to stand on the shop's frontage. In the late 19th century, Peter Dewar had the motto *"Small Profits and Quick Returns"*.

After the Armistice brought WW1 to an end, the firm used the slogan *"Help The Boys To Smoke The Pipe of Peace"*. By the 1930s, *"The Smoker's Mecca"*, was their advertising strapline.

SMOKES
FOR DAD
MAKE SUITABLE
XMAS
PRESENTS

CIGARS,
CIGARETTES
and all
SMOKERS'
REQUISITES

We shall be pleased to
accept orders for Duty Free
Cigarettes and Tobaccos for
H.M. Forces overseas.

PETER DEWAR LTD.
31 Church Street,
21 Ormskirk Street, 20 Bridge Street,
St. Helens.
Telephone 3610   Telephone 3002

Xmas 1939 ad in St Helens News

In 1971 Peter Dewar diversified into men's fashions. The full-page advertising feature in the St Helens Reporter that promoted the new Church Street venture made a point of saying that ashtrays would be "placed at strategic points" round the store. Probably not a huge selling point today!

In the earlier years of the 20th century, Critchley's of Church Street styled themselves as **Chas. A. Critchley**. It was a multi-skilled business that offered to undertake painting, plumbing, decorating and electrical work. *"Critchley's For Class"* was their slogan but in later years it was *"C. A. Critchley – The Hoover Centre"*.

In a St Helens Reporter wedding feature in 1970, Critchley's had this message for grooms – which I expect would be considered somewhat sexist if published today:

Congratulations gentlemen! Now keep her young with Hoover Home Aids. Hoover Junior Cleaner only £26 when you part exchange your old Hoover Upright with foot switch.

In a similar vein during the 1970s, **Griffins** wrote in their newspaper adverts: *"Don't take your wife for granted. (Cash or H.P.) Take her to Griffins."*

What personal feminine gift do you think was being sold that might, perhaps, rejuvenate a flagging marriage? Jewellery, furs, flowers, perfume, maybe? No, furniture! Three piece suites, bedroom units and divans were the specialities of *"The Furniture People of St. Helens"* with a "great walk-round discount" warehouse in Rigby Street and a store in Duke Street.

There have quite a few longstanding furnishers in St Helens. I suppose people will always needs beds, chairs, carpets etc. – and tastes never change all that much.

In 1939, **Gerrards** claimed to have been in the furniture business for ninety-four years with premises then opposite the Theatre Royal in Corporation Street. *"Gerrards For Fine Furniture"* was its simple but effective slogan, adding in the third person:

> *No Competitor Can Injure Their Reputation For*
> *Reliable And Inexpensive Household Goods.*

H. & A. E. Williams was another longstanding St Helens furnisher founded in 1910 by two brothers in a Lowe Street shed. During the '70s, their premises were located in Westfield Street and Corporation Street and run by Ernest and John Williams – who were also undertakers. But in the 1920s, Williams' two shops were in Cotham Street and Duke Street. At that time their ads said:

Crowds Of People Are Delighted With The Bargains They Secure

From 1912 married couple Sam and Sarah Ann Taylor ran **S. and S. A. Taylor's** second-hand furniture stores in Duke Street, North Road and Baldwin Street. *"Sir Ann Taylor – Knighted For Services To Furniture"*, became their slogan, seemingly as a result of customers mispronouncing Sarah Ann. Before WW2 they were simply known as *Taylor's, "The Furnishers Of Distinction"* and in the late 1930s was boasting the largest showrooms in the town.

"They Is Good People To Deal With" was the slogan of furnishers **Chesterfields**. Their premises were in Church Street and during the '50s promised *"3 Huge Floors of Bargains in Contemporary and Traditional Furniture – Lifts To All Floors."* There was also **Edward Astbury**

of Church Street *"The People's Furnisher"* and **Sextons** of Duke Street and College Street – *"Your Stockist of 'G-PLAN' Furniture"*. There were two main stores in St Helens retailing outdoor clothing, footwear and army surplus. **The Great Army & Navy Store**s at 30 Bridge Street claimed to possess the finest stock of parkas in the north. *"There is only one Great Army & Navy Stores and this is it!"*, their ad proudly boasted.

The **Famous Army Stores** at 89 Church Street (at its junction with Hall Street) would dispute that claim. *"It Will Pay You To Pay Us A Visit"* and *"Civility High – Prices Low"*, were their neat slogans.

In its early days, **Oxleys** department store on the corner of Claughton Street and Barrow Street used the strapline *"'Liverpool' In St. Helens"* – meaning that shoppers did not need to travel to the city to obtain value and choice. *"It Pays To Call Often"* was their slogan during the '20s and *"The Quality Stores"* during the '40s. Like Helena House, Oxleys were renowned for their annual Christmas grotto. That usually began during the first week of November with Redgate Boys Silver Band sometimes leading Santa through the town from Shaw Street station to Oxleys store.

The man in the red cloak then took up pride of place in their Fairyland Grotto where there were free balloons and sweets and "bumper parcels" costing 3 shillings. The firm also had a children's department called **Babyland**, which employed the slogan the *"Bargain Spot of St Helens"*. A bad fire struck Oxleys in December 1959, which gutted its old part and destroyed that year's grotto.

Advert for the Oxley prams in the St Helens Reporter of 1923

The St Helens Corporation held monopolies over both the gas and electricity supplies in the town and so their regular advertising could, perhaps, be seen as competing with itself. In January 1939, Radiant House – on the corner of Cotham Street and Ormskirk Street – opened as the **St Helens Gas Showrooms**. At the time of writing, the HoneyRose Foundation is the occupier of the imposing premises.

Radiant House in Cotham Street

The Gas Department's slogans included: *"After All Gas Is Best"* and *"For Even Cooking – Without Even Looking – Use Gas"*.

Whereas the Corporation's electricity department would employ the strapline: *"More Leisure For Pleasure With Electric Cooking"*. Their **Electricity Showrooms** in Bridge Street opened on December 16th 1932 with a two-fold purpose of persuading St Helens folk of the merits of electric power and then to sell them electrical appliances, such as fires and lamps.

Public demonstrations were given each week within their large, lavish rooms, which, according to their brochures, "demonstrate the truth of all that is claimed for this great servant of mankind".

St Helens Newspaper advert from 1946

St Helens Corporation's Electricity Showrooms in Bridge Street

The Electricity Showroom's brightly illuminated front window containing many modern appliances must have looked very impressive at night and bore a large "Made in England" sign.

In the late 1930s, the **LMS Railway** took out ads in the St Helens' papers using the slogan *"Life Is Gay ... Exciting ... On The Sunny LMS Coast"*. The London, Midland and Scottish Railway was encouraging the town's holiday-makers to travel by train – not to the warmer south coast – but remain fairly close to home by commuting to resorts in the north:

> *England's north-west coast calls all who take their pleasures gladly, for here is the very heart of perpetual amusement. Here is the perfect combination of sea and sand and sun and scenery. Here health is thrust upon you unawares by a life-giving tonic air. Here biting winds are outlawed and bronzed men, sun-tanned women, bright-eyed children find a holiday happiness they've never known before.*

This paradise could be experienced at places like Southport, the Isle of Man, Morecambe, Blackpool, North Wales and the Lake District.

By the 1960s and '70s, foreign holidays became more affordable – although some may have been deterred by the extra travel arrangements. Hence **Dixon's World Wide Travel** of Baldwin Street would say: *"Let Us Take The Worry, You Take The Holiday"*.

St Helens Reporter December 21st 1973

The company had been founded in 1948 and in their ads in 1969 used the slogan *"21 Years' Travel Experience Is At Your Service – Entirely Free"*. *"The Sign Of An Active Travel Agent"*, was another of their slogans.

Or you could stay in this country with an organised break in a holiday camp. In 1968 **Phythians Travel Agency** in Westfield Street was advertising a week's stay at Prestatyn Holiday Camp from £9 10 shillings. Or you could: *"See Ireland Through Irish Eyes"* for eight or fifteen days "all in" from £24 10s.

Or you could journey to the moon, maybe.....

On July 18th 1969, with Apollo 11 having launched on its historic mission just two days earlier, the St Helens Reporter published a special advertising feature called 'Moon Time'. Phythians had a large illustration of a rocket in their advert, along with these words:

We can't book you on Apollo 11 but when services to the moon are available Phythians will be the first to know. If you want to go let us know. We will enter your name in our Lunar Flight Register and keep you posted. Until then earthbound mortals can obtain all their Travel and Holiday requirements at Phythians Travel Agency, the only agent in St. Helens which is fully licensed to sell and issue immediately tickets on all international airlines.

Or you could journey to the planets, maybe…..

Helena House Travel Services of Baldwin Street was thinking much further than the moon, writing in the same feature:

All aboard for jet age travel pleasure. Will you require a round trip to Mars in 1980? Or perhaps, just a short trip to the Moon and back? There is no holding back now – nothing is more sure that this is the road that man is taking – The Road to the Planets. Meanwhile, the beauty of our island Earth is open for all to enjoy and see.

Howard Travel of Cotham Street in St Helens was more down to earth in its advertising. The agency was selling short seasonal breaks to places like Dunoon, the Isle of Man, Dublin, Torquay, Bude, Southsea, Ostend etc. *"Go On, Give Yourself A Treat!"*, they urged in their adverts.

There was also **Ellison's Travel Service** of Westfield Street. Its strapline was: *"You Can Relax When You Book With St. Helens Leading Travel Agent"*. And trading from Rexmore House in Cotham Street and later Barrow Street, **Tom Howard's Travel Agent's** said in his ads: *"We Have The Holiday Your Looking For"*.

231

An Ellison's coach pictured in the 1930s

May & Lomax were insurance brokers with premises in Bickerstaffe Street in St Helens. The slogans in their adverts suggested that some rather unusual policies could be taken out with them:

If You Wish To Insure Your Wife Against Having Twins. We Can Arrange It. – If You Wish To Transport Lions To Newcastle. We Can Insure Them.

Wise gardeners save ££'s at A. C. Collins

I am able to sell you a

Lawn Mower

of your own choice cheaper than anyone in the United Kingdom

Known mainly for motorbikes and later electrical appliances, **A. C. Collins** from Brynn Street behind the Town Hall employed the slogan *"Look at My Quality And Prices"*. The firm also sold lawn mowers and made quite a claim:

> *I am able to sell you the lawn mower of your choice,*
> *cheaper than anyone in the United Kingdom.*
> *All I ask . . . Let me quote you.*

If you needed tyres for your car or bike, George Fryer was the man to see. The **Fryer Tyrer Service** of Eccleston Street in St Helens would say *"When Time To Re-Tyre, Remember Fryer"*.

Frank Lennon established **Lennons** as a grocer's around 1915 when he opened a small shop in Park Road in Parr. Later his sons Terence and Dennis inherited the firm. The pair opened their first supermarket in Widnes in 1958 after travelling to America to study the new method of retailing.

Some questioned whether the American style of "pile it high and sell it cheap" would be accepted here – but their supermarket was instantly successful and a second was opened in St Helens in 1959.

1939 advert in the St Helens Reporter

Lennons food stores have used various straplines over the years. In the 1930s their slogans included *"The People's Providers"* and *"A Square Deal For All"*. During the 1950s, *"Lennon's The Big Dividend Grocers – Shop Where Your £ Buys More"* was another regular refrain.

The St Helens Co-operative Stores in Baldwin Street

However, the Co-op was the most famous divi merchant of them all. The St Helens Co-operative Stores was an imposing building built on the site of a former workhouse in Baldwin Street.

When Helena House opened as an extension and eventual replacement of the Stores on May 6th 1958, the St Helens Reporter wrote:

Housewives stood 10 and 12 deep, lining the pavements on all sides of Baldwin Street and Cotham Street on Tuesday, for the opening ceremony of the palatial new building known as Helena House.

Their advertising slogans at the time called Helena House a *"Co-operative Super Store For Super Service"*; *"The Town's Most Modern Building"* and *"The Store For All The Family"*.

On June 6th 1973, when **Nevins** opened their Robins Lane "superstore" in Sutton, they described it as *"The Shoppers Paradise"* and called on housewives to *"Bring Your Hubby"*. The 10,000 sq. ft. supermarket was the 21st store in their chain, which although centred on St Helens, also included shops in Prescot, Whiston, Swinton, Rainhill, Stretford and Widnes.

Michael Nevin had begun the chain when he opened a shop in Park Road and by the late 1920s Nevins claimed to be the biggest retail cash grocer's in the St Helens district. *"Look For The Name Over The Shop"* was one of their main advertising slogans. When Valerie Belshaw interviewed Michael's son Jack Nevin for the St Helens Reporter in 1972, the supermarket's boss said:

See love, the only way to get on in the world today is to take care of people. People matter a great deal. I care deeply about all my employees and I care about the women who shop in my supermarkets.

Supermarkets have in recent times been criticised for displaying tempting sweets and chocolates near their checkouts. However, such treats have not always been seen as unhealthy. What may have been the first advertising feature published in a St Helens newspaper in which a number of retailers and manufacturers took part, appeared in the St Helens Reporter on September 28th 1923.

The subject was sweets and the clear message was that they were good for you, with slogans like *"Get the Toffee Habit"* and *"Sweets Are Energy"*. And if you were worried about tooth decay – well this is what they wrote:

> *Sweets are, in fact, healthful and nutritious....As to their effect upon the teeth – the old belief was that sweets caused decay in a severe form – we have it on the authority of a well-known dentist that nothing is further from the fact.*

The unnamed, well-known dentist from Glasgow was quoted as stating that the notion that sugar caused tooth decay was an "absurd idea". Clearly in agreement was **Roses** of 28 Church Street whose advert in the feature said:

"For High Class Chocolates and Sweets . . . . Go To F. R. Rose"

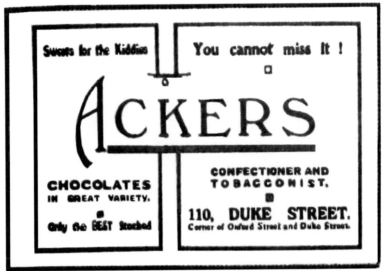

Sweets advertising feature in St Helens Reporter on September 28th 1923

Meanwhile, **Ann Ackers** was offering *"Sweets for the Kiddies"* and *"Chocolates In Great Variety"*. Incidentally, Wrigleys had an advert in the feature for what they were then calling "spearmint chewing sweets" – and not gum. They claimed that their product freshened the mouth, cleaned teeth and aided digestion, recommending its chewing after meals.

In the early 1960s, legalised betting shops were still fairly new and some punters might have had concerns about such places not paying off large wins. So **Bob Collins'** slogans were *"Remember – I Can Pay What I Offer . . . I Do Pay What I Offer"*, and *"Bet In Comfort As You View"*. By the 1970s, the firm – whose head office was in Borough Road and claimed to have been founded in 1905 – was employing the slogan *"Enjoy Your Betting With A Firm Of Repute"* and *"For Service and Integrity Try... [Bob Collins]"*

During the month of December during the 1970s, **F. S. Laughton** of 6/8 Cotham Street promised *"Instant Fun This Christmas"* with a Polaroid; Bullens of 27 Baldwin Street was declaring: *"Books Are Most Acceptable Children's Gifts"* and Tony Sampson of 14 Cotham Street said: *"Get Your Kids-'n-gear This Christmas In Sampson's Sellar"*.

In 1967 **Sampsons** adopted the slogan *"Get The Al Capone Look"*, selling wide-brimmed hats, pin-striped and chalk-striped suits, double-breasted jackets, full-length topcoats, matching silk scarves and dickie bows. To add a touch of realism to their window display, a gun was included.

However, that led to a visit from a sergeant in St Helens Police's Crime Prevention Department who requested that the weapon be removed. Sampsons claimed that the officer had told them that the gun "might corrupt the minds of young people".

During the 1960s and '70s, the Reporter ran an annual "First Baby Contest", with the first dozen "bonny bouncers" born in St Helens after midnight on December 31st awarded a 30-shilling gift.

If the mums bought their pram from Prestts of Duke Street, a free canopy was on offer. In addition, Cholerton's of 166 Duke Street gave the mother of the first New Year's baby a framed photograph of her child and Practical Credit Services of College Street presented a £5 voucher.

And Nevins Grocers gave £1 vouchers to the mothers of the first five New Years babies – that's the equivalent of about £15 in 2022.

Many parents fulfilled their infant's needs by making a beeline to **Baby World**, whose slogan was *"The Town's Most Complete Pram & Toy Specialists"*. George Gornall and Gladys Corns had founded the firm in 1953 in Market Street in St Helens. Within a few years,

Baby World had opened branches in Eccleston Street in Prescot and in Ormskirk and Southport. Then in 1965 Baby World expanded to Duke Street in St Helens. The firm then claimed to be one of only three in Britain that published its own catalogue for its customers. Another shop serving the needs of babies was **Haywards** of 33 Westfield Street. During the '70s they were advertising *"The Best Buys For Baby"*.

During that period **Lilian Rogers** at 30 Duke Street promised *"Fashions For All Ages, Teenage To Outsize"* and **Foster's Florists** of Hardshaw Street, Westfield Street and Ormskirk Street used the strapline: *"For Wedding Flowers Of Charm And Elegance"*. Meanwhile, **Sayers Bakery** would say: *"Weddings Are A Piece Of Cake..." and* **Emmet's Taxi Service** of Corporation Street promised *"Cars For All Occasions"*.

An earlier advertiser of taxi rides had been **Bert Wilcock** of Dentons Green Lane who did not appear to have been the chatty sort of cab driver. His adverts in 1939 promised *"A Ride In Peace At A Reasonable Price"*.

The hairdressers and wig sellers of the seventies included **Chadwick's** of North Road – *"Crown Your Beauty With A New Hair Style"*; **The Hair Boutique**, 15 Prescot Road – *"Why Not Bring Your Man To Sweeney's Den?"* and **The Cut an' Curl Boutique**, 460 Fleet Lane – *"Have A New Hairpieced Wig For Christmas"*.

As to entertainment venues in St Helens, when the **Capitol Cinema** opened on the corner of North Road and Duke Street in St Helens on October 3rd 1929, it used the advertising strapline: *"Be Happy – Visit The Capitol"*. And such a state of euphoria could be inexpensively obtained by paying one of four

The Capitol Cinema in Duke Street

bands of charges. The admission price in the stalls was just 6d; in the grand stalls 8d; 1 shilling in the circle and 1/6 in the grand circle – with children paying half-price.

In December 1956 the Oxford Cinema became the Plaza Ballroom

During the '60s the strapline of the **Plaza Ballroom** in Duke Street was *"St. Helens Premier Beat Venue – The Leading Venue For The Leading Groups"*. Then in the early '70s as the Plaza Theatre Club, it was *"Come To Lancashire's Most Successful Night Club"*. Then there was **The Place** at 57 Ormskirk Street whose slogan was *"St. Helens Only True Disco For The Young"*.

Graphic used by the St Helens Reporter during the 1960s

The 19th Century Newspapers
That Waxed Lyrical

"It is but justice to say that only a few of the sterner sex seemed to have been worshipping too freely at the shrine of the rosy god."

The writing style of journalists has certainly changed over the years. The extravagant, effusive vocabulary often used in 19th century newspaper articles has been replaced by a more direct, informative style, albeit at times sensationalised.

The Plain English Campaign probably approves of this change but it has meant that the diversity and romance of the English language has been curtailed – as well as the need to use dictionaries!

This chapter is dedicated to an era when journalists *(mainly working for the St Helens Newspaper)* decided that spades were not spades but long-handled garden utensils attached to metallic digging heads that reflected the glistening rays of sunlight! I've made that one up – but it leads neatly into my first example…

UNBECLOUDED BRILLIANCY! – From 1882 the London & NW Railway Company held an annual athletics festival at the recreation ground belonging to its Sheeting Stores. The field at St Helens Junction was far from being in an ideal location – with neighbouring factories pumping out smelly fumes into the atmosphere.

In 1889 three thousand spectators lined the ropes to cheer on the competitors. The sun was shining and the track was in good nick, which led to compliments from visitors. That's my plain English version of the event – but this is the St Helens Reporter's description from June 29th 1889:

The eye of heaven flashed with unbeclouded brilliancy...The land, considering that it is surrounded with an atmosphere of chemicals and other oderiferous particles, was in grand condition, and the improvement, compared with previous years, called forth the repeated encomiums of the visitors.

THE GIANT HORSE HAULING HUMAN FREIGHTAGE – The highlight of the annual 3-day Newton Races was Race Friday, as it was known. Many shopkeepers in St Helens closed their premises to allow their staff the opportunity of attending. However, the churches did not approve of the drinking culture at Newton Races and organised counter attractions for schoolchildren and parishioners. These were mainly excursions and this is how the St Helens Newspaper described one journey on June 22nd 1864:

The largest party by train was bound for Southport, numbering nearly two thousand persons. Such an amount of human freightage had to be conveyed in three separate trains, and even then the strength of the giant horse seemed to be tested for a while; but after a few puffs and snorts it hurried them along on the great iron road. A few more groans from its iron lungs; a few more strainings of its iron ribbs [sic], and the party found themselves in rapid motion.

THE SHRINE OF THE ROSY GOD – The newspapers had a variety of ways of describing drunken persons. When in February 1870 Mary Burns was charged with stealing a piece of dripping from the market stall of butcher John Hatton in Exchange Street in St Helens, the Newspaper wrote:

The woman made no defence beyond the obliviousness of drink. On giving a promise to be careful for the future, if she were alive for 50 years, she was let off.

Then on October 18th 1870, James Tierney was fined 10s 6d, including costs, for being a disorderly drunk – or as the St Helens

Newspaper put it, "obstreperous in his cups in the streets of Prescot". And in commenting how only a small number of men had got drunk on Whit Monday 1870, the Newspaper wrote:

It is but justice to say that only a few of the sterner sex seemed to have been worshipping too freely at the shrine of the rosy god.

THE ACME OF ANTICIPATIONS – The annual tea party and ball in aid of St Joseph's RC schools in Peasley Cross was held on October 26th 1868 at the Volunteer Hall in St Helens – with dancing continuing until 1:30am. The St Helens Newspaper could have simply written that there'd been a good attendance and much money was raised. Instead they poetically put:

The good and energetic fathers who exercise a spiritual control over the schools had their project rewarded to the acme of their anticipations.

VIOLENT CONTACT WITH A CRANIUM – The term gatecrasher apparently only came into use during the 1920s – but, of course, uninvited guests had been turning up at events long before then. On January 6th 1872, the St Helens Newspaper described how two Liverpool men had interrupted a workingmen's ball in Prescot:

One of them broke a bottle on a man's head, and not content with this feat, he gave melancholy usage to the secretary for interfering in the interests of order. A large tea cup formed an element in the fight, but collapsed at an early stage from violent contact with the cranium of one of the combatants.

TERPSICHOREAN AMUSEMENT – On September 3rd 1868 the annual tea meeting of Lowe House Church's Women's Guild was held, attended by 60 ladies. After the nosh-up the women enjoyed a dance. That is the short and sweet plain English version of what went on – but this is how the Newspaper said it:

> After a substantial tea some of those who had an inclination for a little Terpsichorean amusement had an opportunity of indulging in their penchant, and the evening passed most agreeably and harmoniously.

RUBBING STONES – I expect many readers will recall the so-called "donkey stone" that housewives would use on their doorsteps. The generic moniker was actually "rubbing stone" but the cleaning product became known by the trade name of a leading manufacturer called Donkey.

When Ann Hulton summoned Mary Donnegan to the St Helens Petty Sessions on September 20th 1869 accusing her of assault, the Newspaper explained that it had been based on a trivial quarrel between the women. This led to the accused using some rubbing stone on Mrs Hulton's face, which, they wrote:

> …had anything but a tendency to produce a polish.

THE QUADRUPED AND THE BIPED – On Whit Monday of 1869, a youth was tasked with driving a bull from the Stanley cattle market to St Helens. The animal was literally being led by the nose, via a cord attached to a ring that passed through its nostrils.

While travelling through Prescot, the bull took a sudden dislike to the cord and began pulling hard at it. In describing its escape on May 22nd, the St Helens Newspaper could have simply said that the cord held by the youth became detached from the bull – but instead they wrote:

> A quiet, but most expressive pantomime was carried on between them for some minutes, and at last, a movement on the part of the quadruped deprived the biped of the link that bound them together.

The Newspaper then explained how the animal had entered a shop on Fazakerley Street, to the horror of the proprietor's wife:

> The bull, dispensing even with the faintest approach to etiquette, was about paying his devoirs [respects] to the lady, when – crash! smash! – the floor yielded beneath his ponderous weight, and the latter half of his person partially disappeared below the level. The treacherous boards, which a moment before presented so smooth a path through the emporium of curiosities, had yielded when least expected, and left the bull in such a state of literal suspense as ought to have spoiled his appetite for holiday keeping. The unlucky animal made very grotesque efforts to recover his footing, but was unsuccessful, until some friendly persons came provided with ropes, and accomplished the restoration of his equilibrium.

THE TEARDROPS OF THE SKY – There was no such thing as paid holidays in 1869. You got paid for the work you did – and nothing else, as cash compensated for your labour. However, a few large firms in St Helens organised an annual outing for their staff. On June 5th 1869, the Ravenhead Plate Glass Works took between 500 and 600 workers and their wives, sisters and "female friends" on an excursion to the Lake District.

Some would likely have been making their first trip out of St Helens and it must have been a real eye-opener – with the murkiness of their hometown temporarily replaced by the beauty of the Lakes. A specially chartered train conveyed the party to Windermere, along with a reporter from the St Helens Newspaper who was obsessed with the weather! Readers were told how a slight shower had begun as the train passed Wigan and worsened as the journey progressed, with a "heavy mist hung like an impalpable curtain between the excursionists and all distant views."

By the time the train reached Windermere the rain was coming down with "mizzling continuity" and as "damping upon the spirits as upon the clothing". But by the afternoon the rain had stopped. The Newspaper then added:

It was half-past two o'clock in the afternoon before the excursionists could conscientiously pronounce the weather fine, and then those who had cared to shelter from the teardrops of the sky poured from all descriptions of conveyances, and directed their course through the rustic village to the lake. Boating being the principal amusement available, boats were hired in plenty, until the waters were enlivened.

AMIABLE MENDICANT – In St Helens Police Court on November 29th 1869, Superintendent James Ludlam – the head of the town's police force – informed the Bench how he was dealing with a rise in beggars. Because of what he described as the "alarming" increase in vagrancy on Saturday nights, a couple of officers had been on the streets in plain clothes to catch offenders. The Newspaper sarcastically described how a man called George Wilson who had been begging in Church Street did not take refusal to donate with good grace:

This amiable mendicant made a habit of cursing the persons who refused him alms, and for this feature in his case he was sent to prison for 14 days.

ELASTIC MIND – As stated in a previous chapter, the most popular medium of advertisement in 1869 was not newspapers – which much of the working class did not or could not read – but posters or handbills that were often called placards. The St Helens Newspaper wrote that during the week prior to Whit of that year:

Our walls were placarded with the announcement of cheap excursions to almost all parts of the country boasting of scenic beauties, and he who possessed time and inclination had many sources of healthful pleasure to make a selection from. The morning looked bright and cheering, and the early trains carried off large numbers of excursionists, some bound to contiguous places, and others bent on opening their summer vacation by a pleasant trip to some healthful locality, where the dust and smoke of our furnace-begift borough may be shaken off by the pure fresh breezes, and the mind depressed by the cares of daily toil, may grow more elastic from rejuvenated health.

DEPRECIATIVE PROCESSES – Anyone could call themselves a professor – but entertainers particularly liked to embrace that moniker. Well, it made them sound more impressive! Although the way that the Prescot Reporter described the act of "Professor" Sinclair on November 6th 1875, he sounded clever enough in his own right without the need of a fancy title. Why, the man used depreciative processes on objects and then restored them to health! Read on for an explanation:

Professor Sinclair gave his ventriloquial, musical, and wizard entertainment at the Town-hall, Prescot, on Tuesday evening, before a fair audience. The several tricks performed by the professor elicited roars of laughter and frequent applause, especially from the juvenile portion of the audience. Hats, watches, and handkerchiefs, borrowed from the audience, were put through apparently depreciative processes, and restored to the owners uninjured, in the most unaccountable manner. The ventriloquial portion of the entertainment was very good, and showed the performer to be an adept in that mysterious art.

THE COLD CHAIN OF SILENCE – When the annual licensing sessions for St Helens and district were held on September 6th 1869, a petition was submitted against Daniel Woods being allowed to retain his licence. He kept a beerhouse in the Market Place but it was far from soundproof and the singing that took place within the house annoyed his neighbours. The St Helens Newspaper described the problem in its own inimitable fashion:

> The house contains a drawing-room, into which the lovers of the lyre are in the habit of going each evening, and fascinating themselves with the latest comic ditties, said ditties being rendered by some very worn-out looking artistes, with a careful attention to forte from beginning to end. It would appear that the music usually discoursed was not of a character to charm those within the radius of its influence, for the present petition was an effort to throw over it the cold chain of silence.

Daniel Woods was allowed to keep his licence upon agreeing to give up his singing room, or, as the Newspaper put it, he gave an assurance that the "warblings shall cease for the future".

THE THREE SCAPEGRACES – Apparently the word scapegrace means someone who has "escaped the grace of God" – a rascal or mischievous person. The Prescot Reporter used the term on December 11th 1875, when they described how three lads had appeared in St Helens Petty Sessions charged with stealing items from a boat:

> THREE SCAPEGRACES – Francis McGurty, a shirtless youth whose clothes but partially covered his body, whose hair was matted like that of an American Indian, and whose skin discovered no trace of any connection with soap and water; Thomas Lyon, another street Arab, and Henry Campbell, said to be the son of respectable parents, but led astray by bad company, were charged with stealing a clock, pair of trousers, a blue guernsey, pair of boots, a cap and other articles of clothing from the flat Elizabeth, lying near to Messrs. Crossfield's chemical works.

The topless Francis McGurty was given two months in prison and Thomas Lyon one month. The 15-year-old Henry Campbell – whose father appeared to be a foreman at a Pocket Nook chemical works and had hired a solicitor for his son – was only fined 20 shillings and costs. It was another example of different standards of justice for those members of families deemed to be respectable – and those who were not.

IN SWEET REPOSE – It was not just women's rows in which the St Helens Newspaper could mock females brought to court. On September 5th 1868 the paper described how Mary Carroll had been sent to prison for a month for simply sleeping in what sounds like a farm building or works shed:

> Mary Carroll, a lass hailing from Liverpool, who was on a summer excursion to the country, was brought up for not securing a decent lodging. Mary was found by a constable, in sweet repose, in an outhouse, and made to exchange her nocturnal resting-place for a police cell. His worship ordered that she be lodged in the Kirkdale refuge for a month.

The report did not tell us what Mary had been doing in the St Helens district. But her "summer excursion" would not have been a holiday and she had probably been seeking work.

PRYING POLICEMAN – There was a similar case in October 1868 when two men described as tramps called James Dumbell and Thomas Waring were charged with vagrancy. The St Helens Newspaper reported how on the previous night both men had entered a barn belonging to a Mr Varley of Gin Lane in Eccleston:

> After coolly improvising a bed with a quantity of straw they found at hand, they quietly composed themselves to sleep. Constable Clarke, who was in a prying mood, took a peep in, and hearing a nasal noise going on briskly he went inside and awakened the sleepers. Dumbell at once surrendered to authority, but Waring, whose temper had been soured by the

interruption to his sleep, struck his disturber a violent blow on the breast. A scuffle ensued in which both men went down together, and the result of which was a victory for the constable.

Dumbell was rewarded for his "quiet conduct" and discharged but his fellow tramp was sent to prison for seven days. Gin Lane later became part of Boundary Road.

A PERFECT BABEL – Back in the 1860s, disputes in St Helens between Protestants and Catholics could end in violence. Meetings held to discuss the question of the Irish church could also prove stormy. On November 4th 1868 such an event was held in St Helens Town Hall, chaired by Rev. Dr Carr *(the Vicar of St Helens)* and featuring a keynote speaker called Brewin Grant. The Liverpool Mercury wrote:

> Between the cheers of the one side and the hootings of their opponents the meeting was a perfect babel of interruptions and confusion. The Lecturer on rising was received with an indescribable variety of noises, which lasted for some time, and prevented his proceeding with his lecture. The services of the police were invoked, and the reverend chairman directed them to remove the "howling wolves," whom he described as the mere "sweepings of the chemical yards," who were only worthy of contempt.

EXPECTORATED INTO THE FACE – Although spitting was a common activity within beerhouses, the act was supposed to take place in spittoons – and not in other beer drinker's faces!

On October 4th 1873, the St Helens Newspaper reported that James Travis had accused John Tatlock of assaulting him in a beerhouse in what the paper sarcastically described as the "fragrant neighbourhood" of Primrose Hill. However, in giving his evidence in court, Travis failed to mention that he had provoked the assault by spitting – or expectorating, as the paper called it – in the face of his opponent:

> Several witnesses were called, whose evidence went to show that the principals fell out about some skittle money. Complainant expectorated into defendant's face, and the latter retaliated by a butt of his head in the stomach of his antagonist which put spitting out of the question for some time. The charge was dismissed.

BESTOWING PHRASES FULL OF STRONG AFFECTION – When Patrick Laffey from Cross Street in St Helens appeared in court in February 1870, the St Helens Newspaper described the 59-year-old as:

> An individual in whom, like Etna, the snows of many winters have not cooled the fire of his blood, though they have left their impression upon his head.

Twelve months earlier, Patrick had appeared in the Petty Sessions along with his two daughters charged with causing a disturbance in the market. This is how the Newspaper then described the case:

> The three defendants, who are relatives, are stall keepers in the market, and in that classic region of animate and inanimate operation, where a little playfulness of tongue is no disability, and above all, no novel characteristic, they are looked upon as a lively trio without whose delightful companionship the slackest business hours would become unsupportably dull. Patrick, in particular, has a happy knack of delivering himself of his opinions of any of his neighbours, with an eloquence and elegance of phraseology that have made him famous within the circle in which he moves. To be sure, his observations have frequently been unfeelingly considered to be slanderous and abusive language.

On the occasion of the disturbance, it had been Patrick's daughters Ellen and Margaret that started rowing – or, as the Newspaper sarcastically put it:

> ...felt a weakness for bestowing phrases full of strong affection upon each other, and they indulged in that species of innocent amusement to their heart's content. While in court, the exuberant Patrick could not restrain his indignation that he should be interfered with by the police, and he gave free expression to his wounded feelings.

Patrick Laffey's solicitor asked the Irishman to quieten down but was told to mind his own business! The magistrates decided to let the threesome off after receiving a promise that they would behave themselves and were no doubt glad to see the back of them!

THE MOST BLOOD-STAINED STORIES – In July 1869 the Newspaper reported on a fight in Parr Street in St Helens between Henry and Margaret Johnson and Elizabeth and Mary Cartwright:

> The quarrel arose amongst the children, and extended to the litigants. It would appear the Johnsons came off second best, for one had a black eye, and the other a well-scratched face. As is usual in these cases, some pieces of pavement, a few pokers, and a great quantity of human hair, were produced, to create effect, and the most blood-stained stories told of each. The witnesses, of whom there were not a few, vied with each other in exaggerating the terrors of that famous fight, which was, by all accounts, one of the most fierce that has disturbed the quiet of the back slums of St. Helens for many a day, which is saying a good deal for its ferocity. Being more noisy and vindictive than the ordinary scrimmages, the whole lot came into court bursting with complaints against each other.

A MERCURIAL TINGE – Some public houses and hotels had newsrooms in which customers clubbed together to share newspapers and periodicals. On November 6th 1869, the St Helens Newspaper described the alarm that was created when the newsroom of the Royal Hotel in Prescot was invaded by a cow:

A fine fat cow was being driven through Fazakerley-street, and when opposite the front entrance to the "Royal," she paused, looked in, and then walked up to the doorway, in the most leisurely and deliberate manner. Several broad steps lead to the level of the hall, but the visitor was in no way abashed at the ascent, which she accomplished with perfect ease. Once in the hall she paused for a few moments, and returned the compliment of staring into the terrified faces which peered out at her from behind the shelter of the "bar," and then, as if having decided upon her course of action, strode straight on, and turned sharply to the newsroom.

The face of the gentleman nearest the door immediately showed a "mercurial" tinge which the study of his favourite Liverpool daily has never given him, and he made "tracks" with the speed of a "courier," in search of a somewhat safer "post." Retiring to the corner he seized the St. Helens Newspaper, and gaining fresh courage, confronted the animal and drove it back with the chivalry of a Spanish matador. There was some surprise as may be expected, at the literary tendencies of the stranger, but Mr. Beaumont, the proprietor, was equal to the occasion, and quietly opening a back door he "persuaded" his visitor to leave.

AMATORY OR MALEVOLENT VALENTINES CARDS – The tradition of sending Valentines Day cards became very popular in the late 19th century – although not all were despatched with romantic overtures in mind. In February 1872 the St Helens Newspaper wrote:

Severe moralists have condemned the custom of sending valentines, because it leads to the transmission of malevolent rubbish for the gratification of jealousy or hatred. It must be borne in mind, however, that the great mass of the missives are of an amatory nature, and therefore perfectly harmless or at least unobjectionable.

Whatever the motivation for sending Valentines Day cards, the practice in the 1870s was clearly popular. The same article revealed that on Wednesday February 14th 1872, the post office had delivered a total of 7,709 items in the town – compared to the average Wednesday delivery of 3,075.

PANTOMIMIC DISPLAY – In July 1870 Margaret Noonan was charged with assaulting Elizabeth Roach outside the Town Hall. Seventeen-year-old Elizabeth said Margaret had used very bad language and threatened her with a knife. The two women from Moss Nook in Sutton had been on different sides in a court case and when they got back home Elizabeth claimed that Mrs Noonan had "raised the place". The St Helens Newspaper could have written that 29-year-old Margaret possessed a weapon but did no harm with it. Instead they wrote that she:

> …vapoured about with a knife, but she fortunately contented herself with pantomimic display.

VOMITED OUT OF THE DOOR – Two likely lads with over thirty convictions between them spent fifteen minutes in Liverpool Road bashing one another. The Newspaper related their pitched battle on August 31st 1872 and used a curious means of describing how one of them had been ejected from a house:

> Patrick Hayes and Joseph Kay were charged with fighting together in Liverpool road, on the 20th instant. Evidence was given showing that they had been in the house of Hayes, which is approached by several steps, and a row arising Kay was vomited out of the door like a football. He fell with a

crash in the street, and Hayes followed up the attack with undoubted vigour. Both men fought in the street for a quarter of an hour, and shed blood very freely. They were bound [over] for two months – in default imprisonment for a month.

The Constable Of Parr In The Year 1700

"Dressed in a tall hat, his portly calves covered by a pair of black stockings, with a musket leaning against the table."

The difficulty of understanding how people lived their lives in the past is magnified as we delve further back in time. Although it is believed that the first newspaper was published in Britain in 1665, high rates of taxation and high levels of illiteracy hampered the industry's development.

As a consequence the newspaper business only began in earnest during the 19th century, with St Helens not having its own paper until 1853. Its unusual title, incidentally, was *"What's Wanted: Containing St. Helens Intelligence"* – adverts and some news, in other words. Not a lot has changed since then!

However, other records have survived which do provide insights into the distant past – and those pertaining to township constables are particularly interesting. Those individuals had many administrative duties to perform, as well as keeping the peace. The St Helens Archive Service holds a number of these faded documents, each with its own idiosyncratic spelling. For example, the constable's book of Billinge from 1668 is signed "trew copie"!

On August 11th 1939, the St Helens News *(as the St Helens Newspaper temporarily rebranded itself)* published a fascinating glimpse into the past after some old documents relating to the work of the constable of Parr had been discovered.

Those dated from around 1700, and although the author of the newspaper article was not identified, it was clearly someone that possessed a good knowledge of the subject. The writer was also a creative individual and with a bit of imaginative licence, was able to bring the work of the constable to life. This is their complete piece:

INTRODUCTION

Years ago, when places like Parr and Hardshaw, Eccleston, and Sutton were districts rejoicing in their own well-defined identity, and St. Helens was almost unheard of, people like beadles, constables and overseers, forerunners of modern local government and its officers, were men of importance and standing. They were characters in an age of individualism, preserving according to their right, law and communal peace, and servants of an order which paved the way to P.A.C. [public assistance / social security], modern constabulary and Town Halls.

Here we roll the years back and show you the Constable of Parr about 200 years ago. If we have drawn upon our imagination a little it is only to make the picture more realistic and to fill in the gaps we found in the calligraphy of a constable of Parr, who was real enough in his day, and who was conscientious in his job according to the faded parchment documents we have used as our authority.

LET US INTRODUCE YOU TO THE CONSTABLE OF PARR

Take a trip to the year 1700! Yes, you can do that with the help of a good imagination and the old documents, discovered in the old Town's Chest, of Parr. The documents – overseers', constables' and doctors' accounts – are preserved in the Library now, and the sheet in which they were found is in the Museum.

Old parchment, brittle, stained and yellow, quaint writing, quaint phrasing – what pictures of byegone days those documents conjure up. Memories lurk between those scrawled lines in faded ink; memories of a life that was just like yours as far as human emotions were concerned; memories of joy and sorrow, romance and tragedy, wealth and poverty. So, back to 1700.

Picture the constable of Parr into whose accounts we will probe. Dressed in a tall hat, his portly calves covered but not concealed by a pair of black stockings, with a musket leaning against the table, he strains mightily at his task of making out the year's accounts for 1688. Our constable is a man of some importance, for are not his duties onerous and his powers many. Do not our businessmen and leading citizens treat him with respect and do not vagabonds who pass through our township hurry on when they encounter his official gaze.

A little pompous he may be, but is that not becoming to one who carried so many of our town's secrets; indeed, it is whispered that he carries on his shoulders the secrets, good and bad, of many of our worthy fellow townsmen, and then, does he not attend the Sessions at Lancaster, Ormskirk, Prescot, Wigan and Warrington, and does he not pay for the repairs to bridges within a radius of twelve miles, and does he not pay the wages of the governor of the "house of correction."?

Oh yes, a worthy man in every respect is our constable – and how seriously he takes his work. See the anxious expression on his face as he peers closely at the parchment over which his quill pen scratches.

His figure looms large in the half shadow cast by the tallow candle, and something like a sigh escapes him as he appends his signature to the accounts he has just finished and sprinkles sand over the ink to dry it. Maybe our faces have betrayed our interest, for with a few well chosen words about betray[ing] official secrets – yes, they had them even then – he hands us his accounts. Here are the items:-

• Paid for the mending of John Brown's muskit – 8d.

• Paid for the coat that I have bought – £2 12s. 6d.

• Paid for the dyed linen for the jacket that I bought at Will Heyes – 1s. 1d.

• Paid for the making of the coatts – 6s. 0d.

Evidently pleased that we are suitably impressed and appreciate the importance of his work our constable pulls open a drawer in his flat-topped desk and hands over a sheaf of accounts for our investigation. Somewhat puzzling are the rather frequent references to payments for repairs to muskits and payments to "soulders," about the year 1688. Then we remember that was the year in which James II abdicated and fled to France, to be succeeded in the following year by William of Orange. The country is only just settling down after the turbulent times of Cromwell and Charles Stuart. Here is another account for 1692, let us see what payments were made then:-

• Paid to the High Constable [of Prescot] for the repair of Stockbridge – £0 4s. 4d. For my gate [expenses] – 6d.
• Paid for the repair of Robbins Bridge – 4s. 4d. For my gate 6d.
• Paid to the High Constable for the wages for the Governor of the House of Correction – £0 2s. 11d. For my gate 6d.

Would future generations ever read these accounts, we wonder. They might, if so doubtless the word "gate" would puzzle them. Doubtless they would refer to books of reference and conclude the "gate" meant journey. Doubtless future generations will be amused at such items as:- "Paid to James Dirke for quartering the soldier that had a pass – £0 1s. 2d."

Our Constable is an honest man, for the money paid out does appear to have been used for the purpose intended, helping "birds of passage" on their way through the township, repairing bridges and other public work. But who was the "jentleman," mentioned in the accounts for 1697:- "Paid for the jentleman's diner at James Hannie's in Chapel-lane – £0 10s. 0d."

Poverty is not unknown in Parr in those days, but we little dreamed that the Constable helped the poor to the extent these accounts for 1700 reveal:- "Disbursed by Matthew Hoult, for the use of the pore of Parr this year, 1700, from Ester to Mickelmas being 26 weeks.

• Paid for shifts [shirts, I think] for Margaret Adamson – £0 3s. 9d.
• Paid for breches for Sam Hill's lad – £0 1s. 0d.
• Paid for tenting James Battersby – £0 9s. 6d."

Proof that the Constable is assiduous in his duties lies in the fact that 6d. has been paid for "a search for a man who had fled from justis pursuant to a warrant," and 3s. "for my gate and expenses in making a search for able-bodied men who had not any lawful calling or visible means of their living." What will future generations assume from the following accounts:-

- Paid for 8 baskets of koolz [coals] for a bonfire – £0 1s. 0d.
- Paid for lighting them and a lode of sticks – £0 6s. 0d.
- Paid for powder – £0 1s. 4d.
- Spent on bonfire at fast day – £0 5s. 0d."

Maybe they will assume it was customary for the Constable and Overseer to light a fire in the streets on certain days for amusement of the townspeople. But probably they will cogitate still more over the following items in the year 1711:-

"For a new pare of stocks and for work don at them and for nales, for mending ye finger post." The way things are going there will be quite a community around the Finger Post, and maybe part of Parr will be called after the Finger Post and perhaps another part after the stocks – after all, not even the Constable knows what the future holds.

Two likely lads try out the old Parr stocks

The Three St Helens Town Hall Fires

"A terrific cheer went up from the huge crowd at the sight of the grey-haired Mr. Pennington fighting back the fire."

Although many places in Britain have suffered serious fires to their municipal seats of government, few have endured three blazes like St Helens Town Hall. I suppose I should really say town *halls*, as the fires of 1871, 1873 and 1913 affected two different buildings. In reporting the latter blaze, the Manchester Guardian wrote: "It is a singular coincidence that the Town Hall in use before the present one was destroyed by fire."

The Corporation Street inferno of 1913 is quite well-known – and so this chapter will mainly focus on the two blazes of the 1870s that destroyed the first hall in New Market Place. However, I will also be describing newly uncovered details of the 20th century blaze that occurred just weeks before the King visited St Helens.

a) THE FIRST TOWN HALL FIRE – May 6th 1871

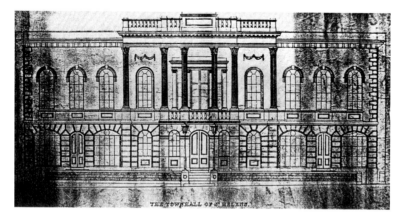

There is no confirmed photograph of the original St Helens Town Hall. A picture that is sometimes touted as showing the old building is believed to instead show some other council offices nearby. We do, though, have the above illustration of the intended structure. The hall in New Market Place was certainly utilitarian in its design. As well as municipal offices, the building included a courtroom, police station and a lock-up *(aka bridewell)* and could easily be converted into a large assembly room to hold dances and dinners. A small public library was also later incorporated.

The Town Hall was built in 1839 as a consequence of magistrates' complaints of the poor court facilities available at the Raven Inn. The town's lock-up was then situated at the old inn in what is now Church Street and so when Prescot magistrates were persuaded to hold court hearings in St Helens, the Raven was the obvious venue. That might seem a strange choice – but inquests and other official meetings were then routinely held in public houses through a lack of alternative accommodation.

However, the shabby lock-up and room space at the Raven left the JPs unimpressed and they told the town's leading citizens that unless new, dedicated premises were soon built, they'd end their monthly sessions in the town. So a meeting was held, which the Manchester Times described on May 5th 1838:

The inhabitants of St. Helen's have had a public meeting for the purpose of entering into arrangements for the erection of a town hall, constable's house, bridewell, &c.; after which a subscription list was opened, and in less than seven days £3,000 was subscribed. Plans are to be forthwith advertised for, and it is expected that early in January next the building will be ready for use. The situation is on the south side of the New Square, which has lately been laid out and flagged in the centre, and which is intended to be used as the Market-place. This square is already nearly built round, with handsome shops and lofty houses four stories [sic] high, all of which are uniform, beautifully stuccoed, &c., and when finished will be one of the handsomest squares in

Lancashire, being hitherto under the superintendence of Mr. Fowden, of Manchester, for the Society of Friends, whose property in St. Helen's is, we believe, rather extensive.

The New Square became known as New Market Place and until building began in the 1830s, it was simply a field around which Bridge Street, Church Street, Market Street and Tontine Street were laid. That is essentially the area where the Church Square Shopping Centre currently stands.

The opening of the Town Hall took place on October 8th 1839, on the same day that St Thomas' church in Westfield Street was consecrated. Four days later the Liverpool Mail described the new building:

> The elevation of the hall is in the modern Italian style...The ground floor is occupied by shops, offices, and a residence for the chief police officer. In the centre is a handsome entrance, and a stone staircase, which leads to the principal floor....The court-room is a remarkably spacious and neat place. It is 65 feet long, 36 feet wide, and 22 feet high....and when the room is required for balls or public dinners, by a very ingenious contrivance the table, forms, witness-box, &c., can be easily deposited below.

The first fire that struck the Town Hall occurred just after 3pm on Saturday May 6th 1871 – and rapidly half the building was reported as having been "wrapped in flames". The blaze was initially discovered at the rear of the hall adjoining a large room and it was some time before the fire brigade arrived at the scene – despite the short distance from their HQ in St Mary's Street.

The crew were summoned by the ringing of a bell and it could take time for them to assemble. The Bolton Evening News wrote that as a consequence of the delay, the flames travelled with "fearful rapidity along the woodwork of the roof", before adding:

The efforts of the firemen did not avail much for a considerable time. The ceiling began to give way, and falling on the floor below set fire to the forms and to an organ worth from £400 to £500. The flooring was partially saved through constant drenching. The office and other parts of the wing [where the police station was located] suffered considerably, and the prisoners had to be removed to the police barracks.

The other wing [where the library was], although nearest the source of the fire, escaped. The danger apparent at one time induced the clearing out of the library, which contained 3,000 volumes. The fire lasted several hours, and was not until eight o'clock that it was completely subdued.

FIRE.—The St. Helen's Town-hall was partially destroyed by fire on Saturday afternoon. The hall, which was situate in the market place, consisted of a central structure and two wings, the latter used as a police-station and a library. The fire commenced in the rear of the large room, and the flames spread rapidly. The ceiling gave way, and, falling on the floor below, set fire to a valuable organ. The wing containing the police-station was much injured, and the prisoners had to be removed. The other wing escaped, but it was so closely threatened at one time that the books of the library were cleared out. The buildings are partially insured. The fire was got under about 8 o'clock, after lasting four or five hours.

Report in The Times from May 9th 1871

The St Helens Newspaper would later write that the "great fire" had gutted the greater part of the building with the large courtroom / assembly room "burned completely out, roof and floor". But what had been the cause of the inferno? Could it have been arson?

The police were certainly convinced that the Town Hall had been torched and six weeks after the event, Thomas May was charged. This is how the Wigan Observer reported his appearance at the St Helens Petty Sessions on June 19th:

It appeared from the evidence given that the accused, who seemed to be slightly deranged, was in the habit of visiting the town hall on Saturdays, when he had the building all to himself. On the date of the fire he was seen in the building shortly before the flames were discovered, but as he was not known he escaped for the time. Last Saturday he was again observed on the premises, and arrested. In his pocket the police found a memorandum book, containing this entry: "The form in the town hall. Town hall, set it on fire." He was remanded for a week.

Was that a note of intent or simply a diary entry by a semi-literate person – as many St Helens folk probably made a record of such a notable event? After seven more days in police custody, no further evidence was obtained against Thomas May and so upon his return to court, the man was discharged.

However, the St Helens Newspaper in their report of the hearing implied that there was still strong suspicion that the young man had been an "incendiary" – we, of course, would say arsonist. Even May's own solicitor, Thomas Swift – who normally fought tooth and nail for his clients – appeared to think him guilty. The paper wrote:

The depositions having been read over, the prisoner was discharged. At the request of Mr. Swift the magistrates called his father forward, and warned him to keep a vigilant watch upon the conduct of his son.

b) THE SECOND TOWN HALL FIRE – July 3rd 1873

Some parts of the municipal centre had escaped the ravages of the fire or been only lightly damaged. So a decision had to be made over whether it should be rebuilt or a new, larger Town Hall constructed, perhaps on another site. St Helens had expanded considerably in the three decades since the building had opened.

The town's official population figures *(within a limited geographical area)* had risen from 14,195 in 1831 to 49,019 in 1871.

And so it was decided that the newly created borough needed a more spacious town hall. Land was acquired in what was then known as Cotham Street – but which would later become Corporation Street. While plans were being drawn up and heated arguments over the cost were taking place, a second fire struck the old building in New Market Place.

estate, in the outskirts of the town.

ANOTHER FIRE AT THE ST. HELENS TOWN-HALL.— The St. Helens Town-hall, which was partly destroyed by fire in May, 1871, was yesterday morning the scene of another conflagration. After the last fire a temporary wooden roof was thrown over the demolished structure, and the premises since then have been used for a police station, public library, and store rooms, by the Corporation. It was in one of the latter rooms that the fire broke out. After an hour's hard work the Corporation Fire Brigade succeeded in getting the mastery of the flames, but not before the whole of the temporary roof of the hall was destroyed. One of the firemen named Ellison, while directing a nozzle upon the

Liverpool Daily Post July 4th 1873

Some of the damage that the first blaze had done had been repaired and the place made useable again – at least on a temporary basis until the new hall could be built. However, the patching up had been largely undertaken with wood.

In November 1871 a fund had been set up in St Helens to aid the sufferers of the Great Chicago Fire. Much of the American city had been destroyed because of its high number of wooden buildings. Even the pavements – or should I say sidewalks – were made of wood, which had allowed the blaze to rapidly spread.

That vast inferno was blamed on a cow kicking over a kerosene lamp while the beast was being milked in a stable. And the second

St Helens Town Hall fire, which occurred just after 6am on July 3rd 1873, had a similar, simple cause. A candle held by a workman came into contact with spilt paint and the building's makeshift wooden ceiling converted the resulting fire into a conflagration. The St Helens Newspaper takes up the rest of the story:

In a few seconds the whole apartment was a mass of fire so fierce and overpowering that it was lucky the men were close to the door and able to escape rapidly, or some of them might have been hemmed in and perhaps destroyed. The roof consisting of the charred beams of the old ceiling, and the temporary wooden covering erected since, furnished good feed for the fire, and was speedily blazing. A messenger hastened to the police and the fire station, with the alarm, and the smoke, which was now arising in dark volumes over the building, attracted others to the spot. There was no lack of water, and the firemen used it liberally.

When they commenced to play the fire gave forth the heat of a furnace, for there was nothing to burn but dry material, which flared up rapidly and burned with intense heat. Nothing but a flooding was of the slightest avail to check the progress of such a fire, and the building was liberally flooded with water. Still the whole of the temporary roof was destroyed, and the floors beneath again encumbered with charred rubbish. The police department was almost wrecked and is at present uninhabitable...Every cell was full of water, the passages were almost roofless, a large gap appeared in the ceiling of the superintendent's private office, and the entire place was despoiled of furnishing.

The reason that the police station at the Town Hall had been "despoiled" of furniture – as the Newspaper put it – was because officers had managed to remove everything portable – including seven prisoners – upon the outbreak of the fire. The flames were extinguished after two hours and the blaze – and the huge volume of water poured upon it – did immense damage to the building. Usually the brigade took some time to get to fires *(as it did with the first Town Hall blaze)* and then struggled to source a water supply. On this occasion the firemen were rapidly on site and, if anything, "played" too much water on the inferno.

Consequently the Town Hall cellars were flooded several inches deep. One of the firemen called Ellison was injured after falling through the roof to the ground floor – but he was not reported to have been seriously hurt.

NEW TOWN HALL.

———

THE FOUNDATION STONE

Of the
NEW TOWN HALL, ST. HELENS,
Will be laid
ON THURSDAY, 6TH NOVEMBER, 1873,
At Two o'clock in the Afternoon, by
HIS WORSHIP THE MAYOR,
(John Marsh, Esq)

After the Ceremony / LUNCH will be served at the Fleece Hotel, the Mayor presiding. Tickets for the Lunch and Admission to the Platform on the laying of the Stone, £1 1s. Tickets for admission to the Platform (only), 2s.

A BALL will be held in the Volunteer Hall, in the Evening. Dancing to commence at Nine o'clock. Gentlemen's Tickets, 7s. 6d ; Ladies' do., 5s each.

An Efficient Band will be in attendance.

Tickets for the Lunch must be taken previous to Saturday, the 1st November.

Tickets may be obtained at Mr Dromgoole's, Mr. Hodson's, and Mr. Foreman's. Printer, Church Street, St. Helens.

Notice in the St Helens Newspaper of October 18th 1873 – the guinea cost of lunch at the Fleece along with platform admission would have been the equivalent of a week's wages for many working class folk

c) THE THIRD TOWN HALL FIRE – June 9th 1913

On April 7th 1920, John Pennington died at his home in Greenfield Road in St Helens. The builder and steeplejack had been considered a hero when the Town Hall tower caught fire in June 1913. The grand building that had opened in 1876 in what became Corporation Street was being renovated in readiness for the visit of King George V. Suddenly a blaze broke out and after being informed of the fire, Pennington dashed from his Dentons Green home to the scene, as the St Helens Newspaper described:

> Mr. John Pennington – who was in his fifties – scaled the ladder to the tower. He dragged a fire hose through blazing timber and a shower of slates and thrust the nozzle through the clock tower to play a jet of water over the flames. A terrific cheer went up from the huge crowd of onlookers at the sight of the grey-haired Mr. Pennington fighting back the fire.

Destruction of Town Hall By Fire St Helens June 9th 1913

A public fund was opened in appreciation of Pennington's efforts and what was described as a handsome sum was presented to him. Speaking to the St Helens Newspaper in 1952, Ralph Pennington, John's son, said that as souvenirs of the event, he still had in his possession a couple of charred scaffold planks that had surrounded the tower as it burnt.

The man who had taken the dramatic picture above of the burning spire collapsing amongst scaffolding had been Thomas Marsh of Keswick Road. At the time of the fire, Mr Marsh had been a pawnbroker in College Street and in its 1952 reminiscences on the blaze the Newspaper wrote:

He dashed along to Victoria Square and took up a position at the Education Office corner, armed with his camera. He took his photograph at ten minutes past ten as the spire collapsed on to the assembly room roof. Mr. Marsh had many copies of the photograph made and says they have been sent to St. Helens people and their friends all over the world.

Many newspapers reported extensively on the disastrous blaze. The headline in the Northwich Guardian was *"Disastrous Fire At St. Helens"*; The Derby Daily Telegraph had *"Fire At St. Helens – Town Hall Destroyed"*; the Yorkshire Evening Post's headline was *"St. Helens Town Hall In Flames"*; the Somerset Guardian had *"Fire At A Town Hall – Tower Falls On Main Building"* and the Widnes Examiner headlined their article *"Town Hall Ablaze – Clock Tower Wrecked At St. Helens – Exciting Scenes"*.

The Daily Mirror in their account of June 10th 1913 described John Pennington as a "brave steeplejack" and added:

> The spire and clock tower soon became a blazing torch, and presently crashed down, causing the fire to spread to the assembly rooms, which were gutted.

On the same day the Manchester Guardian commented how Mr Pennington had occupied a position of "considerable peril", and the "great crowd" that had gathered in Victoria Square had "loudly cheered him for his plucky conduct". The newspaper then assessed the damage done:

> Fortunately the [Council] Chamber was not damaged, and one side of the hall apparently has escaped injury. On the other side, however, which includes the treasurer's department and the police and fire stations, a good deal of damage was done, and the holes observed in the roof after the fire was extinguished showed that the whole of this portion of the Town Hall had had a narrow escape from demolition. Despite the efforts of the fire brigade they were unable to save the roof of the assembly-room, a large

portion of which fell in about twelve o'clock....The spire and clock are entirely destroyed, and much damage, caused by fire and water, has been done to other parts of the building.

As with the previous town hall fires, the water that the firemen had poured onto the blaze did almost as much damage to the building as the flames. The St Helens Reporter of June 10th 1913 went into more detail as to the water damage that had been caused – and the salvaging efforts that had taken place:

Below stairs – that is, the minor departments – were flooded out, and persons with and persons without authority rushed about in a panic of salvage. Books of value, and goods that were merely useless, were hastily grabbed and carried out to be flung into carts, or carried across to the Wesley Church for safe keeping. Whatever these amateur salvage officers lacked in discretion and discrimination, they amply made up in the eagerness of their endeavour. Another visit to the Assembly Hall revealed a pitiable state of affairs.

The numerous hose were still being trained on the beams, loosening pieces of wood and plaster, which fell in an intermittent shower to the floor, which was several inches deep in water. The line of mirrors at the end of the hall was intact, so could be seen when the steam and smoke thinned out and the air cleared. The hall had been arranged with chairs as for a meeting. Many of those were smashed to splinters, and all the while there was a downpour of water such as may be experienced in a heavy shower in the tropics. The water ran out and came down the steps in a cascade. Streams came through cracks in the ceilings from the upper floors. The Council Chamber was well drenched, but was otherwise undamaged. The committee room was the same, and the Town Clerk's department was flooded out.

Four days after the fire a painter from North Road in St Helens called Thomas Hughes appeared in St Helens Police Court charged with obstructing the street with a handcart. However, the Chief Constable, Arthur Ellerington, told the magistrates that he wanted to withdraw the summons against the man "on the principle that one good turn deserves another".

That was because Hughes had volunteered to scale the tower at the Town Hall and try to extinguish the fire – but Ellerington had told him it was too dangerous. That was, presumably, just before John Pennington did exactly the same thing.

Although, Pennington was acclaimed as a hero, it was his firm that was judged to be at fault for starting the blaze in the first place. In today's money the fire had caused somewhere in the region of £2 million worth of damage and a week later an inquiry into the cause of the blaze was held.

What was described as a "considerable number" of witnesses gave evidence to members of the St Helens Watch Committee and they ruled that the fire had been accidentally caused by painters using a blow-lamp to burn off old paint on the tower and spire.

On the same day that the inquiry was held, a short film called *"The St. Helens Town Hall Fire"* began to be screened at the Widnes Picturedrome and, according to the Runcorn Guardian, "aroused much interest". The Kinematograph Weekly of June 19th tells us that the short film had actually been screened in St Helens within hours of the fire occurring:

The disastrous fire which partially destroyed St. Helens Town Hall last week, provided Mr. Helsby Wright, the manager of the Oxford Picture Hall, and Mr. G. Bennett of the Co-operative Hall, St. Helens, with an interesting local topical [film]. The fire, which occurred in the morning of June 13th, was filmed by Messrs. Weisker Bros., of Liverpool, and notwithstanding the fact that it had to be taken to Liverpool (a distance of twelve miles) to be developed, it was finished and brought back to St. Helens in time to be shown the same night. Messrs. Weisker Brothers are to be complimented on their promptitude.

The Oxford Picturedrome in Duke Street would later become the Plaza. As for the speedy filmmaking Weiskers, Leo and his brother Fred were both St Helens lads who started screening films at the Co-operative Hall in Baldwin Street in 1907. The Weisker Bros opened up many cinemas in Liverpool and other Lancashire towns and Leo managed the Hippodrome in St Helens for a while.

Acknowledgements / Credits

St Helens Archive Service

Eccleston Library, St Helens

British Newspapers Archive

Newspapers.com

Findmypast

Most images are from the author's own personal archive or reproduced from newspapers on microfilm at Eccleston Library.

Thanks to Diane Charnock and Gyles Charnock for their proof reading and support.

Newspaper sources: St Helens Newspaper, St Helens Reporter, St Helens Weekly News, St Helens Examiner, St Helens Lantern, Prescot Reporter, St Helens Star, Liverpool Echo, Liverpool Daily Post, Liverpool Albion, Liverpool Weekly News, Liverpool Courier, Liverpool Mercury, Liverpool Mail, (Manchester) Guardian, Manchester Times, Northwich Guardian, Derby Daily Telegraph, Yorkshire Evening Post, Somerset Guardian, Widnes Examiner, Daily Mirror, Daily Herald, Daily Express, Wigan Observer, Bolton Evening News, The Times, Kinematograph Weekly, Evesham Standard, Glasgow Herald and Runcorn Guardian.